THE
MESSAGE
FROM THE
TWO-EDGED
SWORD

THE MESSAGE FROM THE TWO-EDGED SWORD

BETTY MARKLEY POTENZA

XULON PRESS

Xulon Press
2301 Lucien Way #415
Maitland, FL 32751
407.339.4217
www.xulonpress.com

xulon PRESS

ISBN-13: 978-1-5456-7184-9

To my husband and daughter for their great amount of patience and cooperation during the time I spent working on this book.

Also to my mother, who was the first to believe me, and to know that I had to be getting help from the Holy Spirit.

Also to my friend Al, who always showed great interest in what I was writing, and gave encouragement when it was needed. And to my friend Rose, who has been wonderful about taking up what few hours of leisure time she had to type up the final draft for me.

REFERENCES

Unless otherwise indicated, the Scriptures quoted are taken from the Pilgrim Edition of the Authorized King James Version of the Holy Bible, Oxford University Press, New York, 1952.

Books used in researching the subject are the following:

William Barclay, *The Revelation of John,* Volume 1 (The Westminster Press, Philadelphia, 1960).

William Barclay, *The Revelation of John,* Volume 2 (The Westminster Press, Philadelphia, 1960).

H. A. Ironside, *Revelation* (Loiseaux Brothers, Neptune, New Jersey, 1930).

M. R. DeHaan, *Revelation* (Zondervan Publishing House, Grand Rapids, Michigan, 1946).

Clarence Larkin, *Dispensational Truth* (Rev. Clarence Larkin, Philadelphia, 1920).

Merrill F. Unger, *Unger's Bible Handbook* (Moody Press, Chicago, 1967).

William Smith, *Smith's Bible Dictionary* (A. J. Holman Co., Philadelphia).

Alexander Cruden, *Cruden's Complete Concordance* (Zondervan Publishing House, Grand Rapids, Michigan, 1966).

CONTENTS

CHARTS

INTRODUCTION

(Please Read This First)

Through Christ, all things are possible. We say it; but how many of us really believe it? Well, I found out that it is really true. You see, seven months ago I set out to do what normally I would have thought to be an impossible task. And that was to write a book, a detailed interpretation of the Book of Revelation; and in a simple, easy-to-understand language: one that just ordinary, everyday people like myself could understand.

This wouldn't be such an impossible task for a Doctor of Theology, or even ministers who are able to spend possibly years researching the subject. But how could a housewife, who had never even attended an adult Bible class, and who has just recently become truly interested in the Bible, write a detailed explanation of the Book of Revelation? Plus the fact that I had never been interested in writing and knew nothing about it. But circumstances which were beyond my control seemed to be pointing to the fact that God wanted me to do just that. So I began, knowing that it was humanly impossible for me to accomplish such a thing; but also believing that this was what God wanted. I gave Him my time, and depended on Him to show me what to do, and how to do it. I believed that He would, and my faith was not in vain!

The Book of Revelation is mostly a book of judgment. But it is not wrong to be occupied with so many terrible scenes, because all is bright at the end. Jesus is telling us about all these things out of kindness, so that we may be warned ahead of time. In taking Jesus seriously, we can avoid what lies ahead for this guilty world. We should be taking Jesus seriously, regardless; but the fact is that most of us today fall into what is called the "lukewarm" class of Christians—neither "hot" nor "cold" as far as Christ is concerned.

Due to the fact that in many churches the Book of Revelation remains a closed book, or is regarded as not important enough and too difficult to teach, many Christians have been deprived of this warning. In the past, this was not so important; but I believe we are approaching the times spoken of in Revelation, and now it becomes very important. I truly believe that this is why God has caused me to write this book; and to write it in a way that the everyday people can understand it. And I pray that those who read it will get to know the power and feel the closeness of God, as I have.

I'm sure many people will truly enjoy this study of the Second Coming of Christ and the Book of Revelation, because it is so different from what we are used to hearing. But don't be surprised if, as the truth begins to sink in, you find that it makes demands for what at first you feel that you cannot do. You, too, must remember that through Christ all things are possible.

I cannot force you to believe what our Lord has revealed to me. I can only explain it to you to the best of the ability which God has seen fit to give me, and ask that you read this book with a fresh mind, putting aside any previous views that you may have concerning the Book of Revelation. I ask you to study it and test it, using the Bible as the testing ground. This theory that God has shown me has to fit into all situations described in the Bible, to be correct. Of my own knowledge and intelligence, I do not know that it will; but with the same faith that has carried me through this whole book, I believe it will.

THE MESSAGE

FROM THE

TWO-EDGED SWORD

CHAPTER 1

THE BOOK OF REVELATION

There are many prophecies of the future found throughout the Bible; but there is one book in particular which is called prophetic, because it is a prophecy of things to come. And that is the Book of Revelation. Satan has caused this book to be thought of as a deep mystery, which cannot be understood; and as a result, the average Bible-reader knows little or nothing about either its contents or its meaning. This book is supposed to be an unveiling, a revelation. So I think it is time that we found out what Christ is trying to show us.

First of all, let me point out that the Book of Revelation is the one book of the Bible which begins and ends with a blessing pronounced on those who read, hear (meaning understand), and keep what is written therein. So it certainly should be studied!

There are many interpretations of this part of the Bible. And I believe there is some truth in all of them, or the authors would not have been inspired to write them. But they all can't be right, because it is only going to happen one way; and that is, the way that God has it planned. And God is the only one who knows the truth! And it is only through the Holy Spirit that we can find the truth; and I believe without a doubt that He will show it to us. Please join me in this detailed study of the Book of Revelation, in search of the truth.

Rev. 1:1-2. The Revelation of Jesus Christ, which God gave unto him, to show unto his servants things which must shortly come to pass; and he sent and signified it by his angel unto his servant John; who bare record of God, and of the testimony of Jesus Christ, and of all things that he saw.

The true title is given to us in the opening verse, which is the Revelation of Jesus Christ—or the unveiling of our Lord Jesus Christ. God gave it to Jesus, who, by way of His angel, sent it to His beloved, the apostle John. God's purpose in this revelation was to show His servants things which must shortly come to pass. "Shortly come to pass" means that, when the events begin to occur, they will occur rapidly. "Shortly" is translated from the Greek word from which we get our English word "tachometer," which measures velocity.

There are some that question whether this was John the apostle or some other John that wrote this. There is no doubt in my mind that it was the apostle John. Once Jesus said to Peter, "If I want him (John) to live on until I come, what is that to you?" This may not have been what Jesus was referring to; but John did live until he saw Jesus come again in this revelation that Jesus gave him. But really, what is the difference—since Jesus is actually the author? John just wrote what he was told to! John wrote a record of the word of God, and the testimony of Jesus, and everything that he saw.

Rev. 1:3. Blessed is he that readeth and they that hear the words of this prophecy, and keep those things which are written therein; for the time is at hand.

Here we see the blessing which Jesus promises to all who read and understand this prophecy, and keep the things which are written in this book. John wrote this about 1875 years ago, and Jesus said that the time was at hand then; and it still hasn't happened. Why did Jesus say that then? We will go into this a little more later; but John lived and wrote this book in the same time, age, or dispensation that we live in now: that is, the time of the church, the Church Age, or the Dispensation of Grace.

Rev. 1:4-8. John to the seven churches which are in Asia: Grace be unto you, and peace, from Him which is, and which was, and which is to come; and from the seven Spirits which are before His throne. And from Jesus Christ, who is the faithful witness, and the first begotten of the dead, and the Prince of the kings of the earth. Unto Him that loved us, and washed us from our sins in His own blood, and hath made us kings and priests unto God and His Father, to Him be glory and dominion for ever and ever, Amen. Behold, He cometh with clouds; and every eye shall see Him, and they also which pierced Him, and all kindreds of the earth shall wail because of Him. Even so, Amen. I am the Alpha and Omega, the beginning and the ending, saith the Lord, which is and which was, and which is to come, the Almighty.

Versus 4 to 8 make up the salutation of this letter to the seven churches which are in Asia. John writes, "Grace be unto you, and peace from God the Father, who is present all the time; now, in the past, and in the future." And also from God the Holy Spirit, which is symbolized by the seven spirits, pictured before His throne. There are not seven Holy Spirits—just one with seven characteristics, making it complete and perfect. Then with the Father, and the Spirit, we have God the Son, or Jesus Christ as the "faithful witness" when He was here on earth. He is the "first-begotten of the dead" in His resurrected glory; and the "Prince of the kings of the earth" when He comes again to reign. Notice that this pictures Jesus as He was, He is, and as He will be.

3

Now John praises Jesus: "Unto Him that loved us, and washed us from our sins in His own blood. And hath made us kings and priests unto God, His Father; to Him be glory and dominion for ever and ever. So be it."

Then John heralds the good news of the Second Coming of our Lord. Look, He will come with the clouds and every eye shall see Him, and they also which pierced Him, and all nations of the earth shall wail because of Him. Amen. So be it. This tells us how Christ will return, not as a baby like before; but as our glorified Christ descending from heaven. And all will see this miracle. Fifty years ago, they thought only a stupendous miracle could bring this about; but now we know that would be possible, just by switching on our TV set.

John says that Jesus will come with the clouds. Also in Acts 1:11 it describes Jesus being taken up to heaven, and then it says that He will come back in the same way that the apostles saw Him go. There are some who claim that Jesus returned in 1914. Well, if our Lord had returned, everyone, even His enemies, would know about it.—No, this hasn't happened yet!

Now it is the Son who speaks, declaring Himself God. Jesus says that He is the beginning and the ending of all things. He created all things, and He shall end all things on this earth. He is, He was, and is the coming One—the Almighty.

CHAPTER 2

THE VISION

Rev. 1:9-10. I, John, who also am your brother, and companion in tribulation, and in the kingdom and patience of Jesus Christ, was in the isle that is called Patmos, for the word of God, and for the testimony of Jesus Christ. I was in the Spirit on the Lord's day, and heard behind me a great voice, as of a trumpet, saying, I am Alpha and Omega, the first the last; and, What thou seest, write in a book, and send it unto the seven churches which are in Asia; unto Ephesus, and unto Smyrna, and unto Pergamos, and unto Thyatira, and unto Sardis, and unto Philadelphia, and unto Laodicea.

John says that he is not only a brother through Christ, but also through persecution, to those whom he writes. This is because the Roman emperor condemned John to the island of Patmos for witnessing for the Word of God and for the testimony of Jesus.

John was in the Spirit or meditating on the Word of God on the first day of the week, Sunday. If he had been on the mainland, perhaps he would have been in one of the churches mentioned. But he was alone, and suddenly he heard a great voice, which sounded almost like a trumpet, The voice said that He was God, the first and the last; and

5

He tells John to write in a book what he sees, and to send it to the seven churches, which He then lists for John.

This writing of the Book of Revelation took place about 96 A.D.; and John was to send it to the seven churches that God named, so he thought. There were many churches established by then; why were these particular churches named by God? Well, there are several opinions; but I believe it was because the internal conditions prevailing in these churches were suited to portray the state of the whole church in seven distinct periods, from the days of the apostles to the close of the churches' testimony on earth. In other words, the whole Church of Jesus Christ, moving through seven historical stages to complete its history on earth, is what is seen through the seven letters to the seven churches.

Rev. 1:12. And I turned to see the voice that spake with me. And being turned, I saw seven golden candlesticks.

John has heard the voice; now he turns to see the one who spoke to him. The first thing he sees, is seven golden candlesticks, sometimes called lampstands. We are told in verse 20 that they represent the seven churches. This does not mean seven particular churches, or denominations; but God's one, whole, complete church. The number seven means perfect fulness, complete, whole. Remember, God only has one church; man is the one who has divided it up. But even though it is divided, and appears to us as many, it is still only one to God.

Rev. 1:13-14. And in the midst of the seven candlesticks one like unto the Son of man, clothed with a garment down to the foot, and girt about the paps with a golden girdle. His head and His hairs were white like wool, as white as snow; and His eyes were as a flame of fire.

Now John sees Christ, standing in the midst of the candlesticks of His church. Here we are given for the first time some description of Christ. We were never given any descrip-

6

tion of Jesus when He was here as the Lamb, who was slain; just as if God didn't want His Son remembered in that earthy way. But now we see Him in the clothing worn by royalty. He has a robe which comes down to his feet, and He is girt about the breasts with a golden girdle. This is the dress, as described in the Old Testament, worn by high priests and kings. The Lord Jesus Christ is both. As a priest, He must judge the works of His people; as king, He will judge any who rebel and set up His kingdom here on earth.

Christ is further described as having white hair, like wool and as white as snow. The Ancient of Days was described like this from a vision of David in Daniel 7:9. Also, in Isaiah, this description is used:

> Isaiah 1:18. Come now, and let us reason together, saith the Lord: though your sins be as scarlet, they shall be as white as snow; though they be red like crimson, they shall be as wool.

Here, then, we have the symbols of purity and great age, pointing to the fact that He is eternal. "And His eyes are as a flame of fire" speaks of the searching intensity of His judgment. There will be nothing hidden from those eyes.

> Rev. 1:15-16. And his feet like unto fine brass, as if they burned in a furnace; and His voice as the sound of many waters. And had in His right hand seven stars; and out of His mouth went a sharp two-edged sword; and His countenance was as the sun shineth in His strength.

Brass is the symbol of judgment in the Old Testament. The brazen altar which stood before the tabernacle was that on which the fire of God's judgment was burning continually. It was of brass because brass could stand the fire. And here He has feet like brass, for His ways are in righteousness and are unyielding. Everything that is unholy will be stamped out in divine judgment.

7

His voice is as the sound of many waters, a voice of power. When you are at peace with God, the voice is gentle and loving, and you are as a huge ship sitting in the quiet, peaceful waters of a harbor. But, if you resist God, the voice is powerful; and you may be as a tiny ship, struggling in an angry sea.

We are told that He had in His right hand seven stars. His right hand, which is strong enough to uphold the heavens, and gentle enough to wipe away our tears, speaks of His complete control. These seven stars are said to be angels of the church, in verse 20. The Greek word for angel simply means messenger. Sometimes it signifies angels, sometimes men. So these stars are men, ministers of God's Church. "Seven" still means complete. So He holds or controls the ministry of His Church. He did once and He will again when He sets up His Kingdom here on earth.

Out of His mouth went a two-edged sword. We are told in Hebrews 4:12 that this is the Word of God, which is alive, active, and sharp. It cuts all the way through to where soul and spirit meet, to where joints and marrow come together. It judges the desires and thoughts of men's minds.

And His countenance was as the sun shining in His strength. It was the glory of God in the face of Jesus Christ, which is a brighter light than the sun—as if the sun drew its light from Him. Remember Saul of Tarsus, when he was stricken down; he saw a light above the brightness of the sun. And this is what John saw, and he fell at His feet.

Rev. 1:17-18. And when I saw Him, I fell at His feet as dead. And He laid His right hand upon me, saying unto me, Fear not, I am the first and the last: I am He that liveth, and was dead; and behold, I am alive forevermore, Amen; and have the keys of hell and of death.

Not even Moses was allowed to look upon God; for to see God meant death. And John thought that was who this was, and fell at His feet, probably trembling with fear, wondering what would happen. But Jesus put His gentle hand upon

John and told him not to be afraid. He said that He was God; but He was the visible part which John had seen before. He was Christ, who was alive on earth, and was killed. But now, look! He is alive, and will be forever, and He has the keys of hell and of death.

Here we see that Jesus has established God's promise. John sees Jesus alive and as king. The promise that Jesus would live again, and was going back to the Father to be made king, has been kept, according to what John saw. Jesus is not dead, but alive forever, just as we will be if we live in union with Him through the Holy Spirit. Jesus has the keys to hell and death just as He has the keys to heaven and life. He controls the doors to each because He will be your judge.

> Rev. 1:19. Write the things which thou hast seen, and the things which are, and the things which shall be hereafter;

This verse is very important because it is a key to understanding this book of prophecy. It is very clear that John is told to write about three different things:

(a) "Write the things which thou hast seen." This refers to the vision that John has just seen in Chapter 1. But it is now over; it is now spoken of in the past tense—"which was."

(b) "The things which are." This refers to the Church Age, which is covered by the next two chapters. John lived in the Church Age, just as we do—"which is."

(c) "And the things which shall be hereafter." This refers to the Great Tribulations, the Second Coming of Christ, and eventually the new heavens and new earth—"which will be."

There are past, present, and future tenses used in these instructions, revealing that after the present Church Age is complete (seven), we will then have to face what the future holds; which is the Great Tribulation, and the Second Coming of Christ.

Rev. 1:20. The mystery of the seven stars which thou sawest in my right hand, and the seven golden candlesticks. The seven stars are the angels of the seven churches; and the seven candlesticks which thou sawest are the seven churches.

Jesus helps us solve the mystery of the stars and the candlesticks. The stars are the angels of the church; and notice that all the following letters are addressed to the angel of the church. As we mentioned, this could mean either an angel or a man. We know that angels bring messages to men; but Jesus wouldn't have had John send messages to an angel. So the angels of the churches have to be the ministers.

Since seven means whole or complete, the seven stars refer to the whole ministry. The seven candlesticks are the churches, so this refers to the whole Church of Jesus Christ. Gold in scriptures stands for the glory of God, which the church is supposed to take care of. How does the church take care of the glory of God? The church, the children of God, glorify the Father by glorifying the Son. We glorify Jesus with unwavering, genuine faith. But genuine faith is something that has to be worked at. It has to be fed, exercised, and cared for regularly, in order to be strong, healthy, effective, and truly glorify God. And this is a job for every individual, in every church that God has on earth.

CHAPTER 3

THE SEVEN LETTERS TO
THE SEVEN CHURCHES

I certainly want to acknowledge the fact that there are various interpretations on the meaning of these seven letters to the seven churches. Since it is very important that we have the correct interpretation in order to understand the rest of the book, let's take a little time to consider them.

1. Some believe that these are just seven letters to seven churches which really existed at the time that John wrote this book, and are of no importance to us.

But if they were just seven letters to seven churches, with no symbolic meaning, I think it is reasonable to conclude that they would not be in a book of prophecy, which verse three definitely says this is. Also, it has been brought to my attention that it says in verse 11 that John is to write a book—the Book of Revelation; and the book will be sent to the seven churches, not the individual letters. So it seems even more evident that God is sending a message to his whole Church on earth, in John's day, as well as ours. And this message is contained in the seven letters as a whole. Each letter is a part of the message.

2. Some believe that these seven churches described in the seven letters present a picture of seven different kinds of assemblies that are always present during the entire Church Age.

That is to say that all these churches are present all the

time because some of the same characteristics will always be found in various parts of the whole Church, or individuals, as long as the Church is on earth. I agree that some of the same characteristics will always be found in individuals which make up God's Church on earth. But when you consider the full description of each of these churches, I cannot see that the churches of Ephesus, Smyrna, or Pergamos are present now. But even if they were, I fail to see any great prophetic message to the Church, during the entire Church Age, in this interpretation.

3. And I gather that some say that these letters are just personal messages to the individual believers. If this were true, I believe they would have been put elsewhere in the Bible.

4. And some believe, as I do, that those letters to the seven churches represent seven different historical periods that God's whole Church has to go through, from the beginning to the end of its stay on earth, in order to complete its whole history.

That is to say that these seven churches are a progressive picture of the history of the professing Church, from Pentecost to Christ's Second Coming. Each of them describes a certain period of church history. The seven letters to the seven churches could read: "The complete history of the whole Church of Jesus Christ." We must remember that the number seven means "complete" or "whole." Now, this interpretation gives a timetable, and we are able to trace God's Church down through history, and see what part of the Church's history we are living in.

All four of these interpretations can be applied; but let me remind you, Revelation is a book of prophecy! So we must look for a prophetic meaning in the description of these seven churches in Asia. And it seems evident, now that we can look back, that these seven churches are a progressive picture of the history of the professing Church, from Pentecost till sometime in the possibly near future.

12

I believe, without doubt, that this is the way that God intended it to be interpreted. And I will proceed, with this in mind, to interpret the seven letters to the seven churches in detail, using every scrap of evidence which the Holy Spirit sees fit to give me.

God has given us a timetable which He has seen fit to reveal in this day and age. Back in 70 A.D., when Jerusalem fell, the signs of the End Times were surely present, perhaps just as much as they are now. But if this timetable had been revealed at that time, they would have known that Christ wouldn't be back for a long time. And this is true in many other times in history. Some say that every so often a cycle is completed, and the signs are right for the End Times; and some go further and say that this is just another one of those cycles. It is a cycle, but there will never be another one! And, if you interpret the 19th verse of the first chapter, and these letters to the churches as God has revealed them to me, there can be no mistake as to where we are today; or as to what Jesus thinks of His professing Church in the last period of its history.

The Bible talks much about being watchful, waiting, and being prepared to meet Christ on His return, because He will come when you don't expect Him. For over 1900 years this has been said to Christians, and the purpose was to keep them alert and faithful. So God could not reveal this timetable until we were in the last historical period of His Church—the last period before the Great Tribulations, and the Second Coming of our Lord.

I believe it is time we took a good look at ourselves, and gave ourselves some honest answers. What place does God hold in your life? Does God come first, or when it is convenient? What is the true condition of God's Church today, as a whole? Is it made up mostly of people that are willing to serve God in whatever way God wants them to? Are churches today filled with people who live and are guided by the love of Christ seven days a week? Or would you say that,

13

on the whole, Christians of today like to sit on the fence, not being too bad most of the time; but refusing to make any real decisions for Christ? Some are church members, but can't find time to get to church much. Some get to church every Sunday, but forget about Him the rest of the week. When I say on the whole, I'm referring to all denominations that profess Christ as the Son of God. And from my own observations I would say that a very high percentage of the people who claim to be Christians would fall into the "lukewarm" class. They are neither "hot" nor "cold" when it comes to Christ. We are the "Lukewarm Church."

God tells us what He thinks of the Church today in the letter to Laodicea. And He does not say, "I am about to," indicating that He hasn't made up His mind yet, or that there is a chance that He won't spit you out of His mouth. He says, "I will spew thee out of my mouth"—this is future, planned back at the time of creation. And Jesus is going to do it; at the pre-determined time. I do not know how long we have to try and change our image in the eyes of God from the "Lukewarm" church to what He wants; but I know it is a matter of great urgency. I don't mean we can change this period of church history or the timetable; but we can cause individuals to be identified with the Philadelphia part of God's Church that exists today, instead of the Laodicean part.

There is only *one church!* That is the Church of Jesus Christ. And the story of this one church from the beginning to the end can be found in the letters to the churches. Like I have said, these particular early churches describe the different forms or periods that the one Church would go through during its history. The different periods of the Church's history cannot be described as stopping and starting at a particular year, because they merge into one another, and overlap; and gradual change takes place most of the time. Also, some characteristics hold over for many years. But, remember, you have one church moving from one period to another. The description used applies to the Church as a

14

whole, not individuals, or individual churches—God's one Church.

And if you want to try and move the Church of Ephesus to this time, you have to use the complete description Jesus gives of His early church, and make it a distinct part of the whole Church today. I cannot look around and see any part of the one church today that fits the complete description of the Church of Ephesus. Some of the characteristics can describe some individuals, granted; but Jesus is not talking about individuals, but His one Church as a whole.

Try to keep this in mind as we proceed to the letters. God is making us time-travelers, enabling us to watch the spiritual behavior of His Church as it passes through seven (making it complete) distinctly different periods of time. He also is telling us exactly how He feels concerning His Church at each particular time. The dates I use are not accurate; they are there just to represent an approximate time period.

CHAPTER 4

EPHESUS
30-100 A.D.

It is very easy to think of this as just one of the early churches, which it really was; but this not our Lord's intention. He is just using this Church of Ephesus to describe the spiritual behavior of His whole Church at this particular time in church history. To make this picture as clear as possible, let's pretend that this a play with seven acts, and the name of it is "The History of Our Lord's Church." In the play, we shall illustrate changes in the church by picturing it as God's Garden.

ACT 1

Ephesus.—there is a great deal of meaning here, in the name. Many people call this the Loveless Church, which is unjust. Ephesus means full-purposed or desirable! It is said that such a term might be used by a Greek when he refers to the maiden of his choice. I find this very interesting, when you consider that the Church is to be the bride of Christ.

The Church now is like a newly planted garden; first of its kind, planted by Jesus. We have twelve plants to begin with who will help shade and teach the others. But all of the plants that make up the garden are young and tender; and some are quite small and weak yet. And Jesus knows His garden (church) needs much care and protection until they get to be established plants. This gives us a picture of the Church at the beginning.

Rev. 2:1. Unto the angel of the Church of Ephesus write; these things saith He that holdeth the seven stars in His right hand, who walketh in the midst of the seven golden candlesticks.

To the ministers of the church period represented by Ephesus. This message is from the one who controls, guides, and protects the ministry of His Church by means of the Holy Spirit; and who walks among his whole Church, which glorifies God (gold). The true body of Christ glorifies Him, and in glorifying the Son, you glorify the Father. The number seven means whole, or in this case all twelve apostles. Jesus is the center of His Church at this point, and walks among it. Understand, there could be only seven churches, or one hundred or more assemblies or churches; the number is not significant, because all the churches that profess Christ as the Son of God make up God's one or whole Church. Now, in these different churches there are individuals who have the Holy Spirit. These are people who hear (understand) and believe God's Word, and want Jesus as their Lord and Master; and are given the Holy Spirit, which brings them into union with Christ. This is the "True Church," which is only part of the "Whole Church." And there are other individuals that are still growing, and have not received that wonderful gift yet. Then there are those who are not really sincere, and only profess to be Christians. You will find that all three kinds of individuals make up God's whole Church, in all the periods of the church history.

Rev. 2:2-3. I know thy works, thy labour, and thy patience, and how thou canst not bear them which are evil: and thou hast tried them which say they are apostles, and are not, and found them liars: and hast patience, and for my name's sake hast laboured, and hast not fainted.

Now we see Jesus praising his young church. You can tell by all of the praise which Jesus has for His young church that He is proud of them. And notice that the word "patience" has been used twice because they are patiently watching and waiting His return. And He praises them twice for it. I think that is something worth remembering.

Rev. 2:4-5. Nevertheless I have somewhat against thee, because thou hast left thy first love. Remember, therefore, from whence thou art fallen, and repent, and do the first works or else I will come unto thee quickly, and will remove thy candlestick out of his place, except thou repent.

In a comparable short time, Jesus became a little disappointed in His young church. Notice that Jesus does not describe His church now as having a golden candlestick to take away; so, as a whole, His church does not glorify God anymore. This would be from their love lessening. But Jesus is speaking to the church as a whole, not individuals! You don't love me like you did at first—picture love of God as energy, transferred from God's whole Church to one point, where it lights a very large light bulb. At first, a very bright light was produced. But now the light grows dimmer. And God says to go back to the way you were at first, or the light will gradually go out altogether, and the church will actually die (be taken from them by natural means).

It is very easy to think that He is speaking to, or of, individuals here, but consider this: He was satisfied with their love at first, because He told them to go back to it. And when He is satisfied that you really love Him, you will receive the Holy Spirit! Would He be saying to those who had the Holy Spirit that they had left their first love to such an extent that He would take the church from them? No, God does not mean that! Because, once you receive the Spirit, your place in heaven is guaranteed; and this won't be taken away from you. You could lose a crown, but not salvation itself. So He could not be speaking to individuals now or any other time; but to the Church as a whole in this period of church history.

So Jesus sees His church in the very first period of its history dying, unless they turn around and go back. Keep another thing in mind; the Devil also sees the church weakening. Don't be surprised if he doesn't try to help it along!

We pictured the Church as a garden in the very beginning. Let's keep an eye on that and see what changes have taken place. Right now, we see for some reason, the plants have grown very tall, but with thin, spindly stems—perhaps from lack of care. Now, if something isn't done, they will eventually die! There is one thing in their favor, they hate weeds; for there are none around.

Rev. 2:6. But this thou hast, that thou hatest the deeds of the Nicolaitanes, which I also hate.

Even after Jesus complains, He comes back with more praise for His young church. It seems that there were some people that Jesus refers to as Nicolaitans; and He makes it quite clear that He hates them. And the early church is praised because they also hate the deeds of these people. It is debatable as to just who these people are. Some say that they were a sect that said that it was lawful to eat meat sacrificed to idols; they worshipped idols, and did not believe that God created the universe. One thing that we know is that the name Nicolaitans comes from two Greek words meaning "to conquer" and "the people." And some believe them to be some church leaders who wanted to hold office and get power over the people. They distinguished between themselves and the people as "the clergy and the laity."

Rev. 2:7. He that hath an ear, let him hear what the Spirit saith unto the churches; to him that overcometh will I give to eat of the tree of Life, which is in the midst of the paradise of God.

Notice that the first part of this verse appears in all seven letters. In the letters to Ephesus, Smyrna, and Pergamos, which represent the first three periods of church history, it appears next to the last thing in the letters. But in the letters to Thyatira, Sardis, Philadelphia, and Laodicea, which represent the last four periods of the church history, it appears as the very last message in the letter. Jesus is saying—if you really understand the meaning, then pay attention to what the Spirit of Christ says to His Church in this period. This is important information in many ways, as this is past history, from which we can surely learn. But it is more important that we learn about the history that we are involved in, so we can get a better idea of how to cope with it. And I believe that is why Jesus doesn't have these instructions at the most important part of the letter. This period of church history is no longer represented in God's whole Church today.

Now Jesus talks to the individuals of that time, and promises that all who conquer the Devil will be able to eat from the tree of life in Paradise. The only way people can conquer the Devil is through the power of the Holy Spirit, for He is more powerful than the Devil. Even though Jesus sees His church as a whole, declining in their love for Him, there are still many individuals who are receiving the Holy Spirit, and conquering the Devil. And to them Jesus promises eternal life, regardless as to what happens to the Church as a whole. What happened to this period of church history; did they repent?

CHAPTER 5

SMYRNA
100-300 A.D.

The letter to the Church of Smyrna represents the second historical period of God's whole Church. Mind you, this is not a different church; but the same one moving into another time. This pictures the true Christians being persecuted by the Roman Empire. Many of them were thrown to the lions, and many were burned at the stake. Conditions seem to be getting worse instead of better for God's children. The Devil is surely trying to destroy God's Church!

ACT 2

Smyrna—means "myrrh," which is a bitter-tasting resin exuded from certain shrubs. It is used to make incense, perfume, etc. It is frequently mentioned in Scripture in connection with preparing the dead for burial. But myrrh had to be crushed in order to give out its fragrance. You can certainly draw a parallel between this and the church represented by Smyrna. It had to be crushed beneath the iron heel of pagan Rome before it came back to loving God the way it did at first. In Act 1, God told His Church that they must repent, or the church would be taken away from them. But in Act 2, you will see that His Church does repent and, therefore, was not taken away. It would have been a very short history if it had been, and we wouldn't have His Church today.

> Rev. 2:8. And unto the angel of the Church in Smyrna write: These things saith the first and the last, which was dead, and is alive.

To the ministers of the church period represented by Smyrna. This message is from the one who created everything, and shall end everything; and also from the one who was first to be resurrected. Jesus identifies Himself with each period of the Church in a way that connects to their spiritual condition. Here Jesus shows Himself as the conqueror of death, through His resurrection; and reminds them that He prepares the way for them. This indicates that the Church had the Holy Spirit, as a whole; which is the power that true Christians receive from the resurrection.

> Rev. 2:9. I know thy works, and tribulations, and poverty, (but thou art rich) and I know the blasphemy of them which say they are Jews, and are not, but are the synagogue of Satan.

These were the days when the Church of Jesus Christ was hated, outlawed, and persecuted; and they gathered together in caves, catacombs, and other hidden places, risking their lives just to hear the Word of God. In those days, it really meant something to be a Christian. And their faith was stronger then, than probably at any other time in the Church's history. They loved Jesus and were loyal Christians. They were poor in material things; but they were rich spiritually.

Jesus says that He knows what some of the people who claim to be the Children of God are saying. They were Jews nationally; but not spiritually. They bitterly blasphemed Christ as "the hanged one" and opposed Christianity, so that in rejecting the truth their synagogue became that of Satan.

Rev. 2:10. Fear none of those things which thou shalt suffer: behold, the devil shall cast some of you into prison, that ye may be tried: and ye shall have tribulation ten days: be thou faithful until death, and I will give thee a crown of life.

Notice, Jesus has no complaints against His church of this period. He gives them only praise and encouragement!

I believe that it is significant that in the two centuries of Roman persecution, which began with Nero and ended in 312 A.D., there were ten distinct edicts demanding that governors seek out Christians everywhere and put them to death. It ended with Diocletian. Sometimes the persecution would subside for a while when an emperor came to power who did not hate the Christians; but it ended officially in 313 A.D. when the Emperor Constantine issued the Edict of Milan. So, what happens to God's Church in the second period matches up with historical events of the same time.

Continuing to picture the church as a garden, let's see what is happening there. The last time we looked, the plants were tall and spindly; but now look at them! The Devil has come in and cut all our plants off just a little above the ground! Has that Evil One destroyed our garden? Definitely not! Unknowingly, he did just what was needed. And our plants are growing back from the roots, and now they are healthy, strong, little bushy-type plants, with a deep, dark-green color. And once again our little garden gives us a perfect picture of what has happened to God's Church.

God allowed the Devil to persecute His Church in order to purify the faith, and bring His Church back to its first love, or perhaps even greater than its first love. So Satan set out to destroy God's Church; but instead, he really saved it. That sounds familiar when you think of the crucified Christ.

This period of church history has produced the most amazing records of fortitude and faith on the part of the martyrs, who praised God while being burned at the stake; and met the lions quoting Scripture and singing psalms. I am sure this is hard for most of us to even imagine; but the more they suffered for the Lord Jesus Christ, the more joyous they were in their fellowship with Him, and their witness for Him. The testimony of the dying again and again led their very persecutors to receive the Lord as their Savior, because of the convincing power of the truth displayed in the martyrs. It was only the power of the Holy Spirit, and their great expectation and hope of the return of Christ, that enabled these true Christians to die this way. Perhaps if we had a little of both it would be easier to conceive of such a thing happening.

This shows from actions what Jesus meant when He told His Church to go back to the way they loved Him at first. That love was so strong that they would die, rather than be disloyal or give up their faith. That is why I say that Christians today have never known that kind of love for our Lord, so couldn't go back to it—and why the first historical period of God's Church, represented by Ephesus, is not present today. It just doesn't apply. And, while I'm on the subject, I will also say that the second period, represented by Smyrna, is not present today, either.

Jesus says to His young church, which was now being persecuted so severely—be faithful, even if it means death. Happy are those who remain faithful under trials, because when they succeed in passing the test, they will receive the crown of life.

> Rev. 2:11. He that hath an ear, let him hear what the Spirit saith unto the churches; He that overcometh shall not be hurt of the second death.

If you understand, pay attention to what the spirit says to the church of this period. I still say that, since this is not the last thing Jesus says in the letter, it implies that this isn't too important to us now, because this historical period of God's Church is no longer represented.

Jesus tells the individuals of this period that everyone who

26

conquers the Devil shall not be hurt by the second death. Anyone who has been promised the crown of life is guaranteed eternal life. The second death concerns only the lost dead, and is the final separation from God, into torment; which is the punishment of all who have already died physically in unbelief and rebellion against God.

CHAPTER 6

PERGAMOS
300-500 A.D.

The letter to the Church of Pergamos represents the third historical period of God's whole Church. This is one time that the scene changes pretty quickly. For over two hundred years, the Christians have been persecuted; and during this time an unbelievable growth of God's Church was witnessed. Also, we have noted that their great expectation and hope was for the return of Christ. But now, all of a sudden, there was no more persecution. Constantine became emperor of the Roman Empire, and one of his first acts was to liberate the Christians and to stop all persecution. And he decreed that the religion of the Roman Empire must henceforth be Christianity. This sounds great, but is it really? Is the Devil really going to leave God's Church alone?

ACT 3

Pergamos—has two meanings, "marriage" and "elevation" (some just used "mixed marriage"). This will describe God's Church pretty well in this period, when the church was elevated to a place of power and was married to the world. The church and the state were united under Constantine. He issued the edict of Milan in 313 A.D. that stopped persecutions, and he commanded everyone in empire to accept Christianity; and also made all his armies be baptized.

> Rev. 2:12. And to the angel of the Church in Pergamos write: These things saith He which hath the sharp sword with two edges.

To the ministers of the church period represented by Pergamos, this message is from the one who has the word of God, which will either save you or condemn you. Jesus identifies with this period through the sharp two-edged sword, which is the Word of God. As I have already said, it cuts all the way through to where soul and spirit meet, and judges the desires and thoughts of men's hearts. I think Jesus is reminding His Church, since there is so much temptation around that, if they reject the Word now, it will judge them in the last day.

> Rev. 2:13. I know thy works, and where thou dwellest, even where Satan's seat is: and thou holdest fast my name, and hast not denied my faith, even in those days wherein Antipas was my faithful martyr, who was slain among you, where Satan dwelleth.

We see Jesus praising His Church of this period. He says that He knows their works, where they live, and also where Satan's throne is, which indicates that it might be close by. You see, it was at this point in the Church's history that Constantine offered to build beautiful churches; and to give a great deal of money to them. This sounded great, and the church leaders accepted his offer. He also bestowed unwanted honors on the bishops; they sat on thrones with the nobles of the empire.

It was also at this time that the truth of the Second Coming of Christ was given up, due to the change in their circumstances. Christian bishops said, "We have been looking for Christ's reign, but we have been wrong. Constantine's empire is Christ's Kingdom." They actually thought that the Church was already reigning; and this continued until the days of the Reformation. Then the light began to dawn again.

Jesus says that they held fast to His name, and did not deny their faith in Him. Remember, the Church had been purified through two hundred years of persecution. And the people who survived were strong in their faith. So, even though God's true Christians were surrounded by Satan's armies in peace, they were still faithful.

It was in this period of the church history that the Arian controversy was fought out. It was the most tremendous issue that the church had ever been called to face; and for over a century it was a burning question that provoked heated controversy everywhere. And this was the question concerning the Trinity—Father, Son, and Holy Spirit. Were they "of like substance" or "of the same substance?" We believe in ONE GOD, so if they were of like substance, that meant that Jesus was only the greatest being that God had ever brought into existence! But, if they were of the same substance, Jesus was truly God. And, finally, it was settled once and forever, in a public way; and the acknowledged faith of the Church of God held fast His Word, and did not deny His Name. So, I'm sure Jesus had this very much in mind when He was praising His Church.

Knowing that the church leaders fought over this question for one hundred years, it is not surprising that we find it difficult to understand how three persons can be one, and one can be three. But until we can understand it we can believe it by faith. If we could understand all about God, that would mean that He is no greater than ourselves; and who wants to worship such a God? But let me give you something to compare the trinity with, which may help you to get a general picture of the Trinity.

Let's compare the sun with the Trinity—God the Father, God the Son, and God the Holy Spirit. The sun is a great ball, ninety million miles away, which no man has ever seen—not even astronomers. All we see is the light from it; for it is only the light and the chemical power of the sun that comes to earth. By studying the sunlight, astronomers have learned a great deal about the sun.

And so it is with God the Father; no man has seen Him at any time! But we can learn a great deal about Him by getting to know God the Son, Jesus Christ who came to earth. Like the sunshine, He is the Light, and is called the brightness of God's glory. Just as the sunlight is the sun, Jesus Christ is God. For example:

On a cloudy day, the sun suddenly begins to shine. My child exclaims with joy, "There is the sun!", pointing to the floor. She doesn't mean that the great ball in the sky has come into our kitchen; it is the sunlight that she sees. But the sunlight and the sun are one, and we call them both "the sun." Just as God the Father, and God the Son, are one; and we call them both "God."

Then there is the third element in the sun—its chemical power. This is what you feel from the sun, the warmth that causes you to shed your coats in the spring. It is the power which causes those tiny seeds to sprout and grow into nice green plants in your garden. It is the sun!

The Holy Spirit is like that. He is the unseen power from God, which was sent down here to be our helper. It is possible to feel and see the results of His presence. He is a distinct person, yet He is one with the Father and the Son. He is God the Holy Spirit.

So the sun is (a) something which we can't see; (b) it is light; (c) it is a chemical power—just as God is the unseen Father, the Son is the light of the world, and the Holy Spirit is the chemical power.

Rev. 2:14. But I have a few things against thee, because thou hast there them that hold the doctrine of Balaam, who taught Balac to cast a stumbling block before the children of Israel, to eat things sacrificed unto idols and to commit fornication.

The doctrine of Balaam all boils down to worldly compromise—tolerance, laxness, which let worldly (pagan) practices and alliances creep in and corrupt the church. Millions of heathens, including pagan priests, without any real repentance from sin or belief in Jesus as Savior, began to call themselves Christians. The Church thought that it was great that all these people were becoming Christians. She gave up looking for the return of Christ, and settled down to enjoy heathen pleasure and power in the world. It was as if the Church became married to the world. (Remember, God intends that the Church be the bride of Christ). Many heathen customs and ceremonies were soon becoming a part of church services, almost without the true Christians realizing it. The real truth of the Gospel was to be almost hidden under a mass of ceremony, and untruth.

Rev. 2:15. So hast thou also them that hold the doctrine of the Nicolaitanes, which thing I hate.

Notice, Jesus has expressed His hate for this twice now. In the first church it was deeds or acts outside the church: but now it has become a doctrine. We discussed this doctrine in Act 1. Some believe that it all started because certain men lusting for religious power declared themselves above the rest of the people; and if this is the case, it will certainly lead us into the next historical period of the Church.

Let's go take a look at our garden, which is representing the whole Church. Remember, the Evil One did not destroy it when he cut our plants down before. And our little healthy, bushy plants are still there; but someone has been planting some red and yellow plants in here. That is strange, as the Great One who planted this garden said that only green plants were to be planted here. And the gates, which were to be kept locked, have been left open! Oh, here comes the Evil One in disguise, with more of those colorful plants. I'll ask him what he is doing.

"Hello, sir, what are you doing in here?" I questioned.

"Oh, I have come to make your garden beautiful and fragrant, more pleasing to look at," the man answered.

"But aren't you crowding our little green plants?" I ask.

"No, not at all. Don't worry, everything will be fine: just leave it to me," said the man, who smiled, and went his own way.

You must admit that he made it sound good; it seemed reasonable. After all, it will attract more people to the garden. For it looks pretty and more pleasing to the eye; but I know this was not the way it was intended to be. I'm afraid our little garden has run into trouble because they are not keeping with the rules set up by the Great Gardener long ago. And remember, it pictures what is happening to God's Church pretty well. Once more Satan is up to his tricks; he is trying to destroy the Church by worldly patronage (gates open) from the outside, and the introduction of false principles (red and yellow plants) from the inside. Since these plants represent pagan doctrines and man-made rules that crept into God's Church, beginning in this era, we will call them weeds hereafter. Will Satan succeed this time?

Rev. 2:16. Repent: or else I will come unto thee quickly, and will fight against them with the sword of my mouth.

Jesus is saying here: get rid of those evil teachings, or I will come with the sword that comes out of my mouth, and fight against those people in my church who follow those teachings. When? In Rev. 19:15, we see Jesus returning as King, and He has a sharp sword which comes out of His mouth, with which He will defeat the nations. So, in order to be in on that scene, this period of the Church would have to remain the same, and alive till the Great Tribulations, and the Second Coming of Christ—if they didn't repent. Jesus didn't bring this out very plainly because they did repent, and were allowed to fade into the past. Otherwise, they would still be seen today—a church united with the state. When did God's Church repent? It took them about 1000 years, and then the True Church separated themselves from the Mother Church—the Reformation!

> Rev. 2:17. He that hath an ear, let him hear what the Spirit saith unto the churches; to him that overcometh will I give to eat of the hidden manna, and will give him a white stone. And in the stone a new name written, which no man knoweth saving he that receiveth it.

If you understand, pay attention to what the spirit says to the church of this period. This is still not the last thing in the letter, and shows that it isn't so important, because this church is no longer representative in the whole Church today.

Jesus turns to the individuals of that time and says to all that conquer the Devil, I will give the hidden manna, or the Spirit of Christ. In John 6:32, Christ is spoken of as being the true bread which came down from heaven. It is hidden because the unbeliever will not know of it. It was true in those days, and just as true today—unless the Lord is your Master, whom you love, and believe, and obey, the power of the Holy Spirit will remain hidden from you. The white stone speaks of our acquittal in the matter of our sins, which were placed upon Jesus on the Cross. The custom of voting yes, or not guilty, with small white stones; and no, or guilty, with small black stones, is an old custom. It is still used —you have heard of being black-balled out of a fraternity or lodge. The new name on the stone will be the new name that Christ gives to us, to mark a new status, such as he did in the Old Testament: Abram-Abraham, Jacob-Israel.

CHAPTER 7

THYATIRA
500-1000 A.D.

The letter to the Church of Thyatira represents the fourth historical period of God's whole Church. Picture the Church emerging from the last period, joined in an unholy union with the world: the Church compromising principles in order to convert pagans; and heathen ceremonies gradually becoming a part of the church service. And now there is a setting-up of a distinct class of men called clergymen, and the denial of the common priesthood of all believers—which, I believe, led to the Pope being the head of the Church. Some believe that this came from the doctrine of the Nicolaitanes, which Jesus hated; whether it did or it didn't is something we will probably never know. But this I do know: John was rebuked twice for falling down on his knees in front of an angel sent by God. And I class an angel higher than the Pope or any other man on this earth. And, knowing this, I couldn't kneel before a man; but I'm not saying that you shouldn't show respect for your religious leaders. But, let me remind you, we are now referring to the professing Church of Jesus Christ which existed over 1000 years ago. This Church, which Rome became the center of, has greatly improved with age; but at this time people feared the Church because of its power and the terrible burdens that it put on the little people. At one time, the Church controlled a great deal of the known world. And they did not give up that power meekly.

Thyatira—comes from two words meaning "a sacrifice" and "that which goes on continually"; and a suggested interpretation is "continual sacrifice." This certainly seems to apply, as it was during the centuries represented by the Church of Thyatira, called the *Dark Ages,* that the completeness of the finished work of Christ was denied. And to it were added works, ceremonies, rituals, and sacrifices. Look at the praise given this period of God's whole Church. Notice that "works" are mentioned twice in describing the Church, which had turned to a religion of works, and not grace.

Rev. 2:18. And unto the angel of the Church in Thyatira write: These things saith the Son of God, who hath his eyes like unto a flame of fire and his feet are like fine brass.

To the ministers of the church period represented by Thyatira, this message is from Christ, who has eyes, from which nothing can be hid, and who has feet which will stamp out, with divine judgment, all that is unholy. It seems to me that there is a warning already in this message. For some reason Jesus seems to have found it necessary to emphasize His Deity, in connection with this period of His Church. Some believe that it could be because Rome, during this period, accustomed the people to think of Jesus as the Son of Mary.

Rev. 2:19. I know thy works, and charity, and services, and faith, and thy patience, and thy works, and the last to be more than the first.

The Lord gives this period of His Church credit for a great

deal that is good. Remember, from the 7th century, which was the beginning of the papacy, on to the present time, there has been a great deal in the way of good works in the Roman Catholic Church that can't be overlooked. There were nuns and monks who had been ready to lay down their lives for the needy and the sick. There were centuries before Luther when every hospital in Western Europe was simply a Roman Catholic monastery or convent. There are many things that this period of God's Church did that was good, and Jesus sees all and will not forget.

Rev. 2:20. Notwithstanding I have a few things against thee because thou sufferest that woman Jezebel, which calleth herself a prophetess to teach and seduce my servants to commit fornication, and to eat things sacrificied unto idols.

I notice one thing here, that Jesus has almost the same complaint about Jezebel as He had about the followers of the doctrine of Balaam in the last church period. Except, I feel this is worse, because Jesus said that the followers were in the church; but Jezebel is teaching in the Church! Jezebel was the wife of the wicked king of Israel, Ahab; and she caused Ahab to commit idolatry, and to turn from the worship of the true God.

Remember, this period of the church is called the Dark Ages; and it was during these years that the Vandals, the Huns, and the Goths overran Europe, and brought with them their own idolatrous pagan worship. The Church in a spirit of compromise, seeking to win them to professing Christianity, adopted part of the pagan idolatrous religion of these heathens, with the result that there emerged from this age a church that was partly Christian, partly Judaistic, and partly pagan. They speak of idols in connection with Jezebel, and this period; I wonder if this is when the Roman Catholic Church started having all the statues in the church, perhaps for even a different reason, 1000 years ago?

Priests declare that in the "Sacrifice of the Mass" they offer a continual sacrifice for the sins of the living and the dead; but it seems as if they are denying the finished work of Christ on Calvary's Cross—the one, and only, all-sufficient offering for the sins of a guilty world. Perhaps I'm wrong, but I wonder if all the ceremony and the act of sacrificing Christ over and over wasn't a compromised situation with the heathens when they first started doing it in the church, during this period?

God provided a perfect sacrifice for the sins of the world, so that every single person that has genuine faith in Christ will be saved. And nothing, no ceremony performed by man, can add to this, or take anything away from it. Christ has already taken care of that part. The part of the church is to make true believers of the people; this was true from the beginning of the church, and shall be true till the end of it.

Considering that the doctrines of Balaam, of the Nicolaitanes, and the teachings of Jezebel, have found their way into God's Church, I would say that it is really asking for punishment at this point in its history.

Let's go to our garden, which has been representing the whole Church, and see what has happened. When we were there last, the Evil One was there planting colorful plants, to beautify our garden, he said!

Oh, no! Look at this mess! Those plants put here by the Evil One have run wild in our garden! I don't know how I could have thought they were pretty—they look horrible now. Some are tall and hide our green ones, others have grown big around and are sapping all the food out of the soil; and that is weakening our plants. Oh, and these are the worst; they have runners, which are wrapping around our plants and choking them. How will they survive this? There are still a few of our little green plants clear of these horrible weeds; but not for long, I'm afraid. If something doesn't happen soon, the weeds will completely destroy our little garden. What a pity; it was so beautiful once. How could this happen?

Rev. 2:21. And I gave her space to repent of her fornication; and she repented not.

Yes, God's whole Church, in this historical period, did have a chance to change her ways, and go back to the truth—during the Reformation. It was called that because men like Luther, Knox, Calvin, and many others had started out to reform God's whole Church, which was now called the Roman Catholic Church. But, they would not repent!

Rev. 2:22. Behold, I will cast her into a bed, and them that commit adultery with her into great tribulation, except they repent of their deeds.

We have been talking about the church period which was 1000 to 500 years ago. But now Jesus is telling us what He is going to do with that church if they do not repent of their deeds. They will not be allowed to fade into the past; history will change them, but they will be around to be tested, in the Great Tribulations. Also, that He will cause the Church of Rome to be very attractive and inviting; and she will try to seduce the churches of the world into joining her. And all who unite with her will be thrown into the Great Tribulation of the Latter Days, unless they see their error and repent of their deeds. This will be the World Church which Antichrist will influence a great deal in the beginning. Later he will destroy any pretense of worshipping God, and demand that the nations worship him.

Rev. 2:23. And I will kill her children with death; and all churches shall know that I am He which searcheth the reins and hearts; and I will give unto every one of you according to your works.

Jesus will kill the true followers of this church in the latter days (world church) as they worship Antichrist, and will be branded as such. Jesus assures everyone that outward

41

appearances will not change anything, and all will know that He searches the minds and hearts. For each will be dealt with according to what is there, and what they have done.

Notice, this is the first message that Jesus has actually mentioned the Tribulations or His Second Coming. Of course, there is a good reason for that; this is the first period of the Church so far that will still be represented in those days.

Rev. 2:24-25. But unto you I say, and unto the rest in Thyatira, as many as have not this doctrine, and which have not known the depths of Satan, as they speak; I will put upon you none other burden. But that which ye have already hold fast till I come.

Jesus is not only talking to His Church as it was in this period of history, before the Reformation; but also to it as it will be in the latter days. During this period of church history, called the Dark Ages, there were multitudes of true Christians or "light holders" slain; but the "light" could not be put out. A remnant of true believers dared to preserve and spread the truth. To these people, who are His, He says to just hold fast to what you have till He comes.

At some future date, the churches of today will combine to make one church again, under Rome. People will be convinced that it is the right thing to do. Conditions in the world will become so bad that people will be willing to try anything. But in order to do it there will be a lot of good principles compromised. And eventually what is left of the truth will be hidden. But there will be individuals that belong to Christ (the remnant) who will still hold to the truth. And He will lay no other burden upon them. They will not be tested in the Great Tribulation. He says to them, "Just hold fast till I come," because they will be taken up in the rapture.

Rev. 2:26-28. And he that overcometh, and keepeth my works unto the end, to him will I give power over the nations; and he shall rule them with a rod of iron; as the vessels of a potter shall they be broken to shivers: even as I received of my Father. And I will give him the morning star.

Jesus says to all who are alive in the last days, and who were formally connected with the Roman Catholic Church: Unless you receive the Holy Spirit through genuine faith and love for Christ, before the rapture, you will have to remain till the end. If you then conquer Satan, and do God's works until He returns as King, He will give you power over the nations. You will rule with Him when He comes as King during the Millennium, and you will be given the Holy Spirit, which will entitle you to enter Jerusalem, and eat of the Tree of Life.

I would like to bring your attention to the word "end." This is the only place in all the letters that it appears. And I believe it refers to the end of the tribulations, when Christ returns to rule with a rod of iron over the nations. Thus, He must reign until God puts all evil under His feet. This has to be the Millennium reign, as there will be no evil on the new earth. And Satan rules the world now, within allowed limits, which is why sin and wickedness are getting worse.

Rev. 2:29. He that hath an ear, let him hear what the Spirit saith unto the churches.

This verse, which appears in all seven letters, has now been moved to a more important place—the last message in the letter. This is the first historical period of God's Church that is still represented today; and if you understand, it is very important to pay attention to what the Spirit says to the church of this period. Because this could be you they are talking about.

CHAPTER 8

SARDIS
1500-1700 A.D.

The letter to the Church of Sardis represents the fifth historical period of God's whole Church—or I could say, professing Church. God is the only one who really knows who His true Christians are, and man is in no position to judge anyone. Before the Reformation period began, the Spirit began to stir some of the true Christians. It just didn't happen all at once; but the testimony of the remnant of true believers, back in the 14th, 15th, and 16th centuries, began what is called the Renaissance. The Renaissance, which literally means "rebirth," was the name given to this great awakening, which led to the 16th-century Reformation in Europe and to the gloom of the Dark Ages being lifted.

ACT 5

Sardis—means a remnant, or those who have escaped. Many factors were instrumental in bringing about the deliverance of the Church from the Dark Ages. Among these were the discovery of America, the invention of the printing press, and the giving of the Scriptures in printed form to the laity. Up to now, there were a limited number of copies, and they belonged to a few scholars and the clergy. So the Scriptures were unknown to the common people. But, as God had planned thousands of years before, in 1550 the first complete press was finished, which resulted in a new study of the Bible. Lost truths were rediscovered, and unbiblical errors were exposed; thus setting the stage for the Reformation. Next to the early or first period of God's Church, the Reformation period was the most vital part of the history of the Christian Church. It was a revival of primitive Christian faith against the corruption which had found its way into God's Church.

Rev. 3:1. And unto the angel of the Church in Sardis write; These things saith he that hath the seven Spirits of God, and the seven stars: I know thy works, that thou has a name that thou livest, and art dead.

To the minister of the church period represented by Sardis, this message is from the one who has the Holy Spirit and has the ministry. Once more Jesus says that He has the ministry. In the letter to Ephesus, He holds the stars in his right hand; and here He just has them. So Jesus doesn't control the ministry, like in the early church; but they belong to Him. And this certainly means that there is a measure of return to the early principles described here. And I have just described the Protestant Reformation as being just that.

Also, I would like to point out again here that now you see the third period of the Church represented by Pergamos, repenting and separating from those evil teachings of the Nicoliatanes and of Jezebel. So, since God's Church as a whole will not change, we have a split in the Church. Up until now the change covered the whole Church in general.

But the Church whose light had shone brightly while they were fighting to escape the power of Rome fell eventually into a cold, lifeless formalism, which consisted of professing to believe all the doctrine of the Bible, but of failing to carry them out in their own lives. Here, the Church had a chance to really become what God wanted; but they goofed. The Catholic part of God's Church refused to change enough; but there was some reform about fifty years after the Protestant Reformation. The Protestant part of God's Church changed back to the way it should have been—in writing. But they didn't mean what they said, in their hearts, and they did not live their belief, as a whole. But, remember—through every church period there is always the remnant of "true believers," just as in every period of Jewish history there is always the remnant of "true believers." And it will be these two remnants that will reap the reward.

I wonder what has happened to our garden, which we are using to illustrate God's whole Church. Last we saw of it, it looked hopeless. Look, there are seven men leaving the garden. And, the fence on the far side has been taken down; they have expanded the garden. Well, they have dug up all our little green plants that they could from this mass of weeds, and transplanted them over in the new section. It appears as though they are going to leave this old section there. If they remove the weeds now, it will kill the green plants that are left in there.

I can't say that our little green plants look so good. They look like they are alive, as they are still green; but they haven't straightened back up and started to grow as yet. Well, sometimes plants do wilt pretty badly when they are transplanted; maybe with proper care, they will be all right. We will check on them later.

NOTICE, JESUS HAS NO PRAISE FOR HIS CHURCH OF THIS PERIOD, ONLY COMPLAINTS. Jesus says to this church period, your appearance may deceive people, and make them believe that you are alive in Christ, but as a whole you are dead. You are performing beautifully as Christians, but you feel nothing in your heart. You sing the songs of joy; but you know no joy, for my Father has not given you the Holy Spirit.

Rev. 3:2-3. Be watchful, and strengthen the things

which remain, that are ready to die: for I have not found thy works perfect before God. Remember, therefore, how thou hast received and heard, and hold fast, and repent. If therefore thou shalt not watch, I will come on thee as a thief, and thou shalt not know what hour I will come upon thee.

I would like to put in a word about the fact that three out of four versions of the Bible have changed this word "watchful" or "watch." Patiently waiting and watching or being watchful—for the return of Christ is a very important trait of true believers, and only them; and I think it is a mistake to change that word.

Jesus tells this period of His Church to prepare themselves by strengthening the things which remain, which are almost dead. He knows their condition, because they are not righteous before God, which can only be accomplished through the gift of the Holy Spirit, the giver of life. This is a free gift, but to only those who love, and trust Christ enough to humble themselves to the level of a mere servant or a slave to Him. Remember, being a servant to people is not necessarily being a servant to God! You can serve people without serving God: but you can't serve God without serving people.

Jesus also tells them to remember what they have received and heard, and to hold to it and repent. Just what was it that they had received? The Reformation Church received freedom from the evil teachings that had found their way into the Church of Rome. And they heard the true meaning of the Bible through the creeds, and the Reformation leaders. Jesus is not talking to the true Christians here, which are a part of every historical period of God's professing Church. These are only professing Christians; and they will have till the time of the Rapture to repent.

A "true believer" is prepared, and is watchful and waiting for the return of our Lord; for he has nothing to fear. The road may be a little rough prior to His return, but the rewards after that will be well worth it. And Jesus tells His

Church that, if they do not become true believers, He will come on them like a thief; which is how Jesus will come upon the unbelievers when He comes as King.

Rev. 3:4. Thou hast a few names even in Sardis which have not defiled their garments; and they shall walk with me in white: for they are worthy.

There are a few individuals, which are part of the remnant, in His Church of this period that walk with the Holy Spirit, in union with Christ. And they shall walk in white with Him later, for they are worthy. These are the born-again Christians, and they will be kept safe from the Great Tribulations, and be taken in the Rapture.

Rev. 3:5. He that overcometh, the same shall be clothed in white raiment; and I will not blot out his name out of the book of life, but I will confess his name before my Father, and before His angels.

Individuals who repent in time will be kept safe during the Tribulations. The rest of God's children will be tested by the Devil in the Great Tribulations. And, if they conquer, they will receive the same reward, the white robes; but look what they have to suffer first! And Jesus promises not to blot out their names out of the book of life, and to confess their name before God and His angels.

Rev. 3:6. He that hath an ear, let him hear what the Spirit saith unto the churches.

If you understand, pay strict attention to what the Spirit says to the church of this period, represented by Sardis. This is the last message in the letter, because it is very important. The church described here still remains, and can be seen as part of God's professing Church today. You may even be a member of such a church.

CHAPTER 9

PHILADELPHIA
1700-1900

The letter to the Church of Philadelphia represents the sixth historical period of God's whole Church. When the fifth period of God's Church, represented by Sardis, failed to live up to its name, "the remnant," God began to deal again with the faithful remnant within the professing Church. And He called out the Church of Philadelphia, or the sixth historical period of God's Church.

Now that we are beginning to have more than one church period still present, perhaps I'd better explain further. The historical period that the Church is in refers to the description of, by far, the largest part of God's Church at that time.

It is just as if I were to say that I live in a Catholic block or area, because mostly Catholics live here at this time. But there are some Lutherans that live here, too. And, together, they make up the people that live here. But in ten years, this same area could be a Baptist block, Baptist now being the majority; but some Catholics and Lutherans still remain. The block is always described by the name of the majority at the time.

So keep in mind that, even though this is the sixth historical period of God's Church represented by Philadelphia, two

51

other parts of God's Church are still present: those represented by Sardis and Thyatira.

ACT 6

Philadelphia—means "brotherly love." I would say that means to love your fellow man, to help him in all ways possible. But the one thing which is more important than anything in this world is to help him to be a born-again Christian. This must come first, because this means eternal life, and it gives you a true helper and teacher in this life. You must hear and believe the Word of God. You must love and accept Jesus as your Lord and Master; and seriously repent by changing your ways. And He will give you the precious gift of His Spirit, and make you a part of His True Church. This is the most valuable thing that you can receive in your lifetime on this earth. But you must hear and believe—that is the only way! And this historical period of God's Church pictures it in a revival period, when God's servants were concerned about this important need of their fellow man. It started in Europe, and then the British Isles; and by 1800 it had spread to the Western frontier, beginning in Logan County, Kentucky. The truth of the return of the Lord was revived, and as a result, the true Christians were inspired and fired up with their responsibility. And God raised up men full of power, zeal, fire, and passion for souls, in order to awaken the dead Church. And they went through the country calling on sinners to repent, and for saints to awaken to their privileges. So, in this period, missionary fire broke out. Results were seen in new believers, churches, denominations, new colleges, new seminaries, a spread of domestic and foreign missionary work, and formation of numerous Bible societies. Yes, indeed, this surely was a great period for God's Church.

Rev. 3:7. And to the angel of the Church of Philadelphia write: These things saith He that is holy, He that is true, He that hath the key of David, He that openeth, and no man shutteth; and shutteth, and no man openeth.

To the ministers of the church period represented by Philadelphia. This message is from the one who is faithful, and genuinely reliable. Here He is compared with Eliakim, a servant of the House of David, who was holder of the keys to the treasure house. Jesus, the true servant of God, holds the keys to everything in God's great treasure house. He can open the door to the great treasure house of divine truth, which is the Bible. He also has the power to open that door to you, and no man can shut this door. But, on the other hand, in case of an unwillingness to walk in truth, He can shut the door, and no man can open it.

There are many treasures in the Bible which we need to learn about, and believe. Listen to what John says in 1 John 2:27: But as for you, Christ has poured out His Spirit on you; as long as His Spirit remains in you, you do not need anyone to teach you. For the Spirit teaches you about everything, and what He teaches is true, not false. Obey the Spirit's teachings, then, and remain in Christ. (This is quoted from *Good News for Modern Man*).

Many teach that this and many other things in the Bible were meant only for the apostles of that day. And that is why we of today can't do the things that they could do during the Apostolic Period. I do not believe this is true; but it is a much easier answer to millions of professing Christians today, when they ask why it doesn't happen now as it did then. I think the answer is here:

James 1:5-7. If any of you lack wisdom, let him ask of God, that giveth to all men liberally, and upbraideth not; and it shall be given him. But let him ask in faith, nothing wavering; for he that wavereth is like a wave of the sea driven with the wind and tossed. For let not that man think that he shall receive anything of the Lord.

James says, ask and you shall receive, but when you ask, there must not be any doubt as to whether you will receive or not. You must be able to say thank you, knowing that He will answer your prayer. This requires a lot of faith—more than most people have today. Then there are many people with the Holy Spirit, which is the only requirement, who are afraid to exercise their rights—afraid they won't work. But I say to those who have been born again, it works, if you believe it does. Otherwise, I couldn't have begun to write this book. Through Christ, all things are possible; but you must let Him show you, and depend on Him to do so, and HE WILL!

Rev. 3:8. I know thy works: behold, I have set before thee an open door, and no man can shut it; for thou hast a little strength, and hast kept my word, and hast not denied my name.

Jesus is talking about the remnant of true believers of this time, which are represented by the Church of Philadelphia, the largest part of God's professing Church in the sixth period of its history. So far, I have not found one interpretation which I feel is correct, when it comes to this verse. Let's deal with the "open door" that Jesus sets before his faithful church. One author gets through it by saying that this is the missionary age and this church has an open door—open door of mission. Radio and TV have opened up other doors for mission. Another author comes a little closer and says the Lord Himself opens the door for those whom He sends forth. OK. True, there are a lot of doors open to mission work; but all of those doors can be closed by man. Russia is a good example; Germany another. Not only this; we can't lose sight of the fact that Jesus is talking to God's whole Church, represented by Philadelphia at this time, and not individuals —right now. After all, not every individual that is a true Christian is suited for mission work—so where would their open door be? No, this door is open to all born-again Christians! And *no man* can shut it. So, these doors are not the one Jesus is talking about. Keep in mind that this is God's True Church, which He is very pleased with, and He is showing it. He says—I know what you have been doing, and because of it, I have set before you an open door (this connects with the introduction). This door leads to God's treasure house, which Jesus holds the keys for. The Holy Spirit and heaven, and all its rewards are in there! And these are the rewards Jesus gives His true believers, and *no man* can shut this door!

Then He goes on to praise His Church: for you have a little strength. (Different Bible translations again change the meaning. One version says, "I know that you have but little power" means the same? No! Here it says I know you are weak.) Jesus is saying—I'm proud of you, because now you have a little strength; they had none before, so this is a great improvement! And He continues: You have obeyed my Word, you have loved me, accepted me as your Master, and acknowledged that I AM THE SON OF GOD. Jesus has nothing but the highest praise for this part of His whole Church at this time.

Let's go and pay our little garden a visit, and see how it will picture God's whole Church now. I see the section that had so many of those red and yellow weeds in it; and next to them is the section where our little green plants were transplanted. I must say that they don't look any better than they did, still green on the outside; but no strength from within. But there seem to be some missing; perhaps they died. No, look over there on that little hill! My, look at the size of our plants; and the soil is so black over there. Well, of course, once more those seven men have transplanted the little bushy plants that had taken root and started to grow here, over to the new section of the hill, And have left the ones which seem to be fighting a disease. So now we have three sections to our garden.

Let's walk over and take a closer look at the new section. Boy, I just can't get over how big and beautiful they have gotten! Well, what do you know? These larger plants have produced little flowers on them. They look like little stars, and if I didn't know better, I would say that they seem to be giving off light!

Since this period of God's whole Church produced ministers of Christ, giving light to the world, our little garden has painted a beautiful picture of it.

> Rev. 3:9. Behold, I will make them of the synagogue of Satan, which say they are Jews, and are not, but do lie; behold, I will make them to come and worship before thy feet, and to know that I have loved thee.

Of course, Jesus is talking about the future now. We have already seen that these people are Jews nationally; but not spiritually. They are not the remnant which Christ will save and make a new covenant with. They are people who will have to come to Jerusalem once a year to worship the King; and to keep the feast of tabernacles. And, the born-again Christians, are the resurrected saints, which will serve our King in the temple. So, they will know that God has loved us.

> Rev. 3:10. Because thou hast kept the word of my patience, I also will keep thee from the hour of temptation, which shall come upon the world, to try them that dwell upon the earth.

Some have given up on Christ's return long ago; but because you believe I will return, as I told you; and are patiently waiting, and watching for me, I shall keep you from the hour of temptation that shall come upon the world. There is no doubt that Jesus is speaking about the Great Tribulation, which is described at length after the seven letters to the churches in this prophetic book. Jesus is talking to His born-again Christians that will be alive in those days represented by the Philadelphia Church. This is the largest part of the whole church in the sixth historical period, but will be a very small part of the whole church in the Seventh historical period. (I imagine that, percentage-wise, God's record shows that to be true now, in 1973). Like I said, this promise is to believers who are on the earth at the time Jesus separates Himself from the professing Church, because it is so distasteful to Him. (I will spew you out of my mouth). I also will "keep you from" means to "protect someone from something"—rapturing the church (True Church) would do this. And they have some good arguments for this theory. And in all fairness, I must say that, as far as I know, most people that look for the Rapture hold to this theory; that the Rapture will come before the Tribulations. But I have known for some time—in fact, since March 14, 1972—that the Rapture would not occur at this time. And even if I must stand against the world on this point, I will do so. But this is not as important to the True Church as you might first believe, because God will keep us safe, just as He says He will, regardless of how He does it. I refer you to the priestly prayer made by Jesus:

John 17:15. I pray not that thou shouldest take them out of the world, but that thou shouldest keep them from the Evil.

One author, acknowledges this prayer, but says since that "hour" which they are to be kept from is worldwide, and inescapable for all the earth dwellers "kept from" suggests removal from the scene—Rapture. I'm afraid this author missed a very important point. "True Christians" are not these that dwell on the earth; we are not of this world. The Scriptures tell you this in many places:

John 15:19. If ye were of the world, the world would love his own; but because ye are not of the world, but I have chosen you out of the world, therefore the world hated you.

John 17:14. I have given them thy word, and the world hath hated them because they are not of the world even as I am not of the world.

John 17:16. They are not of the world, even as I am not of the world.

Just in case you think that Jesus is just talking about his twelve apostles, here is one of the following verses:

John 17:20. Neither pray I for these alone; but for them also which shall believe on me through their word.

And the Bible also states who those who dwell on the earth are. They are mentioned in Revelation several times, as those whose names were not written in the Book of Life from the foundations of the world, or the beginning of creation. The Children of God were chosen, and our names written in the Book of Life before the foundations of the world. But, mind you, they can be blotted out, before you receive the Holy Spirit. The dwellers of the earth never had their names written in the Book of Life! Another author, at this same point, recognized this, and said, "Careful reading of the various passages in which the term is found, will make it clear that 'the earth dwellers' are in contrast to those whose citizenship is in heaven." But, this second author missed the point in the priestly prayer! So he, too, claims the Rapture is before the Tribulations.

I will not go into any further explanation of the Rapture at this time. The Tribulations are for testing and judgment, and born-again Christians will be kept from it, just as Noah was when God judged the whole world. And it will not be necessary for us to be taken out of the world, no more than it was for Noah; no more than it was for the Jews to be removed from Egypt during the Plagues. The Rapture will occur, but not till a little later.

Rev. 3:11. Behold, I come quickly; hold that fast which thou hast, that no man take thy crown.

Jesus says to the True Church, "Look, I will come suddenly, so hold fast, and stay like you are, so that you don't lose your crown." The crown spoken of here is not their salvation. Salvation is guaranteed, once God gives a person the Holy Spirit. What you do for your Master after you are purchased will determine what extra rewards you will receive. The crown is the reward for your works, which will be judged.

When God gives you the Holy Spirit, after you have heard and believe, this is a stamp of ownership; you are guaranteed salvation. You have been purchased, and are His property. Now you are His servant and you follow His orders!

Ephesians 1:13-14. In whom ye also trust (Christ) *after* that *ye heard* the word of truth, the gospel of your salvation; in whom also *after* that *ye believed* (Christ), ye were sealed with the Holy Spirit of promise. Which is the earnest (guarantee) of our inheritance, until the redemption (when the Lord returns) of the purchased possession, unto the praise of His glory.

Now you have until the Tribulations starts, or until Jesus separates Himself from the professing Church, to conquer and become a true, born-again Christian.

Rev. 3:12. Him that overcometh will I make a pillar in the temple of my God, and he shall go no more out: And I will write upon him the name of God, and the name of the city of my God, is new Jerusalem, which cometh down out of heaven from my God: And I will write upon him my new name.

I am certain that we will serve our King in the Millennium temple, built by man, for the bride shall always be with Christ. But, what is even more important, we shall be a pillar, a permanent part of the temple of God, never to leave it. We will not have to go out from the direct influence of our King, while He reigns on earth. There will be no temple in the Holy City that comes down from heaven. But it is made clear that we shall live in the Holy City on the New Earth, by all the identifying names that Jesus will put on us. We are clearly marked as possessions of Jesus. I really believe that all is involved in this, is beyond our comprehension; but it will be great, and eternal—endless.

Rev. 3:13. He that hath an ear let him hear what the Spirit saith unto the churches.

If you understand, pay close attention to what the Spirit says to the church of this period, represented by Philadelphia. This remains the last thing in the letter because it is so important that you know what is possible; and because this church is still represented. So you can still gain membership into God's True Church. Don't get the idea that I'm referring to a particular denomination. For the True Church is not referring to a church; but to individuals who have heard and believed the Gospel, and have genuine faith in our Lord Jesus Christ.

CHAPTER 10

LAODICEA
1900—TO THE END A.D.

The letter to the Church of Laodicea represents the Seventh historical period of God's whole Church. It is not only the Seventh, it is the last; this will complete the whole history of God's Church. The lukewarmness of today's professing Christians, combined with the increasing influence of Satan, will destroy the Church eventually, which is what Jesus is describing when He says that He will spue us out of His mouth. Perhaps this doesn't seem likely now to some people—how much more unlikely it must have seemed back in the revival period of God's Church! But history has proved how fast outside influences can change things; remember when Constantine became emperor of Rome? We cannot in any way change God's Plans for His Church, which were laid out and set long ago. All that can be done now is to try to change individuals.

ACT 7 (Final Act)

Laodicea—is a compound word and means "the rights of the people" or "people speak." I can't think of another term which applies more to today's affairs. There is always a battle going on about rights. How different it will be some day—right here on earth, when Christ is King. People are becoming so involved in worldly affairs, both difficulties and pleasures, and cutting God out of everything, because to leave Him in might infringe on someone's rights! Well, you go right ahead and worry about those people—help enforce those laws that say, "No prayer in schools." God, Christ, or your religion is not to be discussed at school, or you are subject to having to write 1000 lines! But how are you going to explain to Jesus that you helped cut Him out because of some people's rights? Perhaps Satan will help you; he seems to be doing OK now!

> Rev. 3:14. And unto the angel of the Church of the Laodiceans write: These things saith the Amen, the faithful and true witness, the beginning of the creation of God.

To the ministry of the Church period represented by Laodicea. This message is from the one who has the final word. Christ as judge has here identified Himself with this last period of His professing Church, with a striking contrast. The Amen, the establisher of all God's promises, who has the final say-so on everything. You must go through Him; the faithful and true witness. Then He tells of His sovereignty over all creation. All things were made by Him and for Him.

NOTICE: JESUS HAS NO PRAISE FOR HIS CHURCH OF THIS PERIOD, ONLY COMPLAINTS.

No, Jesus does not praise the church of this period; and in case you have fallen asleep somewhere along the line, this is us that Jesus is describing—a historical period of God's Church when she cares more for the words of man than for the Words of God. Ministers do not tell people of their true condition because the people don't want to hear it, and may criticize them; people don't want to witness because they are afraid of what other people will say or think. The words of man which I speak of are *praise*.

> Rev. 3:15-16. I know thy works, that thou art neither cold nor hot! I would thou were cold or hot. So then because thou art lukewarm, and neither cold nor hot, I will spew thee out of my mouth.

Jesus knows what we are doing. He sees His Church, as a whole, being neither cold towards Him nor being fired up with enthusiasm over Him. We are riding the fence, so to speak. We want to play games with the Devil on one side, but to be able to check with Christ on the other side. Particularly on Sunday, once in awhile; just to let Him know that we still think it was nice of Him to make it so easy for us. And to those who believe that, I say that being a true Christian is not easy! And that easy road is leading straight to hell.

Jesus says that He wishes that we were one or the other, for then He wouldn't have to do this difficult thing. But, because we are lukewarm, He is going to spit us out of His mouth. There is no doubt about it—He is going to, and you can't change it! Oh, the individuals aren't lost yet; for they which are alive when this happens will have a chance to prove whether their faith is genuine or not in the Great Tribulations! And, if they fail this test, they will suffer the Wrath of God, along with the dwellers of the earth. Of course, if they were to become like the church represented by Philadelphia, they wouldn't have any problems. So, everyone today in God's whole Church still has a choice; the door is still open. He has not spit us out of his mouth yet. How long do we have? I don't know; but I do know we do not have enough time left to convert all the lukewarm Christians that will be alive, when the door is closed by Jesus—even if we could. And every minute which is wasted now could add up to tribulation later for someone you know.

Rev. 3:17. Because thou sayest, I am rich, and increased with goods, and have need of nothing: and knowest not that thou art wretched, and miserable, and poor, and blind, and naked.

God's whole Church today appears to be better off than they have been in ages. People have more money, and would rather give a little more, and not be bothered to do any real work for Christ. God's professing Christian Church, as a rule, has nice buildings to meet in, and much money is spent in keeping it that way. Some have almost turned into social centers to attract more people to their church, and this trend will continue; only more so, as time gets shorter. It is great to have large numbers of people in church; but if they are not truly holy numbers, and are there to hear and learn about our Lord, then they are worthless in the eyes of God. A church full of nearly dead people is no good to anyone, unless you can find a way to put life into them. I am not talking about any one church or individual; I am saying that, as a whole, the professing church of today is proud and rather self-satisfied as to their condition.

Jesus says that His Church of this historical period, as a whole, don't know that they are unsatisfactory, inadequate, poor, blind, and naked. I believe that this is the worst condition of all, because as long as people don't know that they are not right with God, they won't do anything about it. People believe that they have it made, so why should they come to church regularly; why should they study the Gospel like their life depended on it? This is too much bother, when there are so many other things that this world provides for them to do. In this modern age, there are more and more things pulling people away from the professing Church, which for the most part is the only place where they hear the word of God. And this will continue to get worse, unless the ministry of this period gives the people a good reason why they must put everything aside and work at becoming true Christians in the eyes of God.

Mind you, Jesus is not speaking to a group of unbelievers outside the Church! He is talking to His professing Christian Church! Now, I am sure, as a whole, the Church has felt that everything was fine between them and God, or surely they would have been doing something about it before now. And just in case you have a tendency to want to believe that Jesus is not talking about us, but someone else, you had better think again, as your life may depend on it. Not just your life on earth, either! Because Jesus is speaking of the largest percentage of His whole Church during the seventh and last historical stage. You are lukewarm! There may be a zeal for organization, but an indifference to the Gospel. The rights of the people alone must be considered; the rights of our Lord are not even thought of. His rules may be too rigid for our comfort; so, we either soften the rules, or find it easier to go on and leave Christ out of this particular area of the Church. Christ created His Church and expects to be the center around which everything revolves. No wonder He sees us as unsatisfactory, and inadequate. We are poor because of our lack of true, genuine faith in our Lord Jesus Christ, which is the key to all things. We are blind and do not know the truth, or the true meaning of the Word of God—due to being poor. We are naked; we do not have the clothing which Jesus provides that covers and destroys our sinful record—due to being poor.

How could Jesus say these things about the largest percentage of His whole professing Church today? What has gone wrong that has let the Church get into this condition, and caused Jesus to look upon us in this manner? Just a century ago, Jesus had nothing but praise for His whole Church. How has Satan led the Church into a false sense of security? Jesus says that the Church does not know that they are unsatisfactory, inadequate, poor, blind and naked! To think that we have been fooled into thinking that we are alright with God! It is a shock to find this out now, when we can still do something—what about those who don't find out until it is too late to do anything? How much greater the shock will be then! Remember, I'm not speaking about every individual, or every church of today; but of God's Church as a whole. But to all I say that there is always room for improvement.

Rev. 3:18. I counsel thee to buy of me gold tried in the fire, that thou mayest be rich; and white raiment, that thou mayest be clothed, and that the shame of thy nakedness do not appear; and anoint thine eyes with eyesalve, that thou mayest see.

Now Jesus gives His whole Church of this period some advice. He says to acquire from Him gold refined or purified by fire, which refers to pure or genuine faith, which glorifies God. Faith is gold—the more you have, the richer you are! Also, acquire the white robes of forgiveness which cover the shame of your sins, so they will not count against you on that Day. And, last, Jesus says to receive the Holy Spirit, who will open your eyes to the truth, so that you may truly see and understand the Word of God.

Rev. 3:19-20. As many as I love, I rebuke, and chasten; be zealous therefore, and repent. Behold, I stand at the door and knock: if any mean hear my voice, and open the door, I will come in to him, and will sup with him, and he with me.

Some believe that God doesn't punish His children here on earth; but He says that He does. Just as a loving Father, He criticizes and disciplines His children; so, therefore, be enthusiastic and turn from sins, and come to Christ as His servant.

Jesus pictured Himself walking among His Church and holding the ministers in His right hand, in the earliest historical period; but now He pictures Himself on the outside of His Church. But He is still extending the invitation to the individuals. He says that if anyone truly believes His words, and opens the door (by his own will), that He, in the form the Holy Spirit, will come in to him, and they will sup together.

Notice that in this letter Jesus turns to the individuals of the time, earlier than usual. This is because His Church as a whole has rejected His invitation, so he is still waiting for some individuals. Now, understand, if you accept His invitation and are reborn with the Spirit, this identifies you with the Philadelphia period of His Church, and your problems with God are over. Yes, you must make peace with God, and then He will give you that peace, which is really beyond all human understanding or description. But if you do not, and are still alive, you will be tested in the Great Tribulations; and in order to pass this test, you may have to prove your faith with your life (martyrdom). It seems to be plain that many will. Is your faith strong enough for this test?

I wonder what has happened to our garden? Let's go and see how it pictures God's whole Church now. The section with the red and yellow weeds is still there, and here is a sign, which reads "Thyatira." There is the section which is green on the outside, but still seems to be struggling with a disease, and won't grow. The sign here reads "Sardis." And here is a new section; the plants here are a mixed color of brown and green, and very small. They don't appear to be dead or alive at this point. Some will probably make it; but it looks as if most of them will die, particularly if they have to endure anything but the best conditions. Here the sign reads "Laodicea"; but I wonder where they came from?

Let's go up on the hill and see the section that was so beautiful the last time we were here. It is separated from these three—and, look, they are starting to build a fence around it. There aren't so many plants now. I see they took all the plants which didn't grow and flower, and put them down in the new patch. What few plants that are left are still just as beautiful as they were before, and still have those little star-like flowers that seem to give off light. Their beauty makes it worthwhile coming to see the garden. And here is a sign that reads "Philadelphia." Oh, here comes the man who is working on the fence!

"Hello, sir. Could you tell me why you are fencing in this little section which is so beautiful?" I ask.

The kindly old gentleman looked at His beautiful plants lovingly and said, "But you have it wrong. I am not fencing it in. I am fencing the other sections out, for this is really my true garden. And this fence will protect it from the Evil One, who keeps trying to destroy my plants."

"But, sir, what will happen to the other three sections?" I asked.

He said, "Any of the plants that really come alive, and grow big enough to flower, before I finish building the fence, will be transplanted over here. But, once the fence is finished they will be left out to fight the Evil One, who is coming in force."

"Thank you, sir, for being so kind, and taking the time to explain all this to me," I said.

He smiled and went back to His garden, and seemed to disappear among His plants.

> Rev. 3:21. To him that overcometh will I grant to sit with me in my throne, even as I also overcame, and am set down with my Father in His throne.

I believe that Jesus is talking to the ones who conquer Satan during the Great Tribulations. And it seems to me that He is making a comparison. He compares those who conquer the Devil, and who are identified with this part (lukewarm) of His whole Church at the end of the Church Age with Himself, who has conquered the Devil at the Cross. And the reward will be of the highest that will be granted —to share His throne. But the test will be supreme! Let's look and compare this verse:

> Rev. 20:4. And I saw thrones, and they sat upon them, and judgment was given unto them; and I saw souls of them that were beheaded for the witness of Jesus, and for the word of God, and which had not worshipped the

beast, neither his image, neither had received his mark upon their foreheads, or in their hands; and they lived and reigned with Christ a thousand years.

So I believe there will be a lot of people who will be required to pay the supreme price to prove their faith is genuine. As for myself, I preferred to prove that my faith was genuine before that time, once I found out about it.

Rev. 3:22. He that hath an ear, let him hear what the Spirit saith unto the churches.

If you understand, pay particular attention to what the spirit says to the church of this period represented by Laodicea. This is the last message that Christ gives to His professing Church. And this will affect you directly if you are still alive at the time of the Great Tribulations.

There are still four historical stages of God's Church represented today by individuals; and this is how you will be judged, not by what church you go to. We might say there are four different types of professing Christians that belong to God's Church: (1) those that follow the doctrine of Rome; (2) those that go through the motions mechanically, without meaning or feeling; (3) those reborn in Christ who let the Holy Spirit lead them; (4) those who are lukewarm who try to sit on the fence and not make any decisions to go either way. This type, which is found in all our different churches (denominations), makes up by far the largest part of God's Church of today. We do not know when the tribulations will start. But if you are alive, and can't be identified with type three, regardless of what church you go to, you will have to deal with them—that is a fact! And, right now, that would be an awful lot of people. What has gone wrong? What are the reasons for the false sense of security? I repeat these things because it is urgent that you recognize what the trouble is.

I have already said that, in order to get the people back

into the churches where they can hear the Word of God, the people have to be convinced that it is of the utmost importance to them. Some people have gotten the idea that church and Bible study are not really important—after all, God understands that we have a lot of other things to do. Grant you, it is true that you do not have to be in a church to worship God; but how much time is spent with God outside the church, generally speaking?

I believe one of the causes behind this attitude of so many is a movement which seems to be within a lot of churches today. And that is religious liberalism, which emphasizes freedom from tradition and authority, and adjusts the beliefs to the spiritual capacities of men. That is to say that a Christian's faith is to bow to human reason. This is not new in the history of the Church. Proud human reason has rebelled against the authority of the Word of God from the very beginning. But in different times in church history, certain trends seem to be present more than at other times.

This liberalism appeals to a lot of people, as they can more easily justify their own actions when they do not have to accept the Bible as the infallible Word of God. It seems that the most used excuse for discrediting and discarding things which are written in the Bible is "that it really was more of a Jewish belief which has influenced the writer and doesn't apply to Christians." It is a dangerous thing to start changing the Word of God; even translating it into terms easier to understand. But to reduce it to human reasoning will be disastrous, as in time the Bible will become just another book. And I'm sure God will not look kindly on the Church for doing that! Believe me, if you honestly seek the truth of the Word of God, you must do so through the Holy Spirit, who will teach you all things. It is good to ask questions with the idea of learning more about God and His Son. But to question the Bible in an effort to discredit it is something else. The Bible is the infallible Word of God; and when I stand before Christ, I don't want to be in such a position as to explain why I tried to discredit it.

Philadelphia

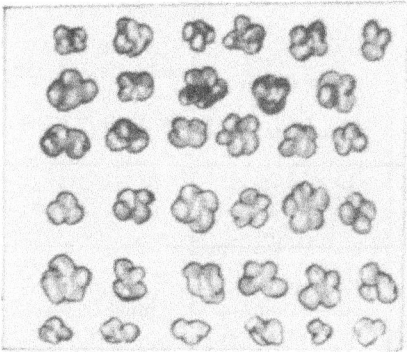

Laoticea

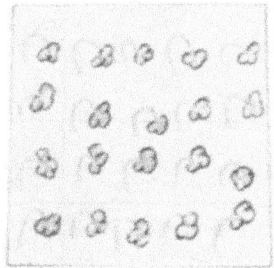

Thyatira

Sardis

Our Garden as it Looks Today
Picturing God's Church

EPHESUS	SMYRNA	PERGAMOS	THYATIRA
desirable	—MYRRH— Must be Crushed	elevated & marriage	Continual- Sacrifice
Jesus Holds Ministry	Jesus is Resurrection	Jesus is the Word	Jesus is Son of God
Praise: Much	Praise: much and understanding	Praise: true even with Satan near	Praise: Many Works
Complaints: Few Lessening of love	**COMPLAINTS:** **NONE**	Complaints: *Teachings* of Balaam and Nicolaitanes	Complaints: tolerate Jezebel idolatry Heathen Practises
Hate *deeds* of Nicolaitanes	IF YOU HAVE EARS, LISTEN NOT LAST	IF YOU HAVE EARS, LISTEN NOT LAST	IF YOU HAVE EARS, LISTEN LAST
IF YOU HAVE EARS LISTEN—NOT LAST Reward-Victorers eternal-life	Reward-victorers Crown of life not hurt by second death	Reward: Hidden manna and white stone	Reward: must endure to END power to rule
Repented	None needed	Repented	Didn't Repent
NOT PRESENT	NOT PRESENT	NOT PRESENT	PRESENT
30-100 A.D.	100-300 A.D.	300-500 A.D.	Will be tested
			500-1500 A.D.

CHURCH HISTORY,

72

SARDIS	PHILADELPHIA	LAODICEA
Remnant-Escaped	Brotherly Love	Rights of People
Jesus has Ministry	Jesus is the Key	Jesus is Sharp Contrast
PRAISE: NONE	Praise: much will Keep Safe from Tribulations	**PRAISE: NONE**
Complaints Reputation of being-alive but are dead	**COMPLAINTS: NONE**	Complaints: Lukewarm Unsatisfactory, Poor, Naked, and Blind
IF YOU HAVE EARS, LISTEN LAST	IF YOU HAVE EARS, LISTEN LAST	IF YOU HAVE EARS, LISTEN LAST
Reward: Walk in white not blot your name out of book	Reward: Many An open door Pillar in Temple New Names	Reward: is Great—Share Throne with Jesus—Test of Faith Supreme
Didn't Repent	None-needed	Didn't Repent
PRESENT	PRESENT	PRESENT
Will be tested	Safe	Will be Tested
1500-1800 AD	1800-1914 AD	1914-END

AT A GLANCE

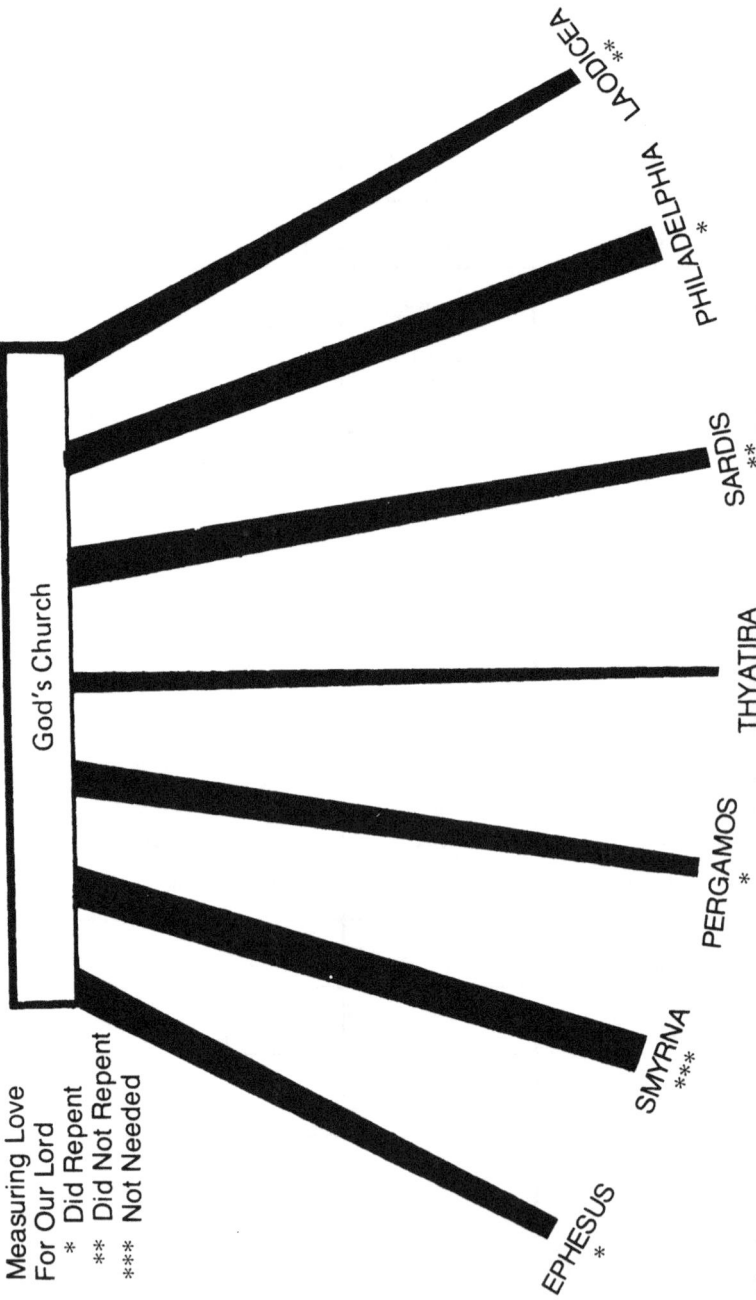

HISTORY OF ONE CHURCH

God's Church

Measuring Love
For Our Lord
    *   Did Repent
   **   Did Not Repent
  ***   Not Needed

EPHESUS
*

SMYRNA
***

PERGAMOS
*

THYATIRA

SARDIS
**

PHILADELPHIA
*

LAODICEA
**

74

CHAPTER 11

THE SEVEN DISPENSATIONS

Before we go into the 4th chapter of the Book of Revelation, I would like to acquaint you with a theory which some people have concerning God's life-plan for His Creation. I don't think this theory can be proven one way or another, but it certainly seems to fit the picture.

Sometimes we stand too close to the trees to see the forest. We have a tendency to just zero in on our part of the picture, and forget about the rest. We need to step back and view the whole picture; then we are able to view our part of it with the proper perspective. And I believe that this theory helps us to that.

This theory points out that, according to the Scriptures, the complete life-plan that God had laid out for His Creation can be divided into seven unequal periods of time, called dispensations or ages. These seven dispensations describe mankind from the creation of Adam to the new heaven and new earth. These ages are marked off in Scripture by some change in God's method of dealing with mankind in respect to sin, and of man's responsibility. I will proceed to run through these seven different ages briefly:

1. *Age of Innocence*—Genesis 1:28-Genesis 3:22.

This one didn't last long! From the creation of Adam until

Adam and Eve were run out of the Garden of Eden, which was their judgment for the sin of disobedience. They ate the forbidden fruit from the tree of knowledge of good and evil.

2. *Age of Conscience*—Genesis 3:23-Genesis 8:22.

Because of the fall of Adam, man had the knowledge of good and evil, or a conscience; and was given the responsibility to do good, not evil. But man failed and became corrupt, and wickedness of man was great on the earth. And the judgment of this Age was the Flood of Noah's day.

3. *Age of Human Government*—Genesis 9:1-Genesis 11:9.

The Flood purified the earth and left eight people still alive. God gave to these people the authority over everything else on the earth. The day came when they decided to build a tall tower with the heavens in its top. (This could have been a temple in which to worship the sun, moon, and the stars! There are temples like this still in Egypt with the signs of the Zodiac pictured around the top). God decided that this was just the beginning of what they would do; and nothing that they purposed to do would be impossible, making them independent of Him! The judgment of this age caused this place to be called Babel because God confused their tongues. They all began to speak different languages, and couldn't understand each other.

4. *Age of Promise*—Genesis 12:1-Exodus 19:2.

God called one man, Abram, from the descendants of the builders of Babel and made a covenant with him. Abraham became the father of the Jewish religion, and circumcision was the sign of this covenant. God will keep His promise to Abraham's true descendants when He returns as King. But this dispensation closed in the judgement of the Egyptian Bondage for the Israelites.

5. *Age of Law*—Exodus 19:3—Matthew 27:35.

God once again came to the aid of His people and picked

Moses to lead them out of bondage. And, out in the wilderness, God gave them the covenant of the Law; and the Israelites said, "All that the Lord has spoken, we will do." But history shows that they went from bad to worse; and they came under judgement again, and were carried away to Babylon. In time Christ came, born of a woman—made under Law. They rejected Him as the Son of God and crucified Him; thus setting the stage for the next dispensation. The Jewish nations were scattered to the four corners of the earth as judgment.

6. *Age of Grace*—Acts 2:1-4-I Thessalonians 4:16.

This also is called the Church Age. This dispensation begins with Pentecost. Salvation is a gift, freely offered to both the Gentile and Jew alike, through faith in our Lord Jesus Christ. I have discussed and described this age in detail in the seven letters to the seven churches. This dispensation will end with the testing of the professing Christians, as their judgment, for their lukewarmness towards Christ.

7. *Age of the Kingdom*—I Thessalonians 4:17-Revelations 21:1.

This dispensation begins when our Lord begins to reign over the earth, after the testing of the Christians; when the kingdoms of this world become the kingdoms of our Lord. This period is commonly called the Millennium, and will last 1000 years. Our Lord will rid this earth of sin and chain up Satan in the bottomless pit while He is doing it.

For six ages man has had to battle the temptation of Satan, so we could always blame him for our failures. But, during the Seventh Age, he will not be allowed to tempt man. This is called by some the Sabbath rest, or the 7th one-thousand-year day for God's creation. And I believe that the Jewish nation calls this the Golden Age.

Hebrew 4:9. There remaineth therefore, a sabbath rest for the people of God.

77

This dispensation will end like all the rest; in judgment! The Great White Throne Judgement, which concerns the wicked dead. This will result in the second death for them.

Then a new earth and a new heaven; and ETERNITY!

We are living in the 6th dispensation—the Church Age, which started with Pentecost and still continues. Notice the chart on the following page. I have pictured the life of God's Creation according to this theory. But the timing of certain events which are to follow the Age of Grace is the way God has showed them to me.

We are living in the 6th Age; now, if we were to divide this age into seven parts, and apply the information given to us by the seven letters to the seven churches, it is clear to see that we are living in the last part of the last age before the Tribulations. To go even further, add the 19th verse of Chapter 1 of Revelation, where John was told to write what was, what is, and what will be hereafter. This just supports the same picture. And then add the fact that number seven means complete. All I can say is that it all fits, and every piece to the picture must fit.

Many times in the past, the signs seemed to be right and the good news of Christ's Second Coming was revived, and it didn't occur! If they had had these two tables, they would have known better; but now that we have them, there is no mistake as to what part of the life-plan of mankind that we are living in. What are you going to do about it?

Here is another thought which has crossed my mind. Our God is a righteous God. He even keeps the battle with the Devil sort of on equal terms. He always deals in truth and fairness. Remembering this, consider the following: God chose the Jews to be His people from Abraham to Christ, which is a period of about 2000 years. In all fairness, don't you think God would give us Christians about the same amount of time? In fact, it seems as though He is going to give us a little less time for our own sake!

Mark 13:20. And except that the Lord had shortened

those days, no flesh should be saved: but for the elect's sake whom he hath chosen, he hath shortened the days.

So we may not have 2000 years before Christ returns, which will begin the New Age. And seven years of testing will take place before that. It has been 1969 years since Christ was born. Due to a mistake in the calendar, He was actually born in 4 A.D. But do we start figuring from this point? Jesus said that He was sent to the lost sheep of Israel. It wasn't till after Pentecost that the Gospel was given to the Gentiles. So our 2000 years might not start till about the year 37 A.D., which would mean that we have been privileged to know God only 1936 years. In that case, we would have a little more time to prepare. But since we do not know how much God is going to shorten our days, we have to stop figuring right there. And nobody will ever know exactly when this will occur. But this was just another thought which makes me believe that we are approaching the days of the Great Tribulations, which precede the Second Coming of Christ—and which causes me to be so concerned about the way that people are neglecting our Lord. It is so easy for me to see these things, because I was doing the same thing a year ago! I speak from experience, not from something that man has taught me.

CREATION
of
ALL THINGS

MAN'S
FALL

Adam

TRANSLATION
of
ENOCH

Noah

TOWER
of
BABEL

BEGIN
o
ISR

Abrah

ISRA

Old
Earth

| 1. Innocence | 2. Conscience | 3. Human Government | 4. Promise |

Curse
&
Death

Flood

Language

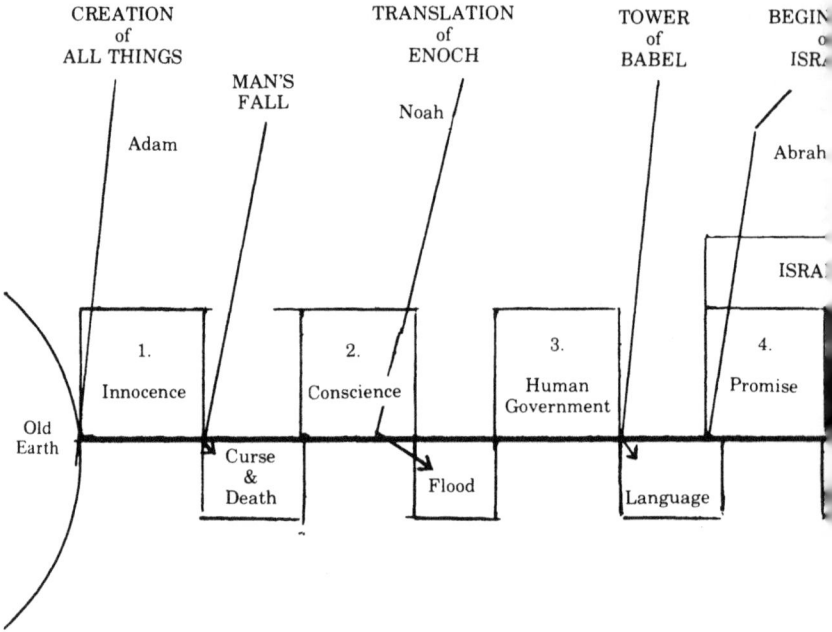

7 Different Periods of Time
7 Failures
7 Judgments

God's Complete Life Plan For His Creation

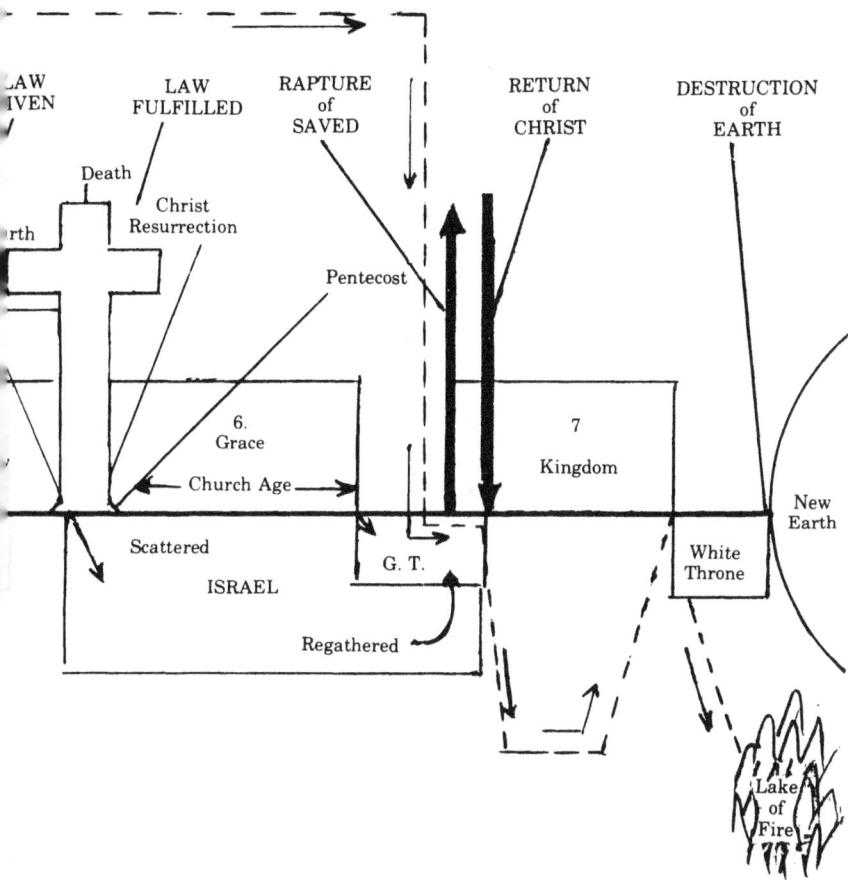

LAW
GIVEN

LAW
FULFILLED

RAPTURE
of
SAVED

RETURN
of
CHRIST

DESTRUCTION
of
EARTH

Death

Christ
Resurrection

Birth

Pentecost

6.
Grace

Church Age

7

Kingdom

New
Earth

Scattered

ISRAEL

G. T.

White
Throne

Regathered

Lake
of
Fire

81

CHAPTER 12

A DOOR OPENED FOR JOHN

Jesus holds the keys to God's great treasure house, as I have pointed out before; and has the power to open any door, to any portion of this treasure house, to any individual He desires to. He opens different doors for different individuals, who are true believers; and He also shuts the door to those who refuse to do His Will or follow His Word. And we see that to His beloved apostle John, Jesus is opening a door that has never been opened to anyone.

Rev. 4:1. After this I looked and, behold, a door was opened in heaven; and the first voice which I heard was as it were of a trumpet talking with me; which said, Come up hither, And I will shew thee things which must be hereafter.

First, let me point out again how important it is to interpret the meaning of the seven letters to the seven churches correctly. John hears a voice saying, Come up here and I will show you what must take place after this. After what? If you have chosen any meaning of the letters other than that it was the complete history of God's whole Church, I don't think you could answer that question. As the church history comes to an end as far as Jesus is concerned (He spits them out of His mouth), He will separate Himself from the Church completely, and thus deal strictly with the individuals from there on. So, when Jesus spews the Church from His mouth, you could say that the Church has become a distasteful thing to Him; and that He wants nothing more to do with it as a whole. And we never see the Church of Jesus Christ again through the rest of this prophetic book. Some use this, saying that it is not mentioned anymore because it was raptured, and no longer on earth. I say that it isn't mentioned any more because Jesus no longer recognizes that He has a professing church on earth: that is, assemblies which claim to have faith in Jesus Christ as Lord and Savior. Therefore, the history of the church comes to an end on this earth.

"Which must be hereafter" certainly indicates a plan made thousands of years ago by God. It has been almost 1900 years since the Book of Revelation was written, and I've shown how the Church has followed its history according to God's plan thus far. And I certainly have no reason to believe that we won't continue to do so.

Up to now, John's vision had been brought down to earth by an angel; many men had received visions of prophecy in this manner in the Old Testament. But, at least symbolically, John is given the honor of being allowed to go up into heaven to continue his vision of what must come to pass; and to later return to earth and deliver it to God's people. Why doesn't Jesus just continue to send the vision down to earth to John, as usual? I believe that Jesus, at least symbolically, puts John's spirit in the best possible place to view what must take place. Jesus is telling us that John can see very clearly what is going on in heaven and on earth, at the same time. Therefore, there should not be any question as to whether a particular part of John's vision actually happens in heaven, and only appears to John as if it happens on earth. We will be switching back and forth quite a bit. Jesus is enabling John to see what is to happen from the end of the Church Age till eternity. Many of the prophets received pieces of this picture through visions and dreams; but Jesus opens the door so John will get a complete picture.

Some say that John represents the True Church being raptured—that John goes up to heaven without dying when Jesus says, "Come up hither." But the whole picture doesn't fit, symbolically or otherwise. Symbolically, John went to heaven without dying; but he also returned to this earth with the same corruptible body, and the same name, to write the Book of Revelation.

> Rev. 4:2. And immediately I was in the spirit; and, behold a throne was set in heaven, and one sat on the throne.

John definitely says that he was in the spirit, so he was not taken up bodily. He may have experienced a sensation of being caught away in his spirit. Or it may be that John's spirit, for the moment, left his body, and was caught away into heaven, to see what Jesus says must come to pass. But, regardless, that special door that was opened for John will not be open for us.

John tells us that the first thing he sees when he arrived in heaven is a throne. And one sat upon the throne. Now John begins to give us a picture of what it is like up in heaven, around the throne of God, and sets the stage for the judgments that are to come. But before we go into that, let's spend a little time on the rapture itself; since we are beginning to mention it. If you happen to be as I was, perhaps you have never heard of it until now.

CHAPTER 13

WHAT IS THE RAPTURE?

I would like to check a few verses which describe the rapture, and discuss it a little at this point. The Second Coming of Christ occurs in two phases: His coming for His saints, and His coming with His saints. The first phase is called the Rapture, and the second phase is sometimes called the Revelation. There is no mystery about the second phase of His coming, except the time, which only the Father knows. Even Enoch, who lived before the Flood, prophesied the coming of the Lord with His saints, according to Jude 14. But, there is certainly a mystery concerning the first phase.

1 Corinthians 15:51-52. Behold, I shew you a mystery; We shall not all sleep, but we shall all be changed, in a moment, in the twinkling of an eye, at the last trump: for the trumpet shall sound, and the dead shall be raised incorruptible, and we shall be changed.

Jesus is telling us something very special here. Not all of God's saints will die; but all of us will be changed in the twinkling of an eye. Just think, in a twinkling of an eye, the dead in Christ will be raised. And changed from a corrupt-

87

ible body to an incorruptible body; from a mortal body which must taste death, to one which will never know death again. And all of us who are fortunate enough to still be living, shall also be changed in the same way. As of now, we must be put to sleep, in order to change bodies, like an operation! But then, it will happen so quickly that it will not be necessary to be put to sleep! Won't that be something? If it weren't for the fact that so many of the people today do not even know about this, I would wish that this would happen tomorrow; but, instead, I pray that God will give us a little more time to get the truth to the people, even if that means that I would have to miss out on the rapture. Jesus is not only telling us what is going to happen here; He is also telling us when, which is the mystery. People try to make this so complicated that they overlook the simple truths, or reject them as being too simple.

> 1 Thessalonians 4:16-17. For the Lord Himself shall descend from heaven with a shout, with the voice of the archangel, and with the trump of God; and the dead in Christ shall rise first. Then we which are alive and remain shall be caught up together with them in the clouds, to meet the Lord in the air; and so shall we ever be with the Lord.

Notice that we meet Him in the air, because He has not come to stay this time.

> Hebrews 9:28—RSV. So Christ, having been offered once to bear the sins of many, will appear a second time, not to deal with sin but to save those who are eagerly waiting for him.

When Christ begins to reign over the earth, and comes as a righteous judge and king, He will rid the earth of sin, just as the flood did in the time of Noah. So it is clear that the Bible is speaking about the Rapture here.

Hebrews 10:35-37. Cast not away therefore your confidence, which hath great recompence of reward. For ye have need of patience that, after ye have done the will of God, ye might receive the promise. For yet a little while, and he that shall come will come, and will not tarry.

We are told here to be patient, and not throw away our confidence in Christ; for it holds a rich reward for us —because, after we have done the will of God, we may receive the promise. It will be a little while yet; then He that shall come will come, but He won't tarry. And according to the two timetables that we have just discussed, that "little while" may soon be expired. And since they are referring to the time when He will not tarry or stay, it has to mean the Rapture.

Rev. 1:7. Behold, he cometh with the clouds; and every eye shall see him, and they also which pierced him; and all kindreds of the earth shall wail because of him. Even so, Amen.

It is a mystery now, as to when and how; but it will not be a secret affair, as some seem to think. He will not come as a thief! A heavenly Bridegroom would not describe Himself as such, when He comes for His Bride—the True Church, true believers, saints, His elect—whichever one you want to call them. His Bride will be expecting Him; will you? And the rest of the people will wail and be fearful of what they see. Everyone will see Him! How? I don't know; but if Jesus says so, that is the way it will be, and He will take care of it.

Matthew 24:29-31. Immediately after the tribulation of those days shall the sun be darkened, and the moon shall not give her light, and the stars shall fall from heaven and the powers of the heavens shall be shaken. And then shall appear the sign of the son of man in heaven: and shall all the tribes of the earth mourn and they shall see the Son of man coming in the clouds of heaven with power and great glory. And he shall send His angels with a great sound of a trumpet and they shall gather together his elect from the four winds, from one end of heaven to the other.

Matthew 24:40. Then shall two be in the field, the one shall be taken and the other left. The women shall be grinding at the mill, the one shall be taken and the other left.

I have tried to show you enough passages from the Bible to prove that there truly is going to be a rapture, and just what it is, before we go on to any more discussion of when it will occur.

As I mentioned, many think that John represents the "True Church" being raptured at this point, before the tribulations begin. Remember, in the Rapture, we will be raised bodily to meet Christ in the air, if we are still alive; and in an instant be made immortal, never to die. John was just raised in spirit.

CHAPTER 14

THE RAINBOW

Now we go back to the throne scene in heaven which John is describing.

Rev. 4:3. And he that sat was to look upon like a jasper and a sardine stone: and there was a rainbow round about the throne, in sight like an emerald.

John says that he beheld a Presence whose glory was like a jasper and a sardine stone. The jasper is described later in Rev. 21:11 as being clear as crystal, and is probably the diamond: the most brilliant of all the precious jewels. The other stone is blood red, and may really be the ruby. Thus the two together give the idea of glory and of sacrifice. Of course the Jews of this day will recall that they were the first and the last stones in the breastplate of the high priest. You see, the high priest in the Old Testament Tabernacle carried on his robe, over his heart, the breastplate of judgment. In it were twelve precious stones arranged in four rows. The first stone was a sardius, the blood-red stone, which had the name of the first-born, Reuben, engraved on it. The last stone in the last row was a jasper, a clear, transparent stone with the name of Benjamin engraved upon it.

Between these were the stones and names of all the other tribes of Israel. Everywhere the priest went in the Holy Place, he bore these stones upon his heart as he interceded for Israel, and averted judgment by constant application of the blood from the Altar of Burnt Offering. Aaron did for Israel in those days, what Christ does for the world today, if they let Him. In the description of the breastplate in Exodus 28:15-21, the red stone comes first, then the jasper; but John reverses the order, and there is a good reason for this.

First, let's examine the meanings of the stones; Sardius, the red stone, spoke of sacrifice and blood (the Cross), and "Reuben" means "behold the son." The jasper was a clear stone speaking of victory; and "Benjamin" means "the son of my right hand." In this order, they point to the Cross, which is the way it would be from the time of Moses. But John sees this in reverse order, as he sees Christ enthroned and looks back to the Cross.

We are also told that there was a rainbow around the throne that looked like an emerald. The emerald was Judah's stone and was green. "Judah" means praise, and green denotes eternal freshness. The first rainbow was what God gave as a sign of a covenant that He made with Noah after the Flood. And this covenant was to never again destroy the earth with a flood; and also, that as long as the earth exists, there will be a seedtime, and a harvest, a summer and winter, and a day and night.

Put yourself back in Noah's time for a minute. Why hadn't there been a rainbow in the sky before? Because there hadn't been any rain! There is no record of rainfall before the flood; but we are told that the earth was watered by a mist or dew that arose from the earth. Can you imagine what the people said and thought when Noah started building the Ark, and telling people that there was going to be a Flood? They would think he was crazy today, and we have a lot of rain sometimes; but then it would have seemed even more impossible! But Noah had faith, and followed, to the letter, what God commanded him to do, and didn't care what other people thought; and he came out a winner. Stop a minute and think about this!

So the rains came, and the storm broke, just as the Wrath of God is coming; but after the storm had passed, the sun again broke through the clouds, and God set the rainbow in the clouds as a sign of His covenant with Noah. Noah represents a group of people, which will mostly be the remnant of Israel, which will pass through the Wrath of God, because they finally put their faith in Christ, after many were sacrificed. And after the Wrath of God rids this earth of a lot of its wickedness, Christ will return to defeat Satan's armies. Christ will then make a new covenant with the people of the earth.

I used Noah as an example once before, in the letter to the Church of Philadelphia, when I said that born-again Christians would be kept safe from the Tribulations, and it wouldn't be necessary to take us out of the world any more than it was for Noah. I was only using Noah as an example there; but here I'm saying that he represents a group of people which will pass through the Wrath of God. Enoch of this age would represent the saints; he was taken up to heaven without dying, before the judgment of God, which was the Great Flood. And so shall the saints be raptured before the Wrath of God comes, which is the judgment that will be poured out on the dwellers of the earth. Notice that I did not say before the Tribulations!

So, in Rev. 4:3, John sees our victorious Christ on the throne with the symbol of an eternally fresh covenant—a green rainbow—around Him, because, when the Lord comes back to earth, He will have a new covenant which will last into eternity. A rainbow always comes after a storm, and Christ will return with this new covenant after the days of judgment. It will mean the dawning of Israel's new day.

CHAPTER 15

THE TWENTY-FOUR ELDERS

Rev. 4:4. And around about the throne were four and twenty seats: and upon the seats I saw four and twenty elders sitting, clothed in white raiment, and they had on their heads crowns of gold.

Some believe this is the clue that says the Rapture will be before the Tribulations. This is the way they deal with it. These twenty-four elders symbolize multitudes of saved worshippers, and are shown here as already having been given a gold crown or rewarded before the Tribulations. Also, that the twenty-four elders will be twelve patriarchs of Israel (such as Abraham, Isaac, Jacob, and Moses) and the other twelve seats will be filled by the twelve apostles.

I believe they are right as to who the elders will be, because in Matthew we see:

Matthew 19:28. And Jesus said unto them, Verily I say unto you, that ye which have followed me, in the regeneration when the Son of man shall sit in the throne of his glory, ye also shall sit upon twelve thrones, judging the twelve tribes of Israel.

I also agree that these are men, not angels, that have been

crowned; as angels are never said to be crowned. But I believe their purpose is to judge the nations. They also use the two following verses to support their idea:

2 Timothy 4:8. (Paul says:) Henceforth there is laid up for me a crown of righteousness, which the Lord, the righteous Judge, shall give me at that day: and not to me only, but unto all them also that love his appearing.

Rev. 22:12. And, behold, I come quickly; and my reward is with me, to give every man according as his work shall be.

They conclude that surely no rewards are given out till He returns for His saints, so there can be no crowned elders in heaven till after the rapture—thus, the Rapture is before the Tribulations!

I don't believe that the twenty-four crowned elders represent the saved ones of all ages—not this age, because the saved peoples of the Church will receive their crowns at the Revelation, or when Christ actually comes as King. At the first judgment! Christ brings his saints with Him clothed in fine linen, assuring their salvation; but their works are yet to be judged, to get their crowns. The twenty-four elders are shown crowned before the Tribulations start, so they could not represent the saved people of this dispensation. The Bible actually sets a time for the rewarding of the saints, the prophets, the servants, and those who fear His name, both small and great. In Rev. 11:18, "that day" which Paul speaks of is when Christ actually comes; and He will have His rewards with Him. Remember, Paul is not one of the original twelve apostles, and he will have to wait to get his reward, just the same as we will. Jesus personally promised a particular reward to the first twelve apostles before the Church Age started. (Remember, each age has its own rules, covenants, and judgments). Therefore, I think it is quite possible that it wouldn't be necessary for the twelve apostles to wait until the first judgment, in order for them to get their crowns. Also, remember, we know that some Old Testament saints have risen.

> Matthew 27:52-53. And the graves were opened; and many bodies of the saints which slept arose, and came out of the graves after His resurrection, and went into the Holy City, and appeared unto many.

So some have already received eternal life, and did not have to wait till the resurrection of this age.

We also see that Lazarus (the beggar) is already in heaven in the story told in Luke 17:22-31. And it came to pass that the beggar died, and was carried by the angels unto Abraham's bosom; the rich man also died and was buried. And, in hell, he lifted up his eyes, being in torments, and seeth Abraham far off, and Lazarus in his bosom. Later the rich man asked Abraham to send Lazarus to tell his brothers about hell, and Abraham said no, that they had Moses, and the prophets to tell them. So this places Abraham, from the Age of Promise, and Lazarus from the Age of Law, in heaven. And Lazarus was just a beggar, not a patriarch. So I believe it is possible that the saved ones of other ages or dispensations are in heaven, and have gotten their rewards. Possibly the resurrection of Christ was a signal for that. But the Church Age has its own rules, just as the Age of the Kingdom will have.

Therefore I believe that the twenty-four elders could represent all the redeemed peoples of past ages. In I Chronicles, Chapter 24, we read something very similar. King David appointed twenty-four elders to represent the entire Levitical priesthood. He had divided the priests into twenty-four courses, each course to serve for two weeks at a time in the temple, which Solomon was to build. You see, there were thousands of priests and they could not all come together at one time. But when the twenty-four elders met, the whole priestly house was represented.

So, perhaps they do represent the priesthood of past ages when John first sees them. But, regardless, they do not represent the saved people of this age, because they haven't arrived yet, not in bodily form.

CHAPTER 16

WHEN IS THE RAPTURE?

I really prefer to wait to present my belief on the Rapture, as it involves so much material which is still ahead. But perhaps it would be better to give you the whole picture now, and let you see how it all fits into place as we go along.

The first thing that we should examine in connection with the Rapture is timing. So I have made Chart A, which shows what is generally believed, and Chart B, which is the way God has shown it to me. Dare I be so contradictive of others who have been schooled in this field? Yes, I shall write whatever God, through the power of the Holy Spirit, chooses to show me.

Let's start with the dispensations: the 6th dispensation ends, and the 7th begins, when Christ begins to rule or reign over the earth. Satan now reigns over the earth and will come into almost direct rule through Antichrist. But this comes to an end with the blowing of the 7th trumpet, as told in the following:

Rev. 11:15-17. Then the seventh angel sounded; and there were great voices in heaven, saying, The kingdoms of this world are become the kingdoms of our Lord, and of his Christ, and he shall reign for ever and ever. And the twenty-four elders, which sat before God on their seats, fell upon their faces, and worshipped God, saying, We give thee thanks, O Lord God Almighty, which art, and wast, and art to come; because thou hast taken to thee thy great power, and hast reigned.

Jesus makes it unmistakenly clear when this occurs —when the 7th trumpet blows! But He also makes something else clear: that He has not come to earth as King yet, which are, and was, and are to come. So the Age of the Kingdom starts from this point!

For the past 3½ years Satan has had his chance to test all the professing Christians. That is, all the people who claim to be Christians, but had not received the Holy Spirit, because of their lack of genuine faith. (Those who have the Holy Spirit have been kept safe and aren't under the power of Satan). Satan appears as Antichrist and the False Prophet. (Compare: Satan, Antichrist, False Prophet to God, Christ, Holy Spirit). And they are allowed to deceive those who dwell on the earth, with their great signs and miracles. The test for God's children will be so great that many will lose their love for Christ. And many who do not will face the supreme test. But, after 42 months, which was the allowed time, Satan's power is taken away. How? His true identity will be revealed by the coming of our Lord in the clouds! Rapture!

2 Thessalonians 2:8. And then shall that Wicked be revealed, whom the Lord shall consume with the spirit of his mouth, and shall destroy with the brightness of his coming.

Rev. 1:7. Behold, he cometh with the clouds; and every eye shall see him, and they also which pierced him, and all kindreds of the earth shall wail because of Him. Even so Amen.

THE GREAT TRIBULATION

CHART A.

JACOB'S WEEK of TROUBLES

AGE of the CHURCH (ended)*				AGE of the KINGDOM

R A P T U R E	* * * * * * * * *	7 SEALS	7 TRUMPETS	7 VIALS	2 n d c o m i n g	MILLENNIUM

3½ yrs.	3½ yrs.	1000 yrs.

7 yrs.

CHART B.

SATAN REIGNS	SATAN FULL P.	OUR LORD REIGNS
JACOB'S TROUBLES	WRATH of GOD	
AGE of the CHURCH	AGE of the KINGDOM	

7 SEALS	7 TRUMPETS	R A P T U R E	7 VIALS	2 n d c o m i n g	MILLENNIUM
1st pains c. birth	Testing		Judgment		Christ is King

3½ yrs.	3½ yrs.	3 yrs.	1000 yrs.

10 yrs.

Repeat-Church of Smyrna	of Repeat-Church Philadelphia
PERSECUTION	BROTHERLY LOVE

As I have stated before, this will not be a secret appearing of Christ, as some seem to believe. The Gospel of the Kingdom will be preached and prophesied all over the world during the 3½ years that Satan is in full power, just prior to this (not the gospel of Grace, but the Second Coming of Christ and his earthly Kingdom). So, when the true Christ appears in the clouds and all peoples of the world see and recognize Him, they will know how Satan has deceived them; and that the Word of God which they heard, and rejected, was true! Antichrist's super-power will come to an end; all who rejected the Word will cry out in fear and sorrow! For now it is too late for most of them.

Yes, the truth about Antichrist will be revealed when the true Christ appears in the clouds! And the Rapture will also take place then.

2 Thessalonians 2:3. Let not many deceive you by any means; for that day shall not come, except there come a falling away first, and that man of sin be revealed, the son of perdition.

All of those which have died in Christ will be raised first. Then all who are still alive, that have proven their faith genuine, and not worshipped the beast or its image, nor received his mark upon their forehead or their hand, will be raptured. This includes the saints, which have been kept safe, during this time of testing. This is the mystery spoken about below:

1 Corinthians 15:51-52. Behold, I shew you a mystery: We shall not all sleep, but we shall all be changed. In a moment, in the twinkling of an eye, at the last trump; (the 7th trumpet) for the trumpet shall sound, and the dead shall be raised incorruptible, and we shall be changed.

Rev. 10:6b-7. That there should be delay, no longer. But in the days of the voice of the seventh angel, when he shall begin to sound (7th trumpet) the mystery of God should be finished, as he hath declared to his servants the prophets.

Luke 21:25-28. And there shall be signs in the sun, and in the moon, and in the stars; and upon the earth distress of nations, with perplexity; the sea and the waves roaring; men's hearts failing them for fear, and for looking after those things which are coming on the earth: for the powers of heaven shall be shaken. And then shall they see the Son of man coming in a cloud with power and great glory. And when these things begin to come to pass, then look up, and lift up your heads; for your redemption draweth nigh.

This is a pretty good description of the 4th trumpet, and tells those that are being tested to hold fast and keep watch because it won't be long. A word of encouragement is given here because the 5th and 6th trumpets are going to be pretty rough. And to the saints Jesus is saying—Be patient a little longer. I imagine, if you had been expecting the Rapture before the Tribulation started, that by now, there could be some who are ready to give up watching for it.

But the Rapture will occur at the blowing of the 7th trumpet, and we have the first resurrection! And all these people are assured of salvation; and are given their white linen robes, and will return with Christ when He comes to set up His Kingdom on earth. Now we have two different groups of people raptured!

Rev. 7:9-10. After this I beheld, and lo, a great multitude, which no man could number, of all nations, and kindreds, and people, and tongues, stood before the throne, and before the Lamb, clothed with white robes, and palms in their hands; and cried with a loud voice, saying Salvation to our God which sitteth upon the throne, and unto the Lamb.

Rev. 7:14b. And he said to me, these are they which came out of great tribulation, and have washed their robes, and made them white in the blood of the Lamb.

"After this" doesn't mean immediately, because in order to come out of the Great Tribulation they had to be in it. I believe these people are the saints that are raptured, as it does not imply that they were tested.

Rev. 7:15. Therefore are they before the throne of God, and serve Him day and night in His temple: and he that sitteth on the throne shall dwell among them.

Compare this with the reward given to the persons presented by the Church of Philadelphia:

Rev. 3:12. Him that overcometh will I make a pillar in the temple of my God, and he shall go no more out.

Here is the second group, and there is no guesswork involved.

Rev. 15:1-3. I saw another sign in heaven, great and marvelous, seven angels having the seven last plagues; for in them is filled up the wrath of God. And I saw as it were a sea of glass mingled with fire: and them that had gotten the victory over the beast and over his image, and over his mark, and over the number of his name, stand on the sea of glass, having the harps of God. And they sing the song of Moses, the servant of God, and the song of the Lamb, saying, Great and Marvelous are thy works, Lord God Almighty; just and true are thy ways, thou King of saints.

Now, this group of people are the ones that were tested and won over Satan during the seven trumpets; and now are in heaven, before the Wrath of God is turned on the earth.

These people were raptured with the saints, and you can tell that there are both Jew and Gentile present, by the songs they are singing. These people were alive and raptured at the sound of the 7th trumpet. Some authors dispose of these people by saying that they all have to endure the supreme test; how else are they going to get them to heaven, since they had the Rapture coming before the tribulation started? I do believe there will be quite a few who are strong enough to hold out even unto death, and will be witnessing and trying to help others until they are killed. And there is another place in Revelation that describes these people.

Rev. 20:4. And I saw thrones, and they say upon them, and judgment was given unto them; and I saw the souls of them that were beheaded for the witness of Jesus, and for the word of God, and which had not worshipped the beast, neither his image, neither had received his mark upon their foreheads, or in their hands; and they lived and reigned with Christ a thousand years.

It is certainly clear that this is not the same group of people that had the harps of God, and were singing songs! John made a definite distinction between these beheaded witnesses, by saying that he saw the souls of them; and those that were raptured alive, he describes them as people. And the rewards are different. No, it is impossible for the Rapture to come at the beginning and get these people to heaven who have proven that they, too, belong to Christ, by enduring the tribulations of testing by Satan, and not worshipping the beast. Leave them here till Christ returns as King? No, for God does not intend that any of His true children from this age should suffer His Wrath.

1 Thessalonians 5:9. For God hath not appointed us to wrath, but to obtain salvation by our Lord Jesus Christ.

Plus the fact that they are seen in heaven before the Wrath

of God begins. Remember, the Wrath of God consists of the seven vial judgements.

You will find that you run into all kinds of problems when you misinterpret, as the Bible is just like a large jigsaw puzzle; when everything is interpreted properly, all the pieces fit together easily. On the other hand, if you try and force your interpretation, it may even seem to fit right at that particular place, but the rest of the pieces of your puzzle will not fit properly.

In case you doubt that only the seven vials are the wrath of God, notice that in the seven trumpets, Satan is not attacking those that worship him—only those who won't! But Jesus makes it quite clear who the seven vial judgments are again, right from the beginning.

> Rev. 16:2. And the first went, and poured out his vial upon the earth; there fell a noisome and grievous sore upon the men which had the mark of the beast, and upon them which worshipped his image.

God has begun to reign; but before He brings His people back, He will cleanse the earth of sinful men. Yes, there will be people who live through this judgment on the world—just as Noah lived through the flood. I know that some of these people will be a remnant of Jews who truly love God but were blind to accepting Christ. God has always kept for His own, down through the generations of time, a remnant of His first chosen people; not because of their works, but because of His mercy. And when the last Gentile has said yes to Jesus, the blinders will be lifted and this remnant of Jews will know Christ. Do not mistake these for Christian Jews, as they will be dealt with in the testing of the Church Age, the same as we will.

Some people seem to think that the tribulations will be mostly against the Jews—possibly because it is referred to as "Jacob's Troubles." Well, this is not true, and I will show you why. Remember that in every dispensation God has had dif-

106

ferent methods of dealing with mankind, and each has its judgment, usually right close to the end of the age. And the Church Age is no different! Their judgment, which is to be tested by the wrath of Satan, is called Jacob's Troubles. Jacob (renamed Israel) was the father of those who were supposed to believe and obey God in the Old Testament—or, in this case, Jacob represents God's children. The Old Testament prophets told about the week of Jacob's troubles, which would occur at the time of the Latter Days, and they were referring to the troubles of God's children. But in this dispensation, God's children are known as Christians instead of Israelites. Remember, when Jacob's Troubles were spoken of in the Old Testament, they had never heard of the word "Christians," so they couldn't use it.

If you still are not convinced, and insist that Jacob's troubles refer to the Jews—or, to be more precise, the descendants of Abraham—then I would have to say that we are descendants of Abraham! God said:

Genesis 17:5. Neither shall thy name anymore be called Abram, but thy name shall be Abraham; for a father of many nations have I made thee. (i.e., not just the Jewish nations.)

Abraham is the Father of all Peoples, in all nations, which believe in Christ. How? He became the father of many nations through his descendant, Jesus Christ. Through the Holy Spirit and Jesus, we, who were once called Gentiles, became the adopted children of God and the descendants of Abraham. But either way that you want to approach the subject, it comes out the same: Jacob represents the Christians in this dispensation.

Notice on the chart that I have a repeat of two historical periods of God's whole Church. I don't know if anyone else has ever come to this conclusion. But this was the way it was pointed out to me; I felt that there was a connection between the historical stage of God's Church, represented by

107

Smyrna, and the Tribulations; but I couldn't make the connection. Then, when I was looking at the chart I had made on the History of One Church, this was brought to my attention. We have two church periods (represented by Ephesus and Pergamos) that repented and were allowed to fade into History. We have three periods (represented by Thyatira, Sardis, and Laodicea) which did not repent, and were being held over to be tested in the Tribulations. And that left two church periods (represented by Smyrna and Philadelphia) which weren't asked to repent—what happens to them? We have a period of great persecution and testing by Satan, and a period of brotherly love—then I saw the connection! This is a description of what lies ahead! I knew the seven seals and the seven trumpets lasted seven years (the week of persecution of God's Children); but I didn't know how long the seven vials would last. But, in the Letter to Smyrna, there is a clue: your troubles will last 10 days. So I have concluded that the whole tribulation period ending when Christ returns to earth as King will last 10 years. And in the New Kingdom we will all, Jew and Christian alike, be united in brotherly love, under Christ.

I have now revealed to you where I was shown that the Rapture would take place, and some of the reasons I was shown to back it up. Try to keep this picture in mind as we continue our search for the truth in the Book of Revelation.

CHAPTER 17

FOUR LIVING CREATURES

Weather was the main factor of the judgment in Noah's time; and I feel that it will play an important part in future events. Try and picture the future in this manner: Pretend you are standing on a high mesa in New Mexico; it seems as though you can see to the ends of the earth! Looking westward, we see a few little storm clouds coming; but beyond that are two huge black clouds. Looking still further, we see a rainbow which is reflecting beautiful colors all over the sky, and the sun is shining in all its glory.

The first black cloud holds the storm that the earth shall feel while being tested by Satan, Antichrist, and the False Prophet. Most of our storms start in the west and move eastward; so it is natural to picture it this way. As it gets nearer, we see the lightning and hear the thunder rolling. The storm cloud passes, and now we can see the lightning in the east, just as we had in the west before the storm. And, behold, the Son of man appears in the sky, first in the east, then in the west, and raptures His people. Now the second dark cloud approaches. It is darker, the lightning is fierce, and the thunder nearly breaks your eardrums! This is a much worse storm, as it is the wrath of God coming to cleanse the earth of sin and wickedness. It passes over the earth, and now we see the lightning in the east, as the storm moves on. And, behold, the heavens open, and there sitting on a white horse is the King of Kings: followed by His saints, who were also on white horses, clothed in fine white linen, white and clean. This, too, is seen first in the east, then in the west. Yes, Christ comes as king to set up His Kingdom on earth.

> Matthew 24:25-27. Behold, I have told you before. Wherefore if they shall say unto you, Behold, he is in the desert; go not forth; Behold, he is in the secret chambers; believe it not. For as the lightning cometh out of the east and shineth even unto the west; so shall also the coming of the Son of man be.

This refers to the Rapture, because Jesus has just warned his disciples about the false Christs and false prophets that will show great signs and wonders. Now He says—Don't be fooled by anyone, because you won't have to look for me when I return. I will be as the lightning flashes across the sky from the east to the west, and every eye will see me. Notice also that the lightning comes from the east, indicating that this occurs after a storm, not before it; as I have brought out in my picture of the future. So this verse tells how and when He will return. True, this could apply also to His actual coming as King; but Christ's warning is not to unbelievers before He comes as King, but to His Bride before the rapture. When He comes as King, it will be as a thief upon the remaining unbelievers; the dwellers of the earth.

I have given you a detailed explanation of the rapture; and now I've tried to give you a picture of the future, in general, as I believe that pictures make it easier to remember. So, try to keep this general picture in mind as we examine more details.

> Rev. 4:5. And out of the throne proceeded lightnings and thunderings and voices: and there were seven

lamps of fire burning before the throne, which are the seven spirits of God.

I believe the lightnings, thunderings, and voices, are telling us that there is certainly a terrible storm brewing, which will burst forth upon the earth. Yes, terrible times are ahead; but let us not lose sight of the rainbow that John has described, around the throne.

We are told that the seven lamps of fire are the seven Spirits of God, which we have discussed earlier, as being one Holy Spirit with seven characteristics, making it complete perfection.

Rev. 4:6. And before the throne there was a sea of glass like unto crystal: and in the midst of the throne, and around about the throne, were four beasts full of eyes before and behind.

The area before the throne symbolizes something which is precious, pure, and covers an immense area. The ordinary glass of the ancient world, was dull: but glass like unto crystal was as precious as gold. And direct or pure light reflecting off this crystal would be more than the eye could stand, like the purity of God. It being called a sea indicates that it covers a great area. Now we have to find something which this describes and fits the picture any and all times that it is used. The sea of glass calls to mind the sea of brass in Solomon's temple. This sea symbolizes, like the laver, the Word of God. The laver contained the water used for priestly cleansing, and we are cleansed by "the washing of the water, by the Word." But this sea will not be needed for cleansing, so it is as crystal; and later we find those who conquered the beast standing on it. It still is the Word of God which abides, stable and sure forevermore, firm and glorious, on which the people of God can stand eternally. Yes, the Word of God is all three—precious, pure, and certainly covering a great area.

Now we come to the "four beasts" around the throne. First

of all, they should be called the "four living ones or creatures," as the word is very different from that used in Chapter 13. In Revelation, we learn that these four living creatures are always found near the throne, and never stop praising and worshipping God. In Revelation 6:1, 6:7, 15:7, we see that they do perform certain other functions and duties. And we do know that they each had six wings and were full of eyes. And for more of description, we continue to:

Rev. 4:7. And the first beast was like a lion, and the second beast like a calf, and the third beast had a face as a man, and the fourth beast was like a flying eagle.

Even though there are definite differences, there certainly is a family resemblance between these living creatures and those in the vision of Ezekiel found in Ezekiel 1:15 and 10:7. In Ezekiel's vision, each creature had four faces—a man, lion, ox, and an eagle. They had only four wings each, and they had four wheels which were covered with eyes. And these four living creatures were definitely identified with the cherubim.

The cherubim appear to be agents of God's judgment; just as in Isaiah 6:2 we see the seraphim, and they appear here as the agents of cleansing by which God purifies His people. And the only thing that is described about them is that they have six wings each. So, considering everything, I believe that the four living creatures are a special order of angelic beings associated with the throne of God, and having the combined characteristics of both the seraphim and the cherubim. John sees them in this way because of what is about to take place on earth; that is the purification by testing and judgment of the earth.

I believe that we have now identified the four living creatures, so let us see what they symbolize.

Rev. 4:8. And the four beasts had each of them six wings about him; and they were full of eyes within; and they rest not day and night, saying Holy, holy, holy, Lord God Almighty, which was, and is, and is to come.

Here, another clue has been given us. They rest not day or night; they never tire of praising God! So let's keep that in mind while we examine the faces:

The Lion—king of beasts, noblest of them all, supreme among beasts.
The Calf, young ox—strongest of the beasts, supreme among cattle.
The Eagle—swiftest of all birds, supreme among birds.
The Man—wisest in all Creation, supreme among all creatures.

Some believe that the four living creatures stand for everything that is the noblest, strongest, wisest, and swiftest in nature. Each of them is supreme in his own particular sphere and world. So, then, the four living creatures represent all the greatness, and the strength, and the beauty of nature; and we see nature praising God. And the ceaseless activity of nature under the hand of God is a ceaseless tribute of praise—which would explain the fact that they rest not day or night from praising God. And they also add the twenty-four elders praising God, and complete a picture of both nature and man engaged in constant praise and adoration of God.

I must say they have created a beautiful picture with this theory, and I would like to be able to accept it, because I'm sure that nature does praise God continually. But let me try to give you a picture just a little different. Remember the whole picture of the throne, and think of it in three tenses—something which was, which is and which will be.

Christ	The Word at Creation	The Lamb at the Cross	King on the Throne
4 Living Creatures	All Creation at the Garden of Eden	4 Angelic Beings	Palestine During the Millennium
Lightning & Thunder	Storm—The Flood	Warning from the Throne	Storm—Testing & Judgment
Rainbow	Covenant with Noah	Green Rainbow about the Throne	New Covenant with All of Israel
24 Elders	12 Patriarchs; 12 Apostles Who Love God	24 Crowned Men	24 Judges or Princes Who Love God

You see, I believe that everything around the throne has three meanings: past, present (in between), and future. Now, let the four living creatures represent all the animals and all the people of God living together in peace, and who never tire of praising our Lord for these indescribable blessings which we were given in the Garden of Eden and lost through sin; but thanks to our Lord Jesus Christ, they will be given to us again when He returns!

Isaiah 11:609. The wolf also shall dwell with the lamb, and the leopard shall lie down with the kid; and the calf and the young lion and the fatling together; and a little child shall lead them. And the cow and the bear shall feed, their young ones shall lie down together; and the lion shall eat straw like the ox. And the suckling child shall play on the hole of the asp, and the weaned child shall put his hand on the cockatrice's den. They shall not hurt nor destroy in all my holy mountain: for the earth shall be full of the knowledge of the Lord, as the waters cover the sea.

So, I believe the four living creatures symbolize all men, and all animals praising God and living together in peace, which will be accomplished in the Millennium.

This symbolizes quite a different relationship from the one that exists now. Think—not only peace between men, but peace between man and animal. This will be a repeat of the Garden of Eden, in that respect. Take notice that many, perhaps all, major events of God's plan for his earth happen twice.

Rev. 4:9-11. And when those beasts give glory and honour and thanks to Him that sat on the throne, who liveth forever and ever, the twenty-four elders fall down before Him that sat on the throne, and worship Him that liveth forever and ever, and cast their crowns before the throne saying, Thou art worthy, O Lord, to receive glory and honour and power: for thou hast created all things, and for thy pleasure they are and were created.

And when the living creatures gave glory, honor, and thanks to God, the twenty-four elders fell down in worship, and cast their crowns before Him; which would indicate their complete submission. These twenty-four elders sit on thrones and have crowns of gold, such as a king or a prince; and would give the appearance of having power. But their actions clearly point out that they have no power of their own; all of their power comes from God, and they submit completely to His will. And they are proclaiming the blessed truth that the one who died on the Cross is worshipped by all in heaven. There can be no mistake as to the Person, for Thou hast created all things. You will find the same message in Hebrew 1:2, John 1:3 as in the following:

Colossians 1:13b-16a. And hath translated us into the kingdom of His dear Son: In whom we have redemption through his blood, even the forgiveness of sins: Who is the image of the invisible God, the firstborn of every creature: for by Him were all things created (and for Him).

All three of these Bible references make it perfectly clear that it was Jesus Christ, the Son, who created all things. And it is He who fills the throne and is the center of worship described here. Jesus Christ, our Lord is God!

Man has learned to do many things and has acquired many powers; but he cannot create! He can alter and rearrange already existing materials; but only God can create something out of nothing. Which boils down to the fact that everything in the world belongs to God.

CHAPTER 18

THE SEVEN-SEALED BOOK

We have just seen the Lord Jesus Christ worshipped as Creator; and now we will see that a higher honor is His: He is worshipped as Redeemer.

> Rev. 5:1. And I saw in the right hand of him that sat on the throne a book written within and on the back side, sealed with seven seals.

We see that the book is in the right hand of Him that sat on the throne. We have just determined that the Son fills the throne; but we must not forget that it is likewise the throne of God the Father, who is our invisible God. And in this situation we have, in the Father's right hand, a book written within and on the back side, and sealed with seven seals.

This book is not a volume such as we know it. It is a scroll made out of papyrus or parchment. This scroll was written on both sides, and sealed with seven seals. This means that the book was rolled up to a certain point, and there was a seal put upon the edge, so that it could not be unrolled until that seal was broken. It was rolled up a little further, and another seal put on, and so on, until there were six seals on the edge of the book; and one seal closing the entire scroll.

So, when the first seal was opened a certain portion of the book was exposed to view; and so with each of the seals.

What is this sealed book? This seven-sealed book is a book of redemption, which must be opened in order for the earth to be redeemed. Until someone who can break the seals and open the book is found, there can be no further revelation.

To understand what a book of redemption is, we must go back to Israel's history in the Old Testament. In Leviticus 25 there are provisions for the redemption of three things: wife, slave, and possessions—land being one of them. I will briefly try to explain the method used. When a man lost his property, he was taken before the judges; and a document was prepared which stated that the land had passed from the debtor into the possession of one to whom he owed the debt. Now, this land could be redeemed by the man himself by paying the redemption price, which was unlikely, for he was now a servant; or it could be purchased back by a relative. The documents, therefore, were written on two scrolls of parchment. On both of these were written the terms of the redemption of the lost land. One scroll was left open in the court of the temple for all to read, but the other was rolled up, sealed with seven seals, and placed in the temple to be brought out only when a kinsman redeemer gave evidence that he was willing and able to redeem it. If he could pay the redemption price and could meet all the conditions of the law, the sealed scroll was produced, and he publicly tore open the seals and invalidated the mortgage; then the man could return to his purchased possession. Later, they began using one scroll and wrote the terms on both sides, within and without. And in Revelation 5, we see the judge of all the earth sitting on His throne, and in His hand is the scroll written on both sides and sealed with seven seals. So I believe this fits the description of the redemption scrolls in the Old Testament.

What is there to be redeemed? Christ paid for the sins of the world, and thus redeemed man over 1900 years ago, when He died on the Cross, and rose again! And it is just as true today as it was then. Those who accept Him as their Lord and Savior have been redeemed. Their accounts have been marked "PAID IN FULL"! But the earth and the creatures of the earth, both vegetable and animal, are still under the curse of man's sin. These also must be redeemed; for Christ is a perfect Redeemer, so everything that came under Adam's sin must be delivered by the redemption of the Last Adam.

Genesis 3:17b-18. Cursed is the ground for thy sake: in sorrow shalt thou eat of it all the days of thy life. Thorns also and thistles shall it bring forth to thee and thou shalt eat the herb of the field.

Genesis 3:14. And the Lord God said unto the serpent, Because thou hast done this, thou art cursed above all cattle, and above every beast of the field, upon thy belly thou shalt go, and dust shalt thou eat all the days of thy life.

Adam lost his inheritance, but God has provided for a plan of redemption so that which Adam lost may be redeemed. The seven-sealed book contains the terms by which Adam's lost estate may be redeemed.

Rev. 5:2-4. And I saw a strong angel proclaiming with a loud voice, Who is worthy to open the book, and to loose the seals thereof? And no man in heaven, nor in earth, neither under the earth, was able to open the book, neither to look thereon. And I wept much because no man was found worthy to open and to read the book, neither to look thereon.

Notice that John sees a strong angel with a loud voice. The angel had to be strong so that the challenge of his voice might reach throughout the whole universe. The call went out to every man already in heaven, every one in the earth and under the earth. Why was it necessary for the call to be so extensive if it is true that the Rapture had already taken place, and all of God's saved ones, alive or dead, were already in heaven? Surely it could be no less than one of God's chosen ones that could open the book! Of course, I believe the answer lies in the fact that the Rapture has not occurred yet, and won't occur until the blowing of the seventh trumpet!

But no man was able to open the book. It had to be a man, not an angelic being, because the inheritance was lost by a human being, and had to be redeemed by one. In fact, in the Book of Leviticus, we are told that one who would redeem a possession lost by a kinsman must meet three definite conditions:

1. He must be a near relative of the one who had lost the inheritance.
2. He must be willing to act as a redeemer.
3. He must be able to pay the price of redemption.

John says that he wept much because no man was found worthy to open and to read the book. What would this mean, if there were no one to redeem the earth; and Satan had the right to rule this world forever, as he has done since Adam forfeited it to him? It would mean that all the prophecies of the Old Testament concerning the reign of Christ on earth and the restoration of creation, and the deliverance of the creatures from the bondage of corruption, as well as the restoration of the nation of Israel to the land of Palestine, would never be fulfilled! God's Word would be untrue; He had promised to do something which He was not able to accomplish! The earth would never be restored to its Edenic fruitfulness and blessing! Thinking about these things, John wept. But his tears were quite unnecessary, just as human worry and grief are often needless. If we had patience to wait and to trust, we would see that God has His own solutions for all situations.

Rev. 5:5. And one of the elders saith unto me, Weep not: behold, the Lion of the tribe of Juda, the Root of David, hath prevailed to open the book, and to loose the seven seals thereof.

Who is this person the elder speaks of, which has won a victory and can open the book? You can identify this person through the Old Testament, but Jesus tells us personally in the following:

Rev. 22:16. I Jesus have sent mine angel to testify unto you these things in the churches. I am the root and the offspring of David, and the bright and morning star.

The Lion of the Tribe of Judah would be the most powerful one ever to come out of that tribe. And Jesus' ancestry can be traced back to Abraham on both his adopted father's side and his mother's side. Joseph's ancestry is traced back to Solomon, son of David—Abraham. Mary's ancestry is traced back to Nathan, son of David—Abraham. So Jesus is the most powerful one to come from the tribe of Judah.

Does Jesus meet the three conditions that the Redeemer must possess?

1. He was the offspring of David and a near relative of humanity.
2. As the root of David, or the creator, He was God and fully able to pay the infinite price of Redemption from the curse of sin.
3. And we shall see that He is willing.

Rev. 5:6. And I beheld, and lo, in the midst of the throne and of the four beasts, and in the midst of the elders, stood a Lamb as it had been slain, having seven horns and seven eyes, which are the seven Spirits of God sent forth into all the earth.

As the elder spoke to John, telling him that the Lion of

121

the Tribe of Judah would open the book, He looks up and sees not a lion, but a lamb. So the titles refer to the same person—the Lord Jesus in His first coming was "Lamb of God," and was rejected and slain; but He is coming again as a lion to punish all those who have rejected Him as the Lamb of God. Everyone will meet Jesus Christ, as the Lamb or the Lion; the choice is yours! If you come to Christ as a lost sinner, repent of your sins, and accept Him as your Lord and Master, and receive by faith the sacrifice He accomplished on the Cross, you will become a child of God and know Him as the Lamb. But if you reject His offer, some day you will meet Him as the Lion and your judge.

The Lamb still bears the marks of having been slain. Here is the picture of the pain and the torment, the shame and humiliation, the death and the Cross, when the Lamb of God was God's perfect sacrifice for the sin of the world. But at the same time it is clothed with the very might of God which can now shatter and break its enemies. The Lamb has seven horns. In the Old Testament horns stand for power:

Deuteronomy 33:17 In the blessing of Moses, the horns of Joseph are like the horns of unicorns: with them he shall push the people together to the ends of the earth.

Zechariah 1:18. Zechariah sees the vision of the four horns which stand for the nations who have scattered Israel.

We also know that seven stands for completeness and perfection; the power of the Lamb is perfect, full, complete. The seven eyes are the seven spirits of God; and this means that the Lord Jesus sees all things and is able, by His Spirit, to look into the hearts of all men, because the Holy Spirit is sent forth into all the earth.

CHAPTER 19

UNIVERSAL WORSHIP OF THE LAMB

The Lamb took the book of redemption from the one who sits upon the throne. Then, starting from around the throne, and spreading outward until it included the whole universe, they worshipped and sang praises to the Lamb. The praise comes in three waves.

> Rev. 5:7-8. And he came and took the book out of the right hand of him that sat upon the throne. And when he had taken the book, the four beasts and twenty-four elders fell down before the Lamb, having every one of them harps, and golden vials full of odours, which are the prayers of the saints.

This is what John actually saw. The four angelic creatures and the twenty-four crowned elders, which represent the heavenly saints of past ages, once again began praising the Lamb. But this time they all had harps and golden bowls of incense, and they began to sing a new song! This must have started an electrified feeling of excitement which spread through the whole universe, following the news that the long-awaited event was about to take place. "The Lamb has taken the book of redemption!"

Rev. 5:9-10. And they sang a new song saying, Thou art worthy to take the book, and to open the seals thereof: for thou wast slain, and hast redeemed us to God by thy blood out of every kindred, and tongue, and people and nation. And hast made us unto our God kings and priests; and we shall reign on the earth.

I believe we are shown this praise in three waves, indicating intervals of time between each wave.

Rev. 5:11. And I beheld, and I heard the voice of many angels round about the throne and the beasts and the Elders and the number of them was ten thousand times ten thousand, and thousands of thousands.

Now the angels join in as the circle of praise gets larger.

Rev. 5:12. Saying with a loud voice, Worthy is the Lamb that was slain to receive power, and riches, and wisdom, and strength, and honour, and glory, and blessing.

There is another interval of time; now the news has traveled to the earth. Christ has returned, redeemed the earth and now sits on His throne.

Rev. 5:13. And every creature which is in heaven, and on the earth, and under the earth, and such as are in the sea, and all that are in them, I heard saying, Blessing, and honour and glory, and power, be unto Him that sitteth upon the throne, and unto the Lamb for ever and ever.

Once again the events around the throne show us the future. When Christ sits on His throne on earth, after he has redeemed not only men but all the creatures of the earth, all creation will praise the Lamb.

In the three waves of praise, you can also see what was, what is, and what will be. The song of the living creatures and of the elders told of the work of Christ in death. The Cross, which we look back on, represents what was. The angels speak of the seven possessions of Christ in His glory as the risen Lord, or what is. And then, the praise of all creation, in the last wave, is certainly what will be. Now that we have taken a quick look into the future, we return to the throne in heaven. And the four living creatures close the event by saying Amen, or so shall it be.

Rev. 5:14. And the four beasts said, Amen, and the twenty-four elders fell down and worshipped Him that liveth for ever and ever.

The glorious day of the Lord is coming when he will receive the praise and worship that he deserves. Jesus Christ will come first in all we do, as he is supposed to now; and not till that happens will all the rest of the problems be solved. And this can apply today to individuals, and tomorrow to all creation!

CHAPTER 20

THE REDEMPTION OF CREATION

I have pointed out that the seven-sealed book was the book of the earth's redemption. After the Rapture, the saints are with Christ; but creation and all the creatures on the earth have not as yet been delivered from the curse brought upon them by the sin of man. The Bible tells us that this creation also must be delivered from the curse of sin.

Romans 8:19-22. For the earnest expectation of the creature waiteth for the manifestation of the sons of God. For the creature was subject to vanity, not willingly, but by reason of him who hath subjected the same in hope. Because the creature itself also shall be delivered from the bondage of corruption into the glorious liberty of the children of God. For we know that the whole creation groaneth and travaileth in pain together until now.

And after the Wrath of God, the Lord will return to His earth to set up His Kingdom, and at the manifestation of Christ and the saints, the entire creation will be redeemed.

Christ died on the cross for several reasons:

1. He saved us, who accept Him as Master, from going to hell.
2. He saved us to reign with Him on the earth.
3. He redeemed the creatures.
4. He redeemed the earth itself.

It is significant that Christ wore a crown of thorns on the cross. Thorns are first mentioned in the Bible in Genesis 3 in connection with the curse of God upon the earth and upon vegetation. So it is believed that the wearing of the crown of thorns is related to that first mention of thorns and thistles, reminding us that all creation shall be delivered from the bondage of corruption.

Isaiah 35:1, 7a. The wilderness and the dry land shall be glad, and the desert shall rejoice and blossom as the rose. And the parched ground shall become a pool and the thirsty land springs of water.

God never made a desert! God pronounced His creation good, and Isaiah tells us that He created the earth not to be void, but to be inhabited. Deserts are the results of the curse upon the ground. Also, the animals shall share in the deliverance of the Redeemer.

Hosea 2:18. And in that day will I make a covenant for them with the beasts of the field, and with the fowls of heaven, and with creeping things of the ground: and I will break the bow and the sword and the battle out of the earth, and will make them to lie down safely.

When Jesus reigns on earth, it will become like the Garden of Eden before the fall. But before this happens, there is work to be done. Now the Lamb has met the conditions at the Cross, and the scroll is given to Him; but Satan refuses to relinquish his claim upon the earth because of man's sin, even though the price that God demanded has been met. He refuses to give up his power; so Christ, the Lamb and the Lion, will take it from him by right and by force.

CHAPTER 21

THE FOUR HORSEMEN

The opening of the seals suddenly starts the period of tribulation on the earth to dispossess Satan and wicked men. The four horses and their riders stand for four great destructive forces which are in the time before the end. The origin of John's vision of the four horses can be found in Zechariah 6:1-8. Here they were the four spirits of God which were to walk to and fro through the earth. The details in John's vision differ; but the principle is the same.

Rev. 6:1-2. I saw when the Lamb opened one of the seals, and heard, as it were noise of thunder, one of the four beasts saying, Come. (Some translations add "and see," but this is not in the Greek text.) And I saw, and behold a white horse and he that sat on him had a bow and a crown was given unto him: and he went forth conquering and to conquer.

With each of the first four seals, one of the living creatures associated with God's judicial government cries "Come"—thus calling forth the first judgments. This is not an invitation to John to come and see; it is a summons to the four horses and their riders.

There are some who tend to believe this is Christ on the white horse because He is described as coming on a white horse in Rev. 19:11-12; but, even though there is definitely a similarity, there are differences. Our Christ came with many crowns already on His head. This rider came, then was given a single crown. Also, remember that Christ as the Lamb is holding and breaking the seals of the book at this time. So it is not Christ, but Antichrist, who imitates Christ. This picture does not tell of the coming of the victor, Christ, but of the coming of the terrors of Antichrist.

This rider has a bow in his hand, and goes forth conquering. He comes on a white horse, which in those days was a symbol of victory. He is crowned and we will learn later that he becomes the Chief Ruler of the Ten Federated Kingdoms of the revived Roman Empire. He is the "Prince which will confirm the covenant with many for one week; and in the midst of the week he shall cause the sacrifice and the oblation to cease"—as we read in Daniel 9:27a.

This shows that Antichrist appears at the beginning of the tribulations or the beginning of the week. Yes, Antichrist will appear, promising peace to the Jews. Remember, the Jewish nation is still looking for the first coming of Christ.

John 5:43. I am come in my Father's name, and ye receive me not; if another shall come in his own name, him ye will receive.

How easy it will be for Antichrist to fool them, believing as they do. At least they have an excuse; we have been given all the information ahead of time. It is all there in the Bible; that book which we use so little.

SECOND SEAL

Rev. 6:3-4. And when he had opened the second seal, I

130

heard the second beast say, Come. And there went out another horse that was red; and power was given to him that sat thereon to take peace from the earth, and that they should kill one another; and there was given unto him a great sword.

Before we go into the second seal, notice on Chart B that I call the seven seals the first pains of childbirth, or just the beginning. I believe there is a very good description of this time in the following. Remember, Jesus was speaking to the Jewish people of that day.

Matthew 24:5-8. For many shall come in my name, saying I am Christ; and shall deceive many. And ye shall hear of wars and rumors of wars; see that ye not be troubled; for all these things must come to pass, but the end is not yet. For nation shall rise against nation, kingdom against kingdom; and there shall be famines, and pestilence, and earthquakes, in divers places. All these are the beginning of sorrows.

Keeping in mind that Antichrist has just made a seven-year peace pact with Israel (one week) which he will break in the midst of the week, or after 3½ years, we can easily see that what is being described in Matthew is taking place in other parts of the world, not Jerusalem. Possibly Antichrist is trying to show Israel that God is punishing those who have hurt her (God is supposed to do that), making them believe even more in him.

In the second seal, there is a red horse and rider which have the power to take peace from the world. Red is the symbol of blood, and the sword, of war; but this is a different kind of warfare, than the bow symbolized. This will not be a world war; it would be described differently in Matthew. There will be small wars going on between nations; but the most damaging will be classified as internal strife: rebellions, revolutions, class-wars, riots of all kinds, resulting in

131

the breaking up of all established order in many countries. I imagine most people think this highly unlikely here; but I believe a severe depression or runaway inflation could give us a big push in this direction.

Rev. 6:5-6. And when he had opened the third seal, I heard the third beast say, Come. And I beheld, and lo, a black horse; and he that sat on him had a pair of balances in his hand. And I heard a voice in the midst of the four beasts say, A measure of wheat for a penny, and three measures of barley for a penny; and see thou hurt not the oil and the wine.

The black horse symbolizes famine. In the Old Testament the phrase "to eat bread by weight" indicates the greatest scarcity.

Leviticus 26:26. And when I have broken the staff of your bread, ten women shall bake your bread in one oven, and they shall deliver you your bread again by weight; and ye shall eat, and not be satisfied.

A measure is about a quart, and is consistently defined in the ancient world as a man's ration for a day. And a penny was the average day's wages for a laborer of those days. Normally, on an average, you could buy about 12 measures of wheat for a penny. So, what John is foretelling, is a situation where wine and oil, or luxuries, were plentiful; but the necessities were scarce and hard to get. And the prices are inflated till only the rich will have sufficient food, at least for a time; and the poor will suffer indescribably.

FOURTH SEAL

Rev. 6:7-8. And when he had opened the fourth seal, I

heard the voice of the fourth beast say, Come. And I looked, and behold a pale horse: and his name that sat on him was Death, and Hell followed with him. And power was given unto them over the fourth part of the earth, to kill with sword, and with hunger, and with death, and with the beasts of the earth.

The fourth horse was pale—a better translation is "livid"—in the sense of being the color of a corpse; and its rider was named Death. A fourth of the population of the earth will die because of internal strife: small wars, rebellions, revolutions, class-wars, riots of all sorts; and from famine, probably triggered by weather conditions. And from epidemics of deadly diseases, which seem to breed in these conditions. And also from hungry animals, attacking human beings. This is a terrible time, but it isn't the end!

CHAPTER 22

THE FIFTH AND SIXTH SEALS

Rev. 6:9-11. And when he had opened the fifth seal, I saw under the altar the souls of them that were slain for the word of God, and for the testimony which they held: And they cried with a loud voice, saying, How long, O Lord, Holy and true, dost thou not judge and avenge our blood on them that dwell on the earth? And white robes were given unto every one of them; and it was said unto them, that they should rest yet for a little season, until their fellow-servants also and their brethren, that should be killed as they were, should be fulfilled.

So far Antichrist has been a man of peace, giving the Jewish nation a false sense of security. All the things that have been happening to the rest of the world are looked at from two points of view. The Jewish nation believes that they are at last being blessed again, and the rest of the world being punished. The rest of the world probably goes on believing that they will work their way out of the mess that they have gotten themselves into, and without the help of God. There have been a lot of people who have died, but from what has appeared to be normal causes for this world:

internal strife, war, famine, pestilence, and hungry animals attacking humans. But there have been no saints martyred up to this point in the tribulations of the End Time!

When the fifth seal was broken, John saw the souls of martyrs under the altar. This sign is explained in Leviticus 4:25: John means that, because of the way in which they died, the Christian martyrs are like the Old Testament sacrifices whose blood was poured out at the bottom of the altar. Now that we know why the martyred saints were pictured that way, the next question which most authors have difficulty with is, who are they, and to what dispensation do they belong? Most authors have placed the Rapture before the Tribulations start; and thus, all the martyred saints of this dispensation have received their new bodies, and you would not see their souls. So they come up with the idea that some saints have already been martyred in this part of the Tribulation. But the Bible doesn't say a thing about this happening yet. As I have stated before, the Rapture has not yet occurred, and those souls of martyred saints are all those that have been killed for the witness of Jesus, and for the word of God, during this dispensation, or during the Church Age; with the exception of the 12 apostles. As I have said, since Jesus personally told them, before this dispensation started, that they would sit on 12 thrones in the New Age, judging the 12 tribes of Israel, I believe they are already there, just as others from other dispensations are. So we see the souls of the martyred saints of this dispensation crying aloud, asking—How long, O Lord, must we wait before you judge, and avenge our blood on them that dwell on the earth?

Many people criticize this, saying that it doesn't seem right for those in heaven to wish to see their persecutors punished. Maybe it isn't so much the punishment that they want to see, but the rewards which they will receive when their blood is avenged in the End Time: an incorruptible body, and getting to reign with our beloved Christ for 1000 years. That is really going to be great, and I don't blame them for being a little impatient. So they were given their white robes, or just a bit of their reward; and were told that they should rest a while longer until the number of those that would be killed, as they were, was fulfilled. So this definitely indicates that there will be more saints martyred in this dispensation—no doubt when Antichrist starts to demand that everyone worship him; and this will not take place until after the first 3½ years.

SIXTH SEAL

Rev. 6:12. And I beheld when he had opened the sixth seal, and lo, there was a great earthquake; and the sun became black as sackcloth of hair, and the moon became as blood.

Please notice that from here on, everytime something important happens, there is an earthquake. And the closer it is connected to Christ, the greater the earthquake. This was a great one!

Now, many people do not think this earthquake should be taken literally, but as a sign or symbol—perhaps the destruction of the present order, political and social, which would result in chaos. But I do believe this earthquake should be taken literally. We have been following right along comparing the seals with Matthew 24:5-8, and it says that there shall be earthquakes in various places. We have taken the rest of the description of the seven seals in Matthew literally; we can't stop with the earthquake just because we don't understand how it could happen and not have complete destruction of the world. An earthquake in modern cities today would break gas, water, electric, and telephone lines. There would be many explosions, and fires from escaping gas, and hot wires; and they would be difficult to put out because of lack of water pressure, together with the chaos and panic that would take over. The smoke would darken the sky, and blot out the sun by day; and it would make the moon appear to be a blood-red disc at night. This could last for days!

There is an interesting phrase used here—sackcloth of hair. This is a coarse cloth made of camel's and goat's hair. It was used for making the rough garments worn by mourners. It therefore became a symbol for sorrow and mourning. This word was used a great deal in the Old Testament because it was something that was practised a lot in those days. But the word is rarely used in the New Testament. So why is a symbol for sorrow and mourning used at this particular place? There is one other place in Revelation that this symbol is mentioned:

Rev. 11:3. And I will give power unto my two witnesses, and they shall prophesy a thousand two hundred and three-score days, clothed in sackcloth. (3½ years.)

The fact that this symbol, which isn't used in the New Testament, appears twice in less than five chapters, leads me to believe that there is an important connection here. Since this book is full of symbols, it is important to match these symbols up to get their meanings.

Rev. 6:13. And the stars of heaven fell unto the earth, even as a fig tree casteth her untimely figs, when she is shaken of a mighty wind.

Now, the seven stars in Revelation 1:20 were seven angels. So, if the stars were angels, it would appear as though a lot of angels fell from heaven at this time.

In the following verses we see the same symbol and the same meaning.

Rev. 12:3. And there appeared another wonder in heaven; and behold, a great red dragon, having seven heads and ten horns, and seven crowns upon his heads. And his tail drew the third part of stars of heaven, and did cast them to the earth.

138

Revelation 12:7-9. And there was a war in heaven: Michael and his angels fought the dragon; and the dragon fought and his angels, and prevailed not; neither was their place found any more in heaven. And the great dragon was cast out, that old serpent, called the devil, and Satan, which deceiveth the whole world: he was cast out into the earth, and his angels were cast out with him.

I believe that not only Satan and his angels were cast out of heaven, but also one-third of the stars, or Michael's angels, were cast down to earth, in this war between the Devil and Michael. This shows us that the Devil is a very strong supernatural power and shouldn't be underestimated.

Rev. 6:14. And the heaven departed as a scroll when it is rolled together; and every mountain and island was moved out of their places.

As I have said, I believe the earthquake is for real. So, if you can, picture people running here and there, trying to find safety during a great earthquake, which could be followed by a series of tremors. Then all of a sudden a tremendous supernatural change takes place in the sky. I haven't been given a clue as to what this might be; but it will startle people on the earth into realizing that God is on His throne watching them, and that Jesus Christ, God's Lamb, is there too. Many of the people who hold with the Post-Milliennialists, which believe that Christ will not come until after the Millennium, will probably think that the world is coming to an end. Anyway, it will be a frightening experience for most of the world.

Rev. 6:15-17. And the kings of the earth, and the great men, and the rich men, and the chief captains, and the mighty men, and every free man, hid themselves in the dens and in the rocks of the mountains; and said to the mountains and rocks, Fall on us, and hide us from the face of him that sitteth on the throne, and from the wrath of the Lamb: For the great day of his wrath is come; and who shall be able to stand?

These verses just point out that the strong and the rich will be in no better shape than the poor and the weak. All peoples on this earth that fear God, because of their wickedness and sin, will now be filled with indescribable terror. But remember—if you have the spirit of our Lord Jesus Christ, fear not, for He has promised to keep you safe, and He will!

CHAPTER 23

GOD'S SERVANTS PROTECTED

Chapter seven of Revelation is a pause, a parenthesis between the sixth and seventh seals.

Rev. 7:1-3. And after these things I saw four angels standing on the four corners of the earth, holding the four winds of the earth, that the wind should not blow on the earth, nor on the sea, nor on any tree. And I saw another angel descending from the east, having the seal of the living God: and he cried with a loud voice to the four angels to whom it was given to hurt the earth and the sea, saying, Hurt not the earth, neither the sea, nor the trees, till we have sealed the servants of our God in their foreheads.

Perhaps this chapter is telling us how God will keep and protect not only the 144,000 Jews, but also the "True Church," until they are raptured.

John says that he saw the angels holding back the four winds of heaven so that they would not blow on the earth, until a certain event takes places. In Daniel's vision, as recorded in the 7th chapter of his prophecy, he beholds "the four winds of heaven" striving upon the great sea, and as a result you have the various world empires coming forth like wild beasts from beneath the restless waves. It seems evident here that the angels are restraining the last wild beasts from making their appearance. John sees another angel descending from the east, having the seal of the living God, and he cries with a loud voice to the angels not to hurt the earth till they have sealed the servants of our Lord.

So, we see God putting His seal on the Jewish remnant, then perhaps the Christian remnant, marking them as possessions. They are to be kept safe during the tribulations till He comes.

The origin of this picture is very likely in Ezekiel 9:1-7. In Ezekiel's picture, before the final slaughter begins, the man with the inkhorn marks the forehead of those who are faithful, and the avengers are told that none who are so marked must be touched.

> Rev. 7:4-8. And I heard the number of them which were sealed; and there were sealed an hundred and forty and four thousand of all the tribes of the children of Israel. Of the tribe of Juda were sealed twelve thousands. Of the tribe of Reuben were sealed twelve thousand. Of the tribe of Gad were sealed twelve thousand. Of the tribe of Aser were sealed twelve thousand. Of the tribe of Nepthalim were sealed twelve thousand. Of the tribe of Manasses were sealed twelve thousand. Of the tribe of Simeon were sealed twelve thousand. Of the tribe of Levi were sealed twelve thousand. Of the tribe of Issachar were sealed twelve thousand. Of the tribe of Zabulon were sealed twelve thousand. Of the tribe of Joseph were sealed twelve thousand. Of the tribe of Benjamin were sealed twelve thousand.

God makes it very clear that these are 144,000 Israelites, 12,000 from each tribe. This has to be taken to mean just what it says. There is not a gentile among them. But, notice, the tribe of Dan is missing.

142

Rev. 7:9-17. After this I beheld, and lo, a great multitude which no man could number, of all nations, and kindreds and people, and tongues, stood before the throne, and before the Lamb, clothed with white robes, and palms in their hands; And cried with a loud voice, saying, Salvation to our God which sitteth upon the throne, and unto the Lamb. And all the angels stood round about the throne, and about the elders and the four beasts, and fell before the throne on their faces, and worshipped God, saying, Amen: Blessing, and glory, and wisdom, and thanksgiving, and honour, and power, and might, be unto our God forever and ever. Amen. And one of the elders answered, saying unto me, What are these which are arrayed in white robes? And whence came they? And I said unto him, Sir, thou knowest. And he said to me, These are they which came out of great tribulation, and have washed their robes, and made them white in the blood of the Lamb. Therefore, are they before the throne of God, and serve him day and night in His temple: and he that sitteth on the throne shall dwell among them. They shall hunger no more, neither thirst any more; neither shall the sunlight on them, nor any heat. For the Lamb which is in the midst of the throne shall feed them, and shall lead them unto living fountains of water: and God shall wipe away all tears from their eyes.

"After this" does not mean immediately; I believe John is looking a little ahead now. He sees a multitude of people, which are the elect gentiles. They are being kept safe right now, but John sees them a little later before the throne. And John again describes the throne scene. As God's plan is being accomplished in the end times, and the realization that the Sabbath Rest is getting nearer, joyous expectation fills the air and we see that more are gathered to the throne to praise our Lord. And also we see the angels are becoming more active in their worship of God.

John is told by one of the elders that these people came out of the Great Tribulations. This is one thing that indicates that John is looking ahead, since the Great Tribulation has not really started yet. This has just been "the beginning of sorrows." And in order to come out of them, they have to be in them, or on earth while they are happening. There isn't any indication that they were tested, though, to see if their faith was genuine. And indeed, they were not, as they are "the True Church"—those whom Christ has already put his stamp of approval on by giving them His Holy Spirit. Christ knows that their faith is genuine, so there is no reason for them to be tested; so He promises to keep them safe while their "lukewarm brethren" are being tested.

Yes, we certainly have washed our robes in the blood of the Lamb and made them pure white. Because we believe what Jesus says is true, we believe He will keep all of His promises, we accept Him as our Master; and we humbly accept the gift the Master gives to His servants. This is the full payment for all our sins, by the human sacrifice of our Lord, and our new birth through the Holy Spirit. The Master pays the debts, receives and destroys our sinful record, and takes possession of His property—His servants! Our Lord is willing to redeem the records of any of God's children; but they have to believe in Him, and accept Him as Master. There are two conditions here to be met, and going only halfway is not good enough, as so many people seem to think today. And tomorrow, it is these people who will have to prove that their faith in Jesus is genuine.

Now the elder tells John that, because of their genuine faith and love for our Lord, these people shall always be near Him, and He near them. They shall serve Him day and night in His temple of the Millennium. Christ shall dwell among them and take care of all their needs. And it shall be good! The 15th verse refers to the Millennium because there will be no light around the Heavenly City, and no temple, in New Jerusalem of the New Earth.

144

Rev. 22:5. And there shall be no light there: and they need no candles, neither light of the sun; for the Lord God giveth them light: and they shall reign forever and ever.

Rev. 21:22. And I saw no temple therein: for the Lord God Almighty and the Lamb are the temple of it.

But, then the elder tells John that this arrangement continues in New Jerusalem on the new earth, because verses 16 and 17 refer to the Heavenly City, where it seems to indicate the presence of both the Lamb and God Almighty. We see this indicated in Verse 22 above, and in several other verses in Chapters 21 and 22. Exactly what this means is not clear; but it is only worded that way when referring to the New Earth. And here the Lamb will feed His bride, and lead her to the living fountains of waters. And God shall wipe away all tears from her eyes. Once the "True Church" is raptured she will be married to the Lamb, and she will always be near Him.

We have carefully examined details of happenings between the 6th and 7th seal; but let's go back and summarize the events. First of all, picture this earth as a battlefield; and the two supernatural enemies are Satan and God. They are fighting over the people, each one trying to get the people to follow them. God uses truth, and Satan uses lies and trickery. God teaches His people the truth; but one of the rules of this war is that Satan be allowed to tempt God's children. In this way Satan gets the opportunity to try to win them over. Also, God is giving man a free will; he has the opportunity to choose. And each of us must make a choice between the two. Jesus said that you could not serve two masters; and He also said that, if you are not for me, you are against me. Regardless of how tempting it is, you just can't continue to sit on the fence!

This is not a one-sided war; any time Satan is showing

great strength, there is a strong witness for Christ in this dispensation. Take the early church and the Reformation periods; Satan persecuted the Christians beyond description, and never was the witness for Christ stronger. In other words, God sort of keeps things even. And this is one reason that I have come to the following conclusion: I believe that the two witnesses of God will make their appearance at the time of the 6th seal. The word "sackcloth," used in describing the moon in the 6th seal, is also used in describing the two witnesses in Revelation 11:3. Here we also see a great earthquake.

Also, it is at this time, that Satan and his angels were with Michael and his angels. And Satan was thrown to earth along with his angels—the stars fell out of heaven. So we see God sending His two witnesses, and giving them great power, which we will go into later. And Satan being thrown out of heaven, he gives his power to Antichrist, and to the False Prophet. Remember, Antichrist has pretended to be a man of peace for 3½ years; but now he gets full power from Satan, in the middle of the week, and breaks his seven-year covenant with Israel. So we have a representation of both supernatural powers put on earth at this time, and both of them will be in power for 3½ years. We will discuss this in more detail later.

Also, at this time 144,000 Jews were given the seal of the living God; and I believe the "True Church" is also given this seal, as we too are the servants of God. Nothing can happen until this sealing is complete. So keep in mind that we have the arrival of God's two witnesses. Satan and his angels also arrived, and the seal of the living God was put on His servants—all from the time of the 6th seal to the 7th seal.

CHAPTER 24

THE SEVENTH SEAL

Rev. 8:1. And when he had opened the seventh seal there was silence in heaven about the space of half an hour.

A very unusual thing happens: there is silence in heaven for a period of time. Even the four living creatures and the twenty-four elders are silent; and we are told that the four living creatures rest not day and night from praising our Lord God. We could say that it was the "calm before the coming storm," which in a way it is. But I believe it was more than that. It was more like the silence of awesome expectation, as if all things in heaven "held their breath." The breaking of the seventh seal concludes the complete opening of the seven-sealed book, so that its full contents are revealed; and they knew that they were about to witness the greatest time of sorrow the world had seen.

Expectation and suspense can be so intense that one dares not breathe. You have heard it said, "It was so quiet you could hear a pin drop"? That is how it was in heaven.

Rev. 8:2. And I saw seven angels which stood before God; and to them were given seven trumpets.

Remember now, we have had the "first pains of childbirth" with the seven seals. Now the seventh seal introduces the "temptations of the Devil," or the 7 trumpets. God is allowing this in order to test the faith of the professing Christians. This would not be necessary if it weren't for the "Lukewarm" condition of God's Church today. This is their final chance to prove their faith. And if you consider worldly pleasures more important than Christ, and insist on the right to be your own master, and refuse to change, it could very well be that the Devil's temptations will be too much for you.

> Rev. 8:3-4. And another angel came and stood at the altar, having a golden censer; and there were given unto him much incense, that he should offer it with the prayers of all saints upon the golden altar which was before the throne. And the smoke of the incense, which came with the prayers of the saints, ascended up before God out of the angel's hand.

Before the Devil can start, prayers of all saints—those in heaven from other dispensations, and those still on earth from this age—were offered to God. Those in heaven might have prayed for their brothers on earth. Those on earth could have prayed for their loved ones who were to be tested, asking God to give them strength; and also thanking Him for their protection during this time of tribulation.

This angel who is seen offering incense would have to be an angel-priest. Many believe that he is Christ who still has a people on the earth for whom to plead. It is true that Christ intercedes for all his saints—we should always pray through Jesus. So it is quite possible that this is Christ. In another of his many roles. And it was as if the offerings of people went up to God wrapped in an envelope of perfumed incense.

> Rev. 8:5. And the angel took the censer, and filled it

with fire of the Altar, and cast it unto the earth; and there were voices, and thunderings, and lightnings, and an earthquake.

After all was prepared, all the servants of God were sealed with His seal, and the prayers of the saints were offered to God, this same angel-priest gave a signal—a signal which broke the silence of heaven. He filled the senser with fire of the altar and cast it into the earth. The suspense was broken, it had begun; voices were heard and storm warnings were given, and an earthquake (not a great one as it was in the sixth seal, when the two witnesses arrived) which announces a major event. I believe this is the exact time that Satan arrives on earth. God would not have permitted him to arrive before His people were prepared, as Satan will not waste any time when he gets here.

Rev. 12:10-12. And I heard a loud voice saying in heaven, Now is come salvation, and strength, and the kingdom of our God, and the power of his Christ: for the accuser of our brethren is cast down, which accused them before God day and night. And they overcame him by blood of the Lamb, and by the word of their testimony; and they loved not their lives unto the death. Therefore rejoice, ye heavens, and yet that dwell in them. Woe to the inhabiters of the earth and of the sea! For the devil is come down unto you, having great wrath, because he knoweth that he hath but a short time.

So I believe Michael and his angels cast Satan and his angels to earth on signal from the angel-priest after they had defeated them in war. So, keep this in mind—the two witnesses came at the sixth seal and Satan at the seventh seal; and each had 3½ years of power.

CHAPTER 25

THE FIRST FOUR TRUMPET JUDGMENTS

Rev. 8:7. The first angel sounded, and there followed hail and fire mingled with blood, and they were cast upon the earth: and the third part of trees were burnt up, and all green grass was burnt up.

Compare the first trumpet with the 7th Egyptian Plague:

Exodus 9:22-26. And the Lord said unto Moses, Stretch forth thine hand toward heaven, that there may be hail in all the land of Egypt, upon man, and upon beast, and upon every herb of the field, throughout the land of Egypt. And Moses stretched forth his rod toward heaven: and the Lord sent thunder and hail, and the fire ran along the ground; and the Lord rained hail upon the land of Egypt. So there was hail, and fire mingled with the hail, very grievous, such as there was none like it in all the land of Egypt since it became a nation. And the hail smote throughout all the land of Egypt all that was in the field, both man and beast; and the hail smote every herb of the field, and brake every tree of the field. Only in the land of Goshen, where the Children of Israel were, was there no hail.

It is plain to see that the 1st trumpet is a repetition of the 7th Egyptian Plague. We take that literally, and I believe we must take the first trumpet literally also.

Rev. 8:8-9. And the second angel sounded, and as it were a great mountain burning with fire was cast into the sea; and the third part of the sea became blood. And the third part of the creatures which were in the sea, and had life, died; and the third part of the ships were destroyed.

It is clear that a literal burning mass falls into the sea. Possibly a meteor will fall into the Mediterranean Sea and destroy a third of the creatures in the sea and one-third of the ships. If you have ever seen the crater that just a small meteor has caused, you wouldn't find it difficult to visualize how extensive the damage would be if a large one were to fall, say, in the area of a large naval fleet. The blood from the killed and injured would discolor a third of the sea.

Rev. 8:10-11. And the third angel sounded, and there fell a great star from heaven, burning as it were a lamp, and it fell upon the third part of the rivers, and upon the fountains of waters; And the name of the star is called wormwood; and the third part of the waters became wormwood; and many men died of the waters, because they were made bitter.

This great burning star called Wormwood will fall from the heavens and poison one-third of the fresh water. Perhaps

152

by exploding in the atmosphere, a meteor could release gases which would be absorbed by the river and poison them.

Rev. 8:12. And the fourth angel sounded, and the third part of the sun was smitten, and the third part of the moon, and the third part of the stars; so as the third part of them was darkened, and the day shone not for a third part of it, and the night likewise.

So far, what has been affected? One-third of the trees and vegetation, one-third of the sea and its creatures, along with one-third of the ships on it, one-third of the rivers or fresh waters. Now one-third of the sun, moon, and the stars are darkened.

Luke tells of this and says men's hearts will be failing them for fear, as the heavens will be shaken. I believe this is more than just a possibility! I have offered some possibilities of what could occur, but no one can be sure of this until it happens. God won't reveal everything to us beforehand. But, however you want to look at it, this will be a terrible time for "Lukewarm" Christians that are alive. It isn't my purpose to frighten you but to warn you, and to encourage you to get off the fence and go all the way for Christ and the shelter He offers.

Rev. 8:13. And I beheld, and heard an angel flying through the midst of heaven, saying with a loud voice, Woe, woe, woe, to the inhabiters of the earth by reason of the other voices of the trumpet of the three angels, which are yet to sound!

This verse introduces the three trumpets to follow, which are distinguished from the four we have already commented upon, as "woe" trumpets. They are called this because they are a more intensified form of judgment than any previously portrayed.

CHAPTER 26

THE FIFTH AND SIXTH TRUMPET JUDG-MENTS

Rev. 9:1-11. And the fifth angel sounded, and I saw a star fall from heaven unto the earth: and to him was given the key of the bottomless pit. And he opened the bottomless pit; and there arose a smoke out of the pit, as the smoke of a great furnace; and the sun and the air were darkened by reason of the smoke of the pit. And there came out of the smoke locusts upon the earth; and unto them was given power, as the scorpions of the earth have power. And it was commanded them that they should not hurt the grass of the earth, neither any green thing, neither any tree; but only those men which have not the seal of God in their foreheads. And to them it was given that they should not kill them, but that they should be tormented five months; and their torment was as the torment of a scorpion, when he striketh a man. And in those days shall men seek death, and shall not find it; and shall desire to die, and death shall flee from them. And the shapes of the locusts were like unto horses prepared unto battle; and

155

on their heads were as it were crowns like gold, and their faces were as the faces of men. And they had hair as the hair of women, and their teeth were as the teeth of lions. And they had breastplates, as it were breastplates of iron; and the sound of their wings was as the sound of chariots of many horses running to battle. And they had tails like unto scorpions, and there were stings in their tails; and their power was to hurt men five months. And they had a king over them, which is the angel of the bottomless pit, whose name in the Hebrew tongue is Abaddon, but in the Greek tongue hath his name Apollyon.

The fifth trumpet certainly cannot be taken literally. This is not a real star—it says "to him was given." This angel has the key to the bottomless pit. He will not be Satan himself or a fallen angel, as God would not trust them with the key to the bottomless pit. And also we see the "same angel" in Revelation 20:1 binding Satan and casting him into the bottomless pit for 1000 years.

The picture of terror mounts in its grim and awful intensity. Now the terrors which are coming upon the earth are beyond nature; that is, they are not simply terrors which come from the forces of elemental nature. From the smoke which emerged from the pit, there came a terrible invasion of locusts. First let us see how bad this would be, in order to evaluate the destruction of what they are a symbol of. Anyone familiar with the locust plagues, or who has had them described to him, knows how the locusts appear in swarms so vast that they seem like a great cloud, actually shutting out the sun and filling the whole air. They devour every bit of vegetation before them. Their destructiveness can best be appreciated from the fact that it is recorded that, in 1866, a plague of locusts invaded Algiers, and so total was the destruction which they caused that 200,000 people perished of famine in the days which followed. All through the Old Testament, the locust is the symbol of destruction. These locusts cannot be taken literally, because they won't hurt the vegetation—only people who do not have the seal of God. These scorpion-type of locusts seem to be a vast army of demons who shall enter into and take possession of the bodies of men, and so torment them that they shall wish to die, but won't be able to. They will bring with them a system of erroneous teachings, damnable heresies which deny the Lord. Like the locusts, they shall shut out the sun; man's true and supreme source of light. They symbolize a spiritual plague in the last days; this Satanic envoy deludes the nations. In II Thessalonians it says that God shall send strong delusion; but our Lord limits Satan's power. They cannot hurt those with God's seal; for if it were possible, they would deceive the very elect.

The detailed description of the locusts actually points out different characteristics of those demons and their evil teachings. I believe that opinions could vary widely here, and it isn't really necessary that we know exactly what they will be like—as destructive as the locust is bad enough! So I'll just take three symbolic descriptions and explain them, to show you what I mean. For instance, their faces were as the faces of men—this could imply intelligence, and these evil teachers make a great appeal to human reason, describing the truth of God as myths or fiction and cunningly-devised fables. Their appeal is to human intelligence—to the mind, rather than to the heart and conscience, as Scripture does.

They had hair like hair of women. In the Old Testament, a woman's hair is her glory, her natural attraction. So their teachings will have a natural attraction and seductiveness to man when presented; but they will prove to have teeth like lions, tearing to pieces those who put their trust in them.

For a limited time, five months, these demons and their teachings will be permitted to dominate those who would not let Christ the Lord reign over them. In His place, Satan himself is worshipped. Satan, the great arch-enemy of God, who has been plotting man's destruction from the very beginning! Satan is their king! (In worshipping Antichrist, the

157

Son of the Devil, you worship the Father, Satan).

Rev. 9:12. One woe is past; and behold, there come two woes more hereafter.

Yes, there is more to come! But if you have survived thus far, and not bowed down to the demands of Antichrist and his army of demons, including the False Prophet, you can no longer be called "Lukewarm Christians"—because you've had to change and let Christ rule, and be your Master, or the Devil would have won you over to him. (I do not speak of the "the dwellers of the earth," as they never had a chance against Antichrist) But, even though you have become faithful to our Lord, it was not soon enough to receive the seal of God. And you still may have to face the supreme test; but rely on Christ for strength and witness for Him till the end, and your reward will be great in just a little while. Hold fast, as He comes soon.

Before we go any further, but without going into too much detail, let me remind you of one thing. The Devil was thrown out of heaven at the seventh seal and gave all his power to Antichrist and the False Prophet; who have been, as the saying goes, "running the show" since then. They had great power and could work great wonders in front of men. Antichrist has proclaimed to be God and demanded worship from all—particularly the Jew. Just as I felt that what was described as the beginning of sorrows took place mostly in different parts of the world other than Jerusalem, I now feel that what is described in the trumpets will be felt worse in the Holy Land. But the power of Antichrist and his armies of demons will extend all over the world.

Just glancing over the five trumpets which we have examined, it rather appears as though Satan tries to use the first four trumpets to scare men half out of their minds, to make them more receptive to the fifth trumpet. On the whole, if people are in bad enough shape physically and mentally, they will accept most anything: particularly when

158

this power seems so powerful, and their teachings so reasonable. The "dwellers of the earth" will worship Antichrist. Many of the "Lukewarm Christians" will turn their backs on our Lord. Luke shows us how effective the methods of Antichrist are, as here are the results of the fifth trumpet:

> Luke 13:12-13. Now the brother shall betray the brother to death, and the father and son; and the children shall rise up against their parents, and shall cause them to be put to death, And ye shall be hated of all men for my sake: but he that shall endure unto the end, the same shall be saved.

Conditions such as these seem unreal to us; but ask someone who lived in one of those countries that Hitler conquered during World War Two.

The demonic locusts were only allowed to hurt, torment, and spread their system of erroneous teachings, but not to kill. But now we see another invasion coming in the sixth trumpet, where one-third of the human race will be killed.

THE SIXTH TRUMPET

> Rev. 9:13-15. And the sixth angel sounded, and I heard a voice from the four horns of the golden altar which is before God, Saying to the sixth angel which had the trumpet, Loose the four angels which are bound in the great river Euphrates. And the four angels were loosed, which were prepared for an hour, and a day, and a month, and a year, for to slay the third part men.

I believe that the fact that these four angels are bound means that they are bad angels and are leaders of, or represent, an army of 200,000,000. They have been kept at the Euphrates, and the very hour of their release is determined; as well as the extent of their destruction. The time when this will happen is pre-set, and nothing will change it. Actually, I believe that Satan's plan to entrap men with his erroneous teachings and unholy philosophies got out of hand, and this war is an unforeseen result of this.

Rev. 9:16-19. And the number of the army of the horsemen were two hundred thousand thousand; and I heard the number of them. And thus I saw horses in the vision, and them that sat on them, having breastplates of fire, and of jacinth, and brimstone: and the heads of the horses were as the heads of lions; and out of their mouths issued fire and smoke and brimstone. By these three was the third part of men killed, by the fire, and by the smoke, and by the brimstone, which issued out of their mouths. For their power is in their mouth, and in their tails: for their tails were like unto serpents, and had heads, and with them they do hurt.

Some seem to believe that this is an army of supernatural demons. But I believe these are men, no doubt infested with hate, desire for killing, for power, and every kind of wickedness. Remember, not all peoples of the world are Christian or Jew; and they will resent this Antichrist fellow trying to take over the world. So I believe that this huge army are great Asiatic hordes, probably led by Russia, which are gathered to invade the Holy Land. But, regardless of whether this army is another demon invasion, or men from the north, the results are the same: one third of the human race will be killed by fire, smoke, and by brimstone or sulphur issuing out of their mouths. There is one question that keeps coming to my mind since I read John's description of this army: how would John describe a massive number of armored tanks of the future, perhaps from a distance?

Rev. 9:20-21. And the rest of the men which were not killed by these plagues yet repented not of the works of their hands, that they should not worship devils, and idols of gold, and silver, and brass, and stone, and of wood: which neither can see, nor hear, nor walk. Neither repented they of their murders, nor of their sorceries, nor of their fornication, nor of their thefts.

It is hard to believe that having one third of mankind killed would have no effect so far as bringing men back to God and repentance. But, on the other hand, how do people react now when things go wrong? Instead of examining themselves, they blame God for letting it happen, and become bitter; and some even turn away from Him. And this is just what happened. They paid no attention to the warning and continued their wickedness.

CHAPTER 27

THE STRUCTURE OF THE BOOK OF REVELATION

Before we go any farther, it is important that we understand the structure of the Book of Revelation. The main body of the book is divided into four sevens: the letters to the churches, the seals, the trumpets, and the vials. Notice also, that after the sixth seal, the sixth trumpet, and the sixth vial, there is a pause from the main action, and more information is given us. You see, so many things are going on at the same time, and it is impossible to tell everything at once. It is just like, say, you are telling a story, and stop now and then, and say, "But wait a minute. There is also something else that is going on right now that we should know about before we go on." Some describe this extra information as parenthetical portions, such as Chapter 7; now we have Chapter 10:—13, Chapter 11, and also later in Chapter 16:15.

Chronologically, when we reach Chapter 11:18, we have actually gone to the establishment of the earthly kingdom spoken of in Chapter 20:4-6; for the seventh trumpet introduces the world kingdom of our God and His Christ, and Verse 18 continues on to very briefly describe what will happen after that, till Antichrist and the False Prophet are destroyed. So from there on it is just a more detailed description of what has already been described, till we get to Chapter 20:6. There are some who believe that Verse 18 takes you to the White Throne Judgment; and I won't argue the point, as I don't believe it is that important.

In other words, from Chapter 4 to Chapter 12, the facts are presented in orderly sequence—or a prophetic outline. And now, starting with the twelfth chapter, it is as if the redemption scroll has been turned over and we get a second view of some events with more details, and are introduced to the seven personages or actors who play major roles during the last days.

CHAPTER 28

THE LITTLE BOOK

Now back to the pause in the action, after the sixth trumpet.

Rev. 10:1-4. And I saw another mighty angel come down from heaven, clothed with a cloud: and a rainbow was upon his head, and his face was as it were the sun, and his feet as pillars of fire: and he had in his hand a little book open: and he set his right foot upon the sea, and his left foot on the earth, and cried with a loud voice, as when a lion roareth: and when he had cried, seven thunders uttered their voices. And when the seven thunders had uttered their voices, I was about to write: and I had heard a voice from heaven saying unto me, Seal up those things which the seven thunders uttered, and write them not.

I don't think there is any doubt that this mighty angel, who was clothed with a cloud, a rainbow on his head, his face like the sun, and his feet like pillars of fire, was our Lord Jesus Christ, Himself. John got a preview of an event close at hand; but couldn't reveal it. The description of the angel is the same as that given of Christ in Chapter 1. It is believed that our Lord is brought before us in this angelic character because at this time He would be dealing largely with Israel, and the true Messiah has not been revealed to them yet. They have believed that Antichrist is the Messiah. Therefore it is but natural that Christ should take the same position that He occupied toward them in Old Testament times. And until the moment of His full manifestation, He is to them the Angel of the Covenant—the cloud that led them from Egypt. When Solomon built the temple and dedicated it to Jehovah, He came in a cloud—and, five centuries later, was seen leaving in a cloud; and he has never returned. This angel has a rainbow wrapped around his head—showing that he brings a covenant with him. Remember, when the full number of gentiles are completed, a new covenant will be made with the Israelites. And of course, his face being as the sun fits Saul's description. Also his feet as pillars of fire links up with being like unto fine brass, as if they were burned in a furnace, found in Chapter 11. So even though He appears as an angel, it is Christ.

Next we are told that He had a little open book in His hand. It is generally believed that this book is the same one that we saw Him take from the hand of the Father on the throne. But nowhere do I find the first book described as "little," such as this one is. So I believe that John is given a limited revelation about a quite small period of time, described in the little book, which at the moment is not to pass on to men. Perhaps it concerns the mystery of God which will be finished when the seventh angel sounds. This we don't know, as God has His secrets in all dispensations, and will reveal them when He is ready. Just like the secret of the seven letters to the seven churches; God couldn't permit their secret meaning to be revealed in the earth church periods, or it would have been disastrous. Those people would have given up, if they hadn't expected Christ's return to be soon.

Rev. 10:5-7. And the angel which I saw stand upon the

sea and upon the earth lifted up his hand to heaven, and sware by him that liveth forever and ever, who created heaven, and the things that therein are, and the earth, and the things that therein are, and the sea, and the things which are therein, that there should be time no longer: But in the days of the voice of the seventh angel, when he shall begin to sound, the mystery of God should be finished, as he hath declared to his servants the prophets.

Christ, in angelic form, makes a gesture of taking possession by putting His feet on the land and on the sea. He was paid the price and followed the requirements in the redemption scroll, which was to give Satan a chance to tempt the people, allowing him full power for three and a half years. He raises his hand in victory and makes an announcement: "There shall be time no longer." This translation has misled many into thinking that this brings us to the end of time, whereas the context makes it very plain that such is not the case. And it is believed to be an inaccurate translation of the original. It is more likely to mean that "there should be no more delay." The point is that the hour of accomplishment has almost struck, and God will not delay the completion of all His plans and the fulfillment of His promises to His people. Six trumpets have sounded, and when the seventh angel sounds, the mystery of God should be finished. While Christ at this time takes formal possession of the earth, actual possession will not be until He comes as King at the close of the Tribulations. This is the time described in the following:

Hebrews 10:37. Yet a little while and he that shall come will come, and will not tarry.

Christ will not stay on earth at this time; He only came to take formal possession of the earth and to gather his servants, which are His possessions, and take them off the earth. And in gathering the complete number of gentiles, He will manifest Himself to the Jewish nation and their eyes will be opened, and they will know Christ and, after nearly 2000 years, realize their mistake. So the mystery of God and His Christ will be finished for the Jew, and the mystery of Christ and His rapture will be finished for the Christian. The dispensation of faith will have come to an end, and the dispensation of sight will have dawned. Those who had pierced Him because they did not believe that He was the Son of God shall mourn when they see that the crucified Nazarene and the Angel of the Covenant are identical.

Rev. 1:7. Behold, he cometh with clouds and every eye shall see him, and they also which pierced him; and all kindred of the earth shall wail because of him. Even so, Amen.

Rev. 10:8-11. And the voice which I heard from heaven spake unto me again, and said, Go and take the little book which is open in the hand of the angel which standeth upon the sea and upon the earth. And I went unto the angel, and said unto him, Give me the little book. And he said unto me, Take it, and eat it up; and it shall make thy belly bitter, but it shall be in thy mouth as honey. And I took the little book out of the angel's hand, and ate it up; and it was in my mouth sweet as honey: and as soon as I had eaten it, my belly was bitter. And he said unto me, Thou must prophesy again before many peoples, and nations, and tongues, and kings.

First of all, let me point out something in this passage which is significant, and applies to all that God has for His children. John is told to take the little book, in fact, twice. This shows us two things: in reaching out to take the little book, John has to exert some effort in order to get this revelation; just as we have to exert some effort in order to understand the Word of God. (Don't misunderstand this). You cannot find the true meaning of God's Word by your efforts alone; far from it. But you have to make the effort first, sincerely and humbly, before God will begin to reveal the truths to you. The other thing this points out is that any revelation from God is never forced on any man; he must take it. God does not force His Word on you, He does not force you to accept Him as Master—it has to be your choice. If you have made that choice and are now one of God's messengers, remember it is now your job to offer the message of God to others; but not to try and force what you believe to be true on others.

John was told to eat the little book that was in the hand of the angel; and that it would be sweet to the mouth but bitter to the belly. There was a similar experience when Ezekiel (Ezekiel 3:1) was told to eat the roll and go speak with God's Words to the house of Israel. John was told to digest or meditate on the contents of this little prophetic book. Prophetic truth is generally sweet and attractive —particularly to those whose interest is just being awakened in it. And if you have really been digesting what you have been reading, you find that it leads to self-judgment, and to separation from evil; and this will always be bitter. In short, God's truth makes demands upon people, and if you conscientiously undertake to walk in the truth revealed, you too will learn something of its bitterness. For John, it was a real privilege to be given the secrets of heaven, and some of the secrets were probably great news for some people; but what would it mean for the rest of them—disaster? It was sweet at first; but then became bitter. It was a two-edged sword; for it was both a message of salvation and a message of damnation. This is always true with the Word of God; a fact which is too often forgotten. Today people hear sermons on the love of God, His mercy, and His goodness, which should be; but also there should be sermons on judgment and damnation, too. God is love, but He is also justice. He is merciful, but He is righteous. He loves sinners, but He hates sin.

John is told that he must prophesy again, as he has done

169

in the previous section, concerning many peoples.

During the Tribulations, as I have mentioned previously, there are times when more than one thing is going on at the same time. If it is just a small incident, there is just a pause, and we are told about it; but if it is something which lasts a long time, John waits until it is convenient, and then back-tracks to pick up that part of the story. And this is just what happens in Chapter 11. Just before the seventh trumpet, we see that the two witnesses of God are killed by Antichrist; and we haven't had a chance to learn anything about them, even though they have been given power for the last three and one-half years. So we now go back three and one-half years, to when God sent His two witnesses to earth. As I have stated before, I believe they arrived at the time of the sixth seal, or just before Satan was thrown out of heaven at the seventh seal, and at which time he gave all his power to Antichrist. Also, remember that the chart showed the seven seals lasting three and one-half years. Antichrist was a man of peace through the "beginning of the sorrows" or the seven seals; and the temple had been rebuilt in Jerusalem, and they worshipped there again. The Jewish people were once again gathered together as a nation, and they felt secure under the rule of Antichrist. This sets the scene for Chapter 11.

CHAPTER 29

THE TWO WITNESSES

Rev. 11:1-3. And there was given me a reed like unto a rod: and the angel stood, saying, Rise, and measure the temple of God, and the altar, and them that worship therein. But the court which is without the temple leave out, and measure it not; for it is given unto the gentiles: and the holy city shall they tread under foot forty and two months. And I will give power unto my two witnesses, and they shall prophesy a thousand two hundred and threescore days, clothed in sackcloth.

The temple of God will be rebuilt in Jerusalem probably before the tribulations start. It was destroyed in 70 A.D., and Israel hasn't had a temple since; because it must be rebuilt on its original site. And on its original site is now the Dome of Rock. The Mohammedans believe the rock formation inside the Dome is the place from which Mohammed ascended to heaven, so it is sacred ground to them also. So, somehow, the Dome of Rock will be destroyed, and the temple rebuilt there. And back at the time of the sixth seal, as we have to go back to pick up this story, John is told to measure this temple and them that worship therein. This shows that our Lord is claiming possession by measuring or surveying the temple, and them that worship there at this time. That is to say that once again God owns a witnessing company, and that will be during the Tribulation period. But John is not to measure the court, for it is given to the gentiles, and the holy city shall they tread under foot for forty-two months. The "gentiles," to the Jew, applied to all peoples except themselves—the ungodly. And Jesus is saying that the heathen will overrun the city for three and one-half years. And at the same time He will give power to His two witnesses, and they shall prophesy for three and one-half years clothed in sackcloth in Jerusalem. Once again, my belief that the two witnesses and Satan will have full power on earth at the same time is substantiated.

There is now the question of who the two witnesses are. I don't think there is any doubt that they are Moses and Elijah. I am not saying that they will be called by those names, though. Elijah came ahead of the Lord before, preaching the Gospel of the Kingdom, as John the Baptist.

Matthew 18:10. And his disciples asked him, saying, Why then say the scribes that Elijah must first come? And Jesus answered and said unto them, Elijah truly shall first come, and restore all things. But I say unto you, that Elijah is come already, and they knew him not, but have done unto him whatsoever they listed. Likewise shall also the Son of Man suffer of them. Then the disciples understood that he spoke unto them of John the Baptist.

I shall continue to refer to them as Elijah and Moses because it really will be them, but called by different names. Just as Christ will be called by another name, when he returns.

Malachi 4:5. Behold, I will send you Elijah the prophet before the coming of the great and dreadful day of the Lord.

It was also those two who appeared to Jesus on the Mount of Transfiguration. And they have miraculous powers like Elijah and Moses. I just don't see how it could possibly be anyone else.

Rev. 11:4. These are the two olive trees, and the two candlesticks standing before the God of the earth.

The two olive trees are the two anointed ones, or the priesthood; and the prophetic testimony which will keep the lampstand, or the worship and testimony, shining for God during this three and one-half years of terror.

Rev. 11:5-7. And if any man will hurt them fire proceedeth out of their mouth, and devoureth their enemies; and if any man will hurt them, he must in this manner be killed. These have power to shut heaven, that it rain not in the days of their prophesy: and have power over waters to turn them to blood, and to smite the earth with all plagues, as often as they will.

These witnesses are immortal until their work is done. Their powers, given them by God, make it impossible for them to be harmed until the set time. This is going to almost be a repeat of the Cross. Notice how similar it is, as we go along. It is said that fire proceedeth out of their mouths and burns up their enemies, and that they have power to shut the heavens so that it will not rain in the days of their prophecy.

II Kings 1:10. And Elijah answered and said to the captain of fifty, If I be a man of God, then let fire come down from heaven, and consume thee and thy fifty. And there came down fire from heaven, and consumed him and his fifty.

The fire will not actually come from Elijah's mouth, just the request—God does the rest.

> I Kings 17:1. Elijah the Tishbite, who was of the inhabitants of Gilead, said unto Ahab, As the Lord God of Israel liveth, before whom I stand, there shall not be dew nor rain these years, but according to my word.

And there was no rain for over three years, and there was a great drought and famine all over the land. Elijah caused this to happen once because the people had forsaken the commandments of the Lord and followed a false god; and I believe it is plain that there will be a repeat of this event.

It is also said that they had the power to turn the waters into blood, and to smite the earth with all plagues, just as Moses did in Egypt.

> Rev. 11:7-8. And when they shall have finished their testimony, the beast that ascendeth out of the bottomless pit shall make war against them, and shall overcome them, and kill them. And their dead bodies shall lie in the street of the great city, which spiritually is called Sodom and Egypt, where also our Lord was crucified.

Now they have been here on earth for three and one-half years, during the testing of the "Lukewarm Christians." They have been walking proof of the power of God, and have been giving testimony concerning the Second Coming of Christ and his Kingdom, which He will set up shortly. They have been God's representatives, and have given strength and encouragement to those Christians who are holding fast to their faith in Jesus Christ. If it had not been for them, none would be saved from this period of testing. For Satan has had his representatives here, too, and they have really made it rough on all the people that would not worship the beast. The beast has wanted to get rid of these two witnesses, no doubt, for some time; but was not able to until the set time—just as in the case of Jesus. At the proper time, Satan finally succeeds; he kills those two pests! It seems as though he has won! He will not permit the people to bury their bodies—he left their bodies lying in the streets for all to see. He wanted everyone to see these men who had claimed to be from God, now dead, just like anyone else. Yes, he had won; of course, he had thought that when he crucified Jesus. Maybe that was another reason he didn't want them buried: he didn't want any stories going around about them being raised to heaven. Yes, he had overcome the two saints; and their bodies lay in the streets of Jerusalem, which spiritually is called Sodom and Egypt. Jerusalem had sunk so low; they had already crucified Jesus Christ, and now were regarding the death of His two witnesses with joy.

> Rev. 11:9-10. And they of the people and kindreds and tongues and nations shall see their dead bodies three days and a half, and shall not suffer their dead bodies to be put in graves. And they that dwell upon the earth shall rejoice over them, and make merry, and shall send gifts one to another; because these two prophets tormented them that dwelt on the earth.

Here, we have a sad picture—joy among the dwellers of the earth because the last testimony for God on earth has been destroyed. Of course they look upon these two witnesses as their enemies, who have tormented them since the day they appeared on the scene. They congratulate one another; now they can live without hearing their voices, which were always questioning their wickedness and prophesying doom for them. And best of all, surely—they have seen the end of all those plagues, and the drought that these two witnesses were responsible for. They called a holiday, and celebrated; making merry and sending gifts to one another. I can imagine that those who feared them most are now among the bravest, with their terrible remarks about them. And the

Christians who were still holding fast to their faith—their feelings were probably similar to those of the disciples when Jesus was crucified. Their leaders were gone!

But the seeming victory for Satan really spells defeat:

Rev. 11:11-12. And after three days and an half the Spirit of life from God entered into them, and they stood upon their feet; and great fear fell upon them which saw them. And they heard a great voice from heaven saying unto them, Come up hither. And they ascended up to heaven in a cloud; and their enemies beheld them.

Let me make a comparison here, before we go into this passage. Their testimony lasted three and one-half years, and after three and one-half days they rose from the dead. Jesus' ministry could have lasted three and a half years, and on the third day he rose. Like Jesus they ascend to heaven in a cloud; but unlike their Master, their enemies saw them.

I believe this to be one of the most terrifying, and the most wonderful, passage in Revelation! Imagine yourself at a funeral home. Someone has died that you hated; and you, with a lot of others, came to the funeral home—not to pay your last respects, but to satisfy your hatred by seeing him dead. And all of a sudden, the dead man arises up out of the coffin and stands before you! I imagine that that, in itself, would cause a few heart attacks. It says great fear fell upon them which saw them. Then they heard a great voice from heaven saying unto them, "Come up hither." Who is the voice speaking to? The great voice, which is Christ, is calling to Moses and Elijah, and all of those which they symbolize! This is the beginning of the rapture!

I believe the Mount of Transfiguration is significant here. As it is found in Matthew 17, Jesus had just said that there were some there that wouldn't die before they had seen the Son of Man coming in His Kingdom; and a few days later, Jesus took Peter, James, and John up on a mountain. And they saw Jesus transformed—his raiment became shining, and there appeared Elijah and Moses talking with Jesus. This scene shows Christ coming into His Kingdom—how it will be when He comes to reign on earth. There will be Christ glorified, as he symbolizes Himself. There will be all those that have died in Christ, symbolized by Moses. And there will be all those that were raptured alive, symbolized by Elijah. Thus Peter, James, and John saw the Son of Man coming into His Kingdom, just as Jesus said: but I don't think they understood it. Of course, we already know that all those that died in Christ and those that were raptured will return to earth with Him—He shall return with His saints. But the fact that Moses and Elijah symbolized those two groups of people then is what I'm bringing to your attention. And it leads me to believe that in the present scene in the tribulation they still symbolize the same two groups of people. And in Revelation 11:12, between the sixth and the seventh trumpets, Moses and Elijah are taken up to heaven!

There is something else here that my attention is drawn to. Why is it brought out so clearly that the two bodies were brought to their feet? And they even mentioned how fearful the people were before they heard the great voice saying, "Come up hither," at which time they ascended up to heaven in a cloud. Could it be that the act of being raised to their feet symbolized those other dead being raised from the grave? For they will rise first:

I Thessalonians 4:16. For the Lord Himself shall descend from heaven with a shout, with the voice of the archangel, and with the trump of God: and the dead in Christ shall rise first. Then we which are alive and remain shall be caught up together with them in the clouds, to meet the Lord in the air: and so shall we ever be with the Lord.

This could be interpreted to mean that the dead shall rise out of the grave first, then, together with those who are

177

alive in Christ, shall be caught up in the clouds to meet the Lord. That is, they all ascend to heaven together, just as Moses and Elijah did. This would explain why their two bodies were brought to their feet first; there is even an indication of a pause, while they mention the fear of the people, before ascending. If Jesus wasn't pointing something out to us, the bodies could have just been seen rising in a cloud.

I must state again that I believe this is the beginning of the Rapture! And once more, as in the past, Elijah and Moses have delivered God's Children from spiritual bondage and physical bondage. In the past Elijah appeared in the darkest day of Israel's spiritual bondage, when they had departed from the Lord under Jezebel and Ahab. God had sent Elijah, the prophet of fire, to deliver Israel from spiritual bondage, just as Moses was called by God to deliver them out of physical bondage in Egypt.

Rev. 11:13. And the same hour was there a great earthquake, and the tenth part of the city fell, and in the earthquake were slain of men 7000, and the remnant was affrighted and gave glory to the God of heaven.

And at the same hour that the two saints were being called up to heaven, or resurrected, there was a great earthquake. As I have mentioned before, an earthquake symbolized an important event, and this is a great one. Notice that this earthquake did not occur when the saints were killed, indicating an angry God whose punishment this was. It came in the same hour as they were resurrected.

There was a mild quake when Christ died:

Matthew 27:51b. And the earth did quake and the rocks rent.

But there was a great earthquake when he was resurrected:

178

Matthew 28:1-2. In the end of the Sabbath, as it began to dawn toward the first day of the week, came Mary Magdalene and the other Mary to see the sepulchre. And, behold, there was a great earthquake; for the angel of the Lord descended from heaven, and came and rolled back the stone from the door, and sat upon it.

What else occurred after the resurrection of our Lord?

Matthew 27:52-53. And the graves were opened and many bodies of the saints which slept arose, and came out of the graves after his resurrection, and went into the holy city, and appeared unto many.

In comparing the two, we have Christ's resurrection, a great earthquake, and Old Testament saints coming out of the graves; then the resurrection of Elijah and Moses, a great destructive earthquake, and, I believe, all the dead saints of this dispensation rising from the grave. Then a rapture of all saints!

This earthquake added to the terror, and after that, the remnant gave glory to God. The only real way to give glory to God is to repent and turn from your evil ways. So, here again, people were won for God by a sacrificial death; this time two witnesses, and by God's vindication of them. I have pointed out right along the similarities, and I must say that this is almost the story of the Cross and Resurrection all over again, in the End Time.

179

CHAPTER 30

THE SEVENTH TRUMPET

We have now completed the parenthesis between the sixth and seventh trumpet.

Rev. 11:14. The second woe is past: and behold, the third woe cometh quickly.

I believe the purpose of this verse is just to re-establish the fact that the second woe is past and that we are back to the place where we stopped, to bring you up to date on a couple of other things that have been happening. The third woe cometh quickly, and is none other than the seventh and last of the trumpets, which ushers in the world Kingdom of our God and His Christ; and it includes the seven vial judgments. It seems like a long time since we discussed the sixth trumpet or the second woe, but I think this verse is also pointing out that the third woe actually follows the second one quickly.

Rev. 11:15-18. And the seventh angel sounded; and there were great voices in heaven, saying, The Kingdoms of this world are become the kingdoms of our Lord, and His Christ; and he shall reign for ever and ever. And the four and twenty elders, which sat before God on their seats, fell upon their faces, and worshipped God, saying, We give thee thanks, O Lord God Almighty, which art, and wast, and art to come; because thou hast taken to thee thy great power, and hast reigned. And the nations were angry, and thy wrath is come, and the time of the dead, that they should be judged, and that thou shouldest give reward unto thy servants and prophets, and to the saints, and them that fear thy name, small and great; and shouldest destroy them which destroy the earth.

I have stated that I believed that the rapture started with the actual raising of Elijah and Moses. Symbolically, they represent those who are to be raptured. The dead shall be risen up first. How long will all of this take? Not very long, as shown in the following passage:

I Corinthians 15:51-53. Behold, I shew you a mystery; we shall not all sleep, but we shall all be changed. In a moment, in the twinkling of an eye, at the last trump; for the trumpet shall sound, and the dead shall be raised incorruptible, and we shall be changed. For this corruptible must put on incorruption, and this mortal must put on immortality.

Rev. 10:7. But in the days of the voice of the seventh angel, when he shall begin to sound, the mystery of God should be finished, as he hath declared to his servants the prophets.

Don't get me wrong; we are not told how many days or hours it will take for the rapture to take place. The dead in Christ shall rise out of the grave first; then, in the twinkling of an eye, we who are alive in Christ shall be changed. My heart jumps with joy at the thought of this possibility. Victory over death and the grave! The following verse will no longer apply:

> Hebrews 9:27. And as it is appointed unto men once to die, but after this the judgment.

So far, to my knowledge, there have only been two men to experience this wonderful happening; but now all of God's "True Children" who are alive at this time will experience it. This is the day we look forward to with great anticipation, because this will just be the beginning of something so wonderful that it is beyond our comprehension. We have never experienced anything so great, so we cannot express it in words. It is not too late to be included in this great event; but you must seek out the true word of God, and accept Christ as your Master in all things, all of the time. It is not easy; you will be criticized, you may lose friends, and you may have to give up some worldly pleasures. But, whatever the price you have to pay now, it will certainly be worth it. And there is something else. All of this petty bickering in the churches today—forget it; it isn't important. Concentrate on "moving ahead in this world, by going back to Christ as your King." Give Him back the reins, and let Him rule as he once did; then there won't be all these problems that people have created for themselves. Let Christ rule in your heart, in your home, in your church, in all places. In surrendering yourself to Christ, you become His property, which He takes care of much better than you can. And take no chances on missing the rapture, if it comes in your life time. And I definitely think that there is a good possibility that I will see these events occur, if God permits me to live a fairly long life.

It does say in Revelation 10:7 that, when the seventh trumpet is blown by the seventh angel, the mystery of God should be finished. I think this will also include that which is described in Revelation 11:19. Everything will be opened for all to see. So, from the sixth trumpet through the seventh trumpet, a lot of things are happening, and in very rapid succession; or even at the same time.

We have been discussing what has been taking place on earth; but Verse 15 takes us back to heaven and the throne scene. As the seventh trumpet sounds, there is great joy in heaven because, as they say, the kingdoms of this world have now become the kingdoms of our Lord and His Christ, who shall reign forever. The power over the earth which Satan holds has been taken away from him; Christ has taken formal possession of his property. I believe John saw a preview of this and other events surrounding it in the "little book." And the twenty-four elders worshipped God, giving thanks to the Almighty, who was, who is, and who is to come. This points out that Christ is yet to come, in person, to reign. He will not taken actual possession until He is seen coming on the white horse with His armies of saints following Him. But first He has work to do. He must get all His saints off the earth: those who have been kept safe during the testing period, those who have passed the test, and those who died in Christ during this dispensation, or the Church Age.

> Matthew 24:30. And then shall appear the sign of the Son of Man in heaven and then shall all the tribes of earth mourn, and they shall see the Son of Man coming in the clouds of heaven with power and great glory. And he shall send his angels with a great sound of a trumpet, and they shall gather together his elect from the four winds, from one end of heaven to the other.

Yes, Christ took control of His property, and through the rapture he gathered his possessions and brought them up to heaven—to get them out of the way while he does a little house-cleaning on his earth. His possessions, or his servants, are temples which house his Spirit, and this prevents the Devil from having everything his own way, even now. And

Elijah and Moses really are a picture of this during the three and one-half years that Satan has had almost direct power through Antichrist and the False Prophet, which now comes to an end! Because, when the two prophets and the saints are taken out of the way in the Rapture, Christ will appear in the clouds, revealing who Antichrist really is. And Satan's term of power will come to an end at the seventh trumpet.

Rev. 1:7. Behold, he cometh with the clouds and every eye shall see him, and they also which pierced him: and all kindreds of the earth shall wail because of him.

Antichrist became so powerful because he convinced most of the world that he was God. The Jews thought He was the Messiah; those who hadn't received the truth of Christ before thought he was a God, probably; and many Lukewarm Christians thought he was Christ—returning. I would say the Jewish people at least had an excuse for not recognizing Antichrist as Satan; but the Christians had no excuse whatsoever! But now our Lord appears, the eyes of Israel are opened—they see the horrible mistake that they have made. We saw them, the remnant, repenting, and giving glory to God, back in Revelation 11:13.

The 18th verse is a summary, in the form of a very brief sketch, as to all that is still to come between now and the establishment of the Kingdom. So we leave the present and take a look into the future: Christ has just taken control, starting His eternal reign; and He is about to start pouring out His wrath on the angry nations, "the dwellers of the earth." For this is the time for judgment of the dead in Christ that are living. The seven vial judgments, which are the wrath of God, will cleanse the earth of wickedness. And then Christ will return with His uncrowned saints. Then it will be time to reward His servants, the prophets and the saints, and all who fear His Name. And Antichrist and the False Prophet will be destroyed by being cast alive into the lake of fire.

Now we shall return to the present to conclude the trumpets:

> Rev. 11:19. And the temple of God was opened in heaven, and there was seen in his temple the Ark of his testament: and there were lightnings and voices, and thunderings, and an earthquake, and great hail.

The temple of God in heaven was open, and there is seen in the temple the Ark of the Covenant—which brings to mind the covenant that God made with His chosen people, Israel. Now to the repenting remnant of Israelites that we saw, this will be a great day, after they get over the shock! For a minute, consider what they have experienced recently:

1. The two witnesses killed.
2. The witnesses raised to their feet, then ascended up in the clouds.
3. A great earthquake that killed 7000 in Jerusalem.
4. Saw Christ in the clouds.
5. They repented and gave glory to God.
6. Then—they saw the Ark of the Covenant, and without dying.

This is a sign from God to the "Chosen Israelites" that once again a relationship has been established between them. After all these years of silence, God has spoken to them again. How happy they will be to know that God has not rejected them forever! Many Jews will appear to come back to God at this time; but not all the descendants of Abraham are children of God. And only the chosen ones will remain faithful during the terrible judgments to come.

The fact that God fully displayed this most secret place to ordinary people means that the glory of God is going to be fully displayed. We are leaving the dispensation of faith; the seventh trumpet marks the end of that. The Millennium has started; the Day of Judgment on earth has started. This is a terrifying time for the enemies of God. The seven vial judgments are to come next, which will complete the third woe. After the Ark of the Covenant is seen, we have the same description as in the seventh seal, except that hail is added at the end. The lightnings and voices and thunderings are storm warnings of the coming events. And I believe the earthquake again marks a major event: the time when Christ takes control. Thus Satan's reign of power, which lasted three and one-half years, ends now, because Christ has raptured the Christians and enlightened the Jews. Remember, Satan came into power at the seventh seal and loses power at the seventh trumpet—three and one-half years. The witnesses came at the sixth seal and were raptured at the sixth trumpet—three and one-half years. And great hail is added this time, which indicates that the coming judgments will be even worse than the ones described in the seventh seal.

CHAPTER 31

THE WOMAN, THE DRAGON, AND THE MAN CHILD

John stops telling us about the Tribulations at this point, in order to acquaint us with the characters that play major roles in them. We have already been introduced to the two witnesses; now here is a woman.

Rev. 12:1-2. And there appeared a great wonder in heaven; a woman clothed with the sun, and the moon under her feet, and upon her head a crown of twelve stars: and she being with child cried, travailing in birth, and pained to be delivered.

A great wonder implies a miracle and leads us to believe there is something supernatural about this woman. Her description certainly connects her with the Israelites. And she is about to bring forth a child, and is suffering to be delivered.

Rev. 12:3-4. And there appeared another wonder in heaven: and behold, a great red dragon, having seven heads and ten horns, and seven crowns upon his heads. And his tail drew the third part of the stars of heaven, and did cast them to the earth; and the dragon stood before the woman which was ready to be delivered, for to devour her child as soon as it was born.

Here is a dragon who is Satan, and who is to conquer one-third of the angels of heaven in a war in heaven later. But now he waits before this woman who is about to give birth, ready to devour her child.

Rev. 12:5. And she brought forth a man child, who was to rule all nations with a rod of iron: and her child was caught up unto God, and to his throne.

This verse covers thirty-three years. There is no doubt that the man child is Jesus. And from the beginning, Satan tried to destroy the Son of God, through different people and in different ways. He thought that he finally did; but God had raised Jesus back to heaven and his throne.

Rev. 12:6. And the woman fled into the wilderness, where she hath a place prepared of God, that they should feed her there a thousand two hundred and threescore days.

We now jump from the time Christ died until the time of the Tribulations, which is what John is telling us about. We have just been told a few important events in this woman's history to help us identify her. We are told here that she is kept safe in a place prepared by God, for three and one-half years: kept safe from the dragon, or Satan, who will be after her.

Now we have all the facts, so let's try and identify this woman. Some believe that she is Mary, the Mother of Jesus Christ, as the man child is identified as Christ. But I believe the woman symbolizes something more than one individual. I believe that it would more likely be a particular group of people. And, considering her description, most people say that she is the nation of Israel, who is suffering to be delivered; and who also gave birth to Christ. I believe that is only partly true; to say that the nation of Israel gave birth to Christ is too broad a statement. For Christ came out of a very select group of Israelites.

Romans 9:6b. For they are not all Israel which are of Israel. (Not all the people of Israel are the chosen people of God.)

And it was from the Chosen People, a particular group of Israelites, or a community of the chosen ones of God, that Jesus sprang in His human lineage. So I believe this woman stands for that community of the chosen ones of God. Out of that community, Christ came; and it is this community, which has undergone terrible sufferings at the hands of this hostile world, which is ruled by Satan. They did not suffer because they were Jews, or because there were black or red; but because of their belief in God, and our Lord Jesus Christ. This community is a continuous thing. We tend to forget that the first followers of Christ, later called Christians, were Jews. And the chosen ones of Israel, of that day, knew Jesus and loved Him, when they saw him and heard his words. Chosen people are children of God, making God their Father.

John 8:42-44a. Jesus said unto them, if God were your Father, you would love me, for I proceedeth forth and came from God neither came I of myself, but he sent me. Why do ye not understand my speech? Even because ye cannot hear my word. Ye are of your father the devil, and the lusts of your father ye will do.

John 8:47. He that is of God heareth God's words: ye therefore hear them not, because ye are not of God.

191

As I said, this community of the chosen ones of God is something that continues and passes down through time. Up until Saul was chosen by God to bring the Gospel to the gentiles, this community was made up of all Israelites. But later, it was made up of individual Israelites and individual gentiles. This community of chosen people still exists today: in the past, it was not all of Israel, and today it is not all of the church.

Matthew 22:14. For many are called, but few are chosen.

You must have genuine faith and love for our Lord, if you want to be among the community of the chosen ones of God, and be symbolized by the woman in the last days. I believe that I can now state that this woman symbolizes the "True Church" or "born-again Christians" of this age, just as she symbolized the "chosen ones of Israel" in the last age—or perhaps a better name would be the "remnant."

Let's apply this identification of the woman to the verses about her: The moon beneath her feet speaks of the reflected glory of the Old Covenant with the remnant; while the sun, in which she is wrapped, tells of the New Covenant with the True Church. The remnant who was to bring forth the child cried for many years to be delivered. And Satan waited to destroy the Christ child. When He was born, Satan tried to destroy Him through Herod's efforts, when he had all the little boy babies killed. Satan tried to destroy Jesus in the desert through temptation. He tried again at the Cross. But God raised Him to heaven and to His throne.

About 2000 years later, the True Church flees into the wilderness where God has prepared a place for her for three and one-half years, while Satan is in direct power through Antichrist, and until the Rapture.

CHAPTER 32

MICHAEL AND THE DRAGON

Rev. 12:7-12. And there was war in heaven: Michael and his angels fought against the dragon; and the dragon fought and his angels, And prevailed not; neither was their place found any more in heaven. And the great dragon was cast out, that old serpent, called the Devil, and Satan, which deceiveth the whole world: he was cast out into the earth, and his angels were cast out with him. And I heard a loud voice saying in heaven, Now is come salvation, and strength, and the kingdom of our God, and the power of his Christ: for the accuser of our brethren is cast down, which accused them before our God day and night. And they overcome him by the blood of the Lamb, and by the word of their testimony; and they loved not their lives unto the death. Therefore rejoice, ye heavens, and ye that dwell in them. Woe to the inhabiters of the earth and of the sea! for the devil is come down unto you, having great wrath, because he knoweth that he hath but a short time.

Now our attention is turned from the earth to heaven; and Michael, the leader of the heavenly hosts, is now introduced.

Since the beginning, and it will be to the end, we find a record of conflict between two mighty forces: between God and Satan, between good and evil, between the seed of the woman and the seed of the serpent.

Genesis 3:15. And I will put enmity between thee and the woman, and between thy seed and her seed, it shall bruise they head, and thou shalt bruise his heel (said God to the serpent).

This conflict has been going on for nearly 6000 years; and I believe we are near the final great battle which will end in victory for God and all that is good, and defeat for Satan and all that is bad. Other wars of our history have been but mere skirmishes, as a result of this one. This war started in Genesis and the end is described in Revelation, which is only fitting.

The Scriptures seem to teach that Satan has limited access to heaven; he is said to accuse men before God day and night. Paul tells us that Satan is the prince of the power of the air. And now the time of his judgment is drawing near. We are told that there is a war going on in heaven between Michael and his angels, and Satan and his angels. In Verse 4 we see that many angels of Michael fell in battle with Satan. But Satan lost, and he was told that there is no more a place in heaven for him. And at the right time, which I believe was at the time of the seventh seal when Christ gave the signal by casting to earth a censer filled with fire of the altar, Satan and all his angels were cast to earth. Then a voice of praise was heard in heaven because the accuser of God's children had been cast out of the heavens at last. The final battle was beginning. It won't be long now till Christ will reclaim His possession and reign over His creation. The accuser of our brethren, who were martyred, has been cast down. And there was great joy, for you might call this the cleansing of heaven. But woe to those on earth! For the Devil comes to earth with great wrath because he knows his time is short.

Remember, Antichrist made a seven-year peace pact with Israel, and up till now has been their "protector." We will find that he has gained control of the re-formed Roman Empire of ten nations; and at the end of three and one-half years, he becomes a cruel dictator who demands worship as if he were God. This is when Satan is cast to earth and gives his power to Antichrist, at the end of what is described in Matthew as "the beginning of sorrows," or the seven seals.

> Rev. 12:13-17. And when the dragon saw that he was cast unto the earth, he persecuted the woman which brought forth the man child. And to the woman were given two wings of a great eagle, that she might fly into the wilderness, into her place, where she is nourished for a time, and times, and half a time, from the face of the serpent. And the serpent cast out of his mouth water as a flood after the woman, that he might cause her to be carried away of the flood. And the earth helped the woman, and the earth opened her mouth, and swallowed up the flood which the dragon cast out of his mouth. And the dragon was wroth with the woman, and went to make war with the remnant of her seed, which keep the commandments of God, and have the testimony of Jesus Christ.

Satan had failed to destroy Christ; but he thinks that he has another chance. He can attack the woman or the "True Church," which is the body of Christ. The born-again Christians, which have the Spirit of Christ, are one with Him; and it doesn't make any difference whether they are Jew or Gentile, black, white, red, yellow, rich or poor, weak or strong. Neither color, race, or the fact that you belong to a particular church, nor baptism alone, will make you a part of that body! The opportunity is there; but you must take advantage of it. You must have genuine faith, believe in Him, trust Him, and love Him as your MASTER, who provides all and gives you the power to be Sons of God. Jesus will do everything He promises for those whom He has given His Holy Spirit, because of their faith. I tell you this, not because it has been taught to me by man; but from personal experience. And I say to all "Lukewarm Christians," which I was not more than seven months ago, "You don't know how much you are missing." And I am not speaking of after you are dead, or even in the last days; I'm talking about right now—it is truly unbelievable!

And Satan thinks he is going to hurt the woman; not as long as Jesus has anything to say about it! But he tries; Satan cast out water as a flood after the woman, so he might cause her to be carried away. But the earth helped the woman; it opened her mouth and swallowed up the flood. Satan seeks to persecute her by that which comes from his mouth; this could be a number of things. Some say it is an army of men searching out Christians; whatever it is, the earth or nature will come to help her. And the woman will be given two wings of a great eagle to take her to a safe place. The two wings of a great eagle recall how the Lord delivered Israel from Egypt, and bore her "on eagle wings." He who delivered his people from Egypt and cared for them in the wilderness will in that terrible day deliver his "True Church" from the wrath of the dragon, and protect them in the wilderness.

Some believe that this wilderness is actually the wilderness of peoples. But I believe the chosen ones, particularly around Jerusalem, will, under the guidance of God, flee to the wilderness or mountains. This actually happened just before the final disaster came in A.D. 70, and I believe they will do it again.

There was an impregnable ancient city called Petre located in Edom. It was located in the mountains; and it looked as if it was in the crater of a volcano, and had but one entrance. I'm sure that this city was still there in the early nineteen hundreds; but I can't find anything on it now. Even so, I believe that this will be their city of refuge. Jesus

196

instructs His people in the following:

> Matthew 24:15-16. When ye therefore shall see the abomination of desolation, spoken of by Daniel the prophet, stand in the holy place (whoso readeth, let him understand). Then let them which be in Judea flee into the mountains.

So, when Antichrist receives his power from Satan, he will break his covenant and become a cruel dictator. And when he or his image stands in the temple, it is time for those in Judah, the chosen ones, to seek the protection of the mountains.

Unable to hurt the chosen ones of God, of this age, who are to be kept safe for these three and one-half years, Satan turns his wrath on the rest of her seed, which will be the rest of the church. Going back to the seven letters to the seven churches, we see that the last four letters represent parts of the Church which are still present today. The letter to Philadelphia represents the only part of the Church today which will be kept safe; the rest of the Church will have to face the wrath of the Devil if these events occur during our lifetime. Please stop and consider the price you will pay for not taking Jesus seriously; for trying to ride the fence, because it is more comfortable there, *now*.

CHAPTER 33

THE TWO BEASTS

In Revelation 13 we have a detailed description of two great powers who will arise in the Tribulation period. During this brief time of the world's greatest sorrows, Satan will make his last great attempt to defeat the program of God through these two powers. These two great powers will be two men, called "beasts" because of their viciousness and cruelty of their reign. To help us to understand how all this comes about, we should become familiar with a dream of King Nebuchadnezzar, which Daniel interpreted in Daniel 2; and also a vision of Daniel's, in Daniel 7.

In Daniel 2, the king had seen a great image with its head of gold, chest and arms of silver, belly and thighs of brass, legs of iron, and feet of iron and clay. These different parts of the image represent the stages of gentile world-domination which began with the captivity of Judah and will end at the Second Coming of Jesus Christ. First there was Babylon, followed by Medo-Persia, Greece, and finally the Roman Empire. The two legs of iron that represent Rome indicate that the Roman kingdom would be divided into two parts. And so it was; history records the division into Western and Eastern Roman Empires, and seemingly it disintegrates during the centuries when democracy dominates. But the Roman Empire will be revived in the end times and play a prominent part. The two feet and the ten toes of the image, which are a mixture of iron and clay, show us the final form of the restored Roman Empire. It shows us that there will be ten separate nations coming together. Some seem to believe that this pictures man's attempt to mix the iron of imperialism with the clay of democracy. The time is coming when people will get tired of the constant conflict, and they will attempt to take everything into their own hands. This is already beginning to happen, and you can expect conditions to get worse, all over the world. It will get to a point where people will be willing to try anything. Eventually, ten countries of today, which were included in the Old Roman Empire of John's day, will form a federation. Later Daniel saw a great stone cut without hands out of a mountain, which smites the image in its feet and grinds it to powder. And the stone became a mountain which filled all the earth. Christ is that stone.

Daniel 7 also records a vision which tells us the same thing, but in a different way. Daniel saw four beasts rising in succession. The first was like a lion, the second like a bear, the third like a leopard, and the fourth was a monstrosity. Daniel describes it as dreadful and terrible and strong exceedingly, and it had great iron teeth, and it had ten horns. These four beasts mentioned in Daniel 7 are the same as the four parts of Nebuchadnezzar's image of which we saw in Daniel 2. Here they are called the kingdoms of Babylon, Persia, Greece, and the Fourth Kingdom. The last beast has ten horns, just as the image had ten toes. The beast representing the Fourth Kingdom is the Roman Empire; but from the ten horns, we see that Daniel foresaw that it would eventually be divided into ten separate but federated kingdoms. And, as Daniel was looking at the horns, there came up among them another little horn; before whom there were three of the first horns plucked up by the roots. This could mean that when Antichrist rises to power he destroys three kings out of the original ten in the federation.

Then John sees that in this horn are eyes like the eyes of man, and a mouth speaking great things. This little horn, which is a powerful king, will speak great words against God, and shall think to change times and laws. And he shall have power for three and one-half years. Also it says that this king was different than the others. Daniel also foresaw Antichrist come out of the sea of nations or the federation. Now if Antichrist did destroy three kings of the ten nations federation, he had to replace them; because later they are to receive power as kings for one hour with the beast. In the first seal we do see Antichrist coming on a white horse and a bow in his hand, which meant he had been victorious in battle. But we have no way of knowing who he had fought against. But, regardless, he became head of the ten-nation federation.

Now we return to Revelation and see John's vision of the beast:

> Rev. 13:1-2. And I stood upon the sand of the sea, and saw a beast rise up out of the sea, having seven heads and ten horns, and upon his horns ten crowns, and upon his heads the name of blasphemy. And the beast which I saw was like unto a leopard, and his feet were as the feet of a bear, and his mouth as the mouth of a lion: and the dragon gave him his power, and his seat, and great authority.

The *beast* that John sees has a double meaning; it *represents both* the *revived Roman Empire* and its *imperial head*. Sometimes this beast pictures the man, sometimes his empire; he will so thoroughly control his empire, once Satan gives him power, that either is true. John's beast has *seven heads*, which also has a double meaning; they refer to the "City of Seven Hills" or Rome.

> Rev. 17:9. And here is the mind which hath wisdom. The seven heads are seven mountains, on which the woman sitteth.

And in Daniel 2 we saw that the great stone which was cut out without hands smote the ten toes and destroyed them. The stone is Christ, and He shall set up His Kingdom after this.

Daniel 2:35b. And the stone that smote the image became a great mountain, and filled the whole earth.

So I would say that a great mountain refers to a king and his kingdom here, and Revelation 17:9 says that the heads are mountains. Thus, I also believe that the seven heads give us a picture of all the kings which stand for different kingdoms from Daniel till the Stone Kingdom of Christ. These are the seven heads:

1. Babylonian Kingdom—Nebuchadnezzar
2. & 3. Medo-Persian Kingdoms—with 2 kings, Darius and Cyrus
4. Grecian Kingdom—Alexander the Great
5. Grecian Kingdom—divided between 4 generals at the death of Alexander
6. Roman Kingdom—Caesar Augustus
7. Revived Roman Kingdom—10-nation Federation —Antichrist (first three and one-half years)

And John's beast has ten horns with ten crowns on them. This is the ten-nation federation represented by the ten crowned kings.

John describes the beast as like a leopard, but with feet of a bear and mouth of a lion. This shows that the Roman Kingdom kept characteristics of the past three kingdoms. Long ago, it was a boast of the Roman conquerors that they never destroyed a civilization, but absorbed into their own great commonwealth everything that was best of the various nations. This will also be true with the Revived Roman Empire; it will incorporate everything which man has learned to value throughout all of the other empires before it. This will also be true with its imperial head, Antichrist; he will have all the abilities and powers of all the great kings before him, which will make him the most conspicuous and prominent of men. For three and one-half years he will pose as a great humanitarian, the friend of man, and the special friend of the Jewish race; and he will persuade them that he has come to usher in the "Golden Age" as pictured by the prophets, and they will receive him as their Messiah. But, after three and one-half years, the dragon will have been cast to the earth; and he who is Satan will give this man his power, his position and great authority. Paul calls Antichrist the "son of perdition," which is not without significance. The name is used but twice in the Scriptures. In John 17:12, in the priestly prayer, Christ called Judas the son of perdition.

Notice that John sees the beasts in reverse order compared as to how Daniel saw them. Once again, it shows that John is looking back, where Daniel is looking forward. Also notice that the largest part of this beast, the body, is represented by the leopard, which is Greece. So it may be that the Revived Roman Empire and Antichrist will be linked more with the former Grecian Empire than the others.

Rev. 13:13. And I saw one of his heads as it were wounded to death; and his deadly wound was healed; and all the world wondered after the beast.

The seventh head or king, which is Antichrist, will receive a deadly wound, probably at the hand of an assassin. Remember, this is a man who has just simply fascinated the people of the world; not a man such as Nero or Hitler whom people hated and feared. Now he has been killed; but he is brought back to life, probably by the False Prophet, and all the world wonders about him. They already thought he was "too good to be true," and now with a little help they believe that he must be a God, the Messiah, or Christ coming the second time. Some will believe that it is impossible to bring anyone back to life, so this explanation couldn't be right. It happened many times in the Bible, and the scientist expects to be able to do this in the future—which is why some bodies are being prepared, frozen, and kept in cold storage, instead of being buried, at this time!

Rev. 13:4. And they worshipped the dragon which gave power unto the beast; and they worshipped the beast, saying, Who is like unto the beast? who is able to make war with him?

We glorify God by glorifying the Son. In these days they will worship Satan by worshipping Antichrist, which is the son of perdition. They will marvel at the fact that he couldn't even be killed, and will conclude that there is none on earth like him. Antichrist with the help of the False Prophet, which we take up next, will cause the people to feel so happy and secure at this time.

Rev. 13:5-7. And there was given unto him a mouth speaking great things and blasphemies; and power was given unto him to continue forty and two months. And he opened his mouth in blasphemy against God, to blaspheme his name, and his tabernacle, and them that dwell in heaven. And it was given unto him to make war with the saints, and to overcome them: and power was given him over all kindreds, and tongues, and nations.

As far as the Great Tribulations are concerned, we have reached the end of the first three and one-half years, and the end of the seven seals. Now Satan has given his power and authority to Antichrist, which accounts for the great change that takes place in him. Before he received the deadly wound, he was a nice guy; but after his recovery, he became devilish, proud, demanding of people's worship, denying the power of God and his Christ, denying the existence of heaven, other than what he can make right here on earth, and closing any churches which profess to still worship God. For the first three and one-half years he has acted as the elected head of the ten-nation federation; but now he will throw off all restraint and declare himself emperor. He has made a covenant with the Jewish people, of which Isaiah 28:15 speaks as a "covenant with Death and Hell." Now he breaks this covenant with the Jews and desecrates the temple by setting up the "Abomination of Desolation," which is an idol-image. He will make war on Moses and Elijah, who are the saints that God sent down to witness for Him during these three and one-half years. And when the time is right God will permit this horrible beast of a man and his army of followers to overcome the two saints and kill them. They have hunted out and killed many Christians, all over the world, who have refused to worship Antichrist. But his great power will only last three and one-half years, which will be drawing to a close with the death of Moses and Elijah.

Rev. 13:8. And all that dwell upon the earth shall worship him, whose names are not written in the book of life of the Lamb slain from the foundation of the world.

This does not mean that all peoples which inhabit the earth will worship him. It means that all the people living at that time, whose names were not written in the Book of Life at the beginning of Creation, shall worship this beast, who is the Son of Satan. In the Book of Revelation there is a definite destinction made between God's children, whose names are written in the Book of Life at the time of creation, and the dwellers of the earth, whose names were not written in the Book of Life. We are told by Paul in Ephesians 1:4 that God has chosen us in Christ before the foundations of the world, so that leaves another group of people whom God did *not* choose, and their names were not written in the Book of

Life of the Lamb. I believe that Jesus is telling us about this very thing in his explanation of the parable of the wheat and the tares:

> Matthew 13:37-39. He answered and said unto them, He that soweth the good seed is the Son of Man: The field is the world; the good seed are the children of the kingdom; but the tares are the children of the wicked one; The enemy that sowed them is the devil; the harvest is the end of the world; and the reapers are angels. As therefore the tares are gathered and burned in the fire, so shall it be in the end of this world.

I believe the day of judgment or the day of the harvest starts when Christ takes control of His creation, which is at the 7th trumpet, and will last 1000 years. Remember what Peter said:

> Peter 3:8. But, beloved, be not ignorant of this one thing, that one day is with the Lord as a thousand years, and a thousand years as one day.

For 1000 years Christ separates the good from the evil, and rids the earth of all evil, including death. And at the end of the day, the wicked are thrown in the lake of fire. Just before the new heaven and new earth is described in Revelation, we read:

> Rev. 20:15. And whosoever was not found written in the book of life was cast into the lake of fire.

In Matthew 13 we were told that the Lord planted the good seed, and the devil planted the bad seed, or the tares, which will be destroyed. Here Jesus is saying the same thing again:

> Matthew 15:12-14. Then came his disciples, and said

unto him, Knowest thou that the Pharisees were offended, after they heard this saying? But he answered and said, Every plant, which my heavenly Father hath not planted, shall be rooted up. Let them alone; they be blind. And if the blind lead the blind, both shall fall into the ditch.

The Pharisees were not physically blind. Who are the blind that he refers to?

II Corinthians 4:3-4. But if our gospel be hid, it is hid to them that are lost: in whom the god of this world hath blinded the minds of them which believe not, lest the light of the glorious gospel of Christ, who is the image of God, should shine unto them. (Satan prevents them from seeing the light of Christ.)

Let me make one thing clear. God has the master plan for the whole universe, and sets limits to what Satan can do now; but Satan is the prince of this world, and will be until Christ returns. Thus he blinds the minds of his followers to the Gospel—those that he planted on this earth, those that are lost, and whose names were never in the Book of Life of the Lamb. They are the dwellers of the earth and subjects of the prince of this earth, Satan! This idea—that this earth is inhabited by the children of God, planted by God, and to whom God gives a free choice; and by children of the Devil, planted by the Devil, who are blinded and not given a choice—is very disturbing to our human minds. But, since evidence supporting this idea has been pointed out to us throughout the Bible, I can't ignore it.

Before continuing, I would like to point out something that was accidentally brought to the surface. (I said "accidentally" because I didn't plan it). Reread the part where I said that the Day of Judgment would last 1000 years. If this is a fact, and I believe it is, do you realize what this means? Those that believe that Christ will not return until the Day of Judgment, and those that believe that He will return and reign on earth for 1000 years (millennium), believe the same thing!

Followers of Satan are not the only ones that are lost. Many children of God, those who names were written in the Book of Life, are lost because they do not love and believe in Christ, and value the things that this world provides so much that they don't want to give them up. Some really mean to take Jesus seriously; but they put it off for a number of reasons until, many times, it is too late. Satan is delighted when he can claim one of God's children. And God is overjoyed when one of His lost is brought back to the fold. And Jesus has this to say:

Rev. 3:5a. He that overcometh, the same shall be clothed in white raiment; and I will not blot out his name out of the Book of Life.

Therefore:

1 John 2:15-17. Love not the world, neither the things that are in the world. If any man love the world, the love of the Father is not in him. For all that is in world, the lust of the flesh, and the lust of the eyes, and the pride of life, is not of the Father, but is of the world. The world passeth away, and the lust thereof: but he that doeth the will of God abideth forever.

So much time is spent today accumulating worldly goods and participating in worldly pleasures, that many do not have any time left for the most valuable thing of all. In the past many have died, and will regret it; and perhaps many today will live to regret it.

Rev. 13:9-10. If any man have an ear, let him hear. He that leadeth into captivity shall go into captivity; he that killeth with the sword must be killed with the sword. Here is the patience and the faith of the saints.

After saying that all the dwellers of the earth shall worship the beast, Jesus turns back to the children of God and says—if your ears have been opened to the word of God, listen. The days ahead will be terrible for the children of God that are being tested. The True Church or saints will be kept safe, but even at that, they will have to show patience and faith, regardless of how things seem to be. Jesus gives the Christians a warning: you will be hunted and persecuted; but you are not to take up the sword against this enemy of Christ. For them that kill with the sword, must be killed with the sword. Right can never be defended by doing wrong; thus the gospel of love can never be defended by the methods of violence. The Christians must win this battle with the world by presenting to all men the unchanging loyalty to Christ, which will not be moved by the fear or the favor of men. This is true today and certainly will be true in the Great Tribulations.

Now John tells us about the second beast:

Rev. 13:11. And I beheld another beast coming up out of the earth; and he had two horns like a lamb, and he spake as a dragon.

The first beast came out of the sea of nations; but this beast comes out of the land. It is described as having two horns like a lamb. Because "lamb" is used here, many believe that this beast is Antichrist, for he is supposed to imitate Christ. But the description of the Lamb in Chapter 5:6 says that the Lamb had seven horns, not two. This second beast speaks as a dragon, and he has a name. He is called the "False Prophet" three times in Revelation. Remember the order in which we have been introduced to the Satanic Trinity—Satan, then 2 different beasts. Compare that order with the following:

Rev. 16:13. And I saw three unclean spirits like frogs come out of the mouth of the dragon, and out of the mouth of the beast, and out of the mouth of the false prophet.

Rev. 19:20. And the beast was taken, and with him the false prophet that wrought miracles before (in his sight) him, with which he (Satan) deceived them that had received the mark of the beast, and them that worshipped his image. These both were cast alive into a lake of fire burning with brimstone.

Rev. 20:10. And the devil that deceived them was cast into the lake of fire and brimstone, where the beast and the false prophets are, and shall be tormented day and night for ever and ever.

Matthew 24:24. For there shall arise false Christs and false prophets, and shall shew great signs and wonders, insomuch that if it were possible, they shall deceive the very elect.

This makes it clear that there are two different individuals; so Antichrist and the False Prophet cannot be the same, as some believe. And the order in which they are spoken of is always the same, which leads me to believe that Antichrist is the first beast, and the False Prophet is the second beast.

Rev. 13:12. And he exerciseth all the power of the first beast before him, and causeth the earth and them which dwell therein to worship the first beast, whose deadly wound was healed.

This beast had the same powers that Satan gave the first beast. And he used them, and caused the dwellers of the earth to worship the first beast, who he had brought back to life, after it had received the deadly wound. This has to be the False Prophet, because here we see that he causes people to worship the first beast. Antichrist will exalt himself, not someone else.

> II Thessalonians 2:3b-4. And that man of sin be revealed, the son of perdition; Who opposeth and exalteth himself above all that is called God, or that is worshipped: so that he as God sitteth in the temple of God, shewing himself that he is God.

Antichrist will be a king and rule over a kingdom and exalt himself, claiming to be God. But the False Prophet is not a king. He does not exalt himself; he exalts Antichrist, or the first beast. His relation to Antichrist is the same as the Holy Spirit's relation to Christ. He also has the power to give life, and in this he imitates the Holy Spirit.

> Rev. 13:13-14. And he doeth great wonders, so that he maketh fire come down from heaven on the earth in the sight of men, And deceiveth them that dwell on the earth by the means of those miracles which he had power to do in the sight of the beast; saying to them that dwell on the earth, that they should make an image to the beast which had the wound by a sword, and did live.

The False Prophet will be a miracle worker; and one of the miracles that he will perform is that he will bring down fire from heaven. We know that Satan, who gives his power to his two witnesses, is able to do this from Job 1:16, where Satan, having secured permission from God to touch all that Job had, brought down fire from heaven and burned up Job's sheep and servants.

The False Prophet deceives them that dwell on the earth with these miracles that he had power to do in the sight of the Antichrist. And he told them that dwell on the earth that they should build an image to the beast which had received the deadly wound, but now lived. They were probably eager to do so, just to honor him. We saw back in the 4th verse that they already worshipped the first beast. So they built the image, and the False Prophet performed another miracle.

Rev. 13:15. And he had power to give life unto the image of the beast, that the image of the beast should both speak, and cause that as many as would not worship the image of the beast should be killed.

When John wrote this, and even 100 years ago, this would seem like an impossible thing. It could only be a miracle. But today, considering all the computerized equipment, and the fact that man can make a machine do almost anything, I don't think it would be too difficult to make this image appear to be alive, to move, to talk: and to demand that all who would not worship it be put to death.

This image reminds us of the "Golden Image" that Nebuchadnezzar commanded to be made and put up in the "Plain of Dura," before which, at the sounding of musical instruments, the people were commanded to bow down and worship. And those who disobeyed were cast into a burning fiery furnace (Daniel 3:1-30).

There will be many who will refuse to worship the image of Antichrist, even under the penalty of death. But there will be many more of God's Children who will take the easy way out because of fear for their life, and lack of faith in God.

Rev. 13:16-17. And he causeth all, both small and great, rich and poor, free and bond, to receive a mark in their right hand, or in their foreheads: And that no man might buy or sell, save he that had the mark, or the name of the beast, or the number of his name.

The False Prophet, realizing that it would be impossible to

hunt out everyone who wouldn't worship the image and kill them, devised another plan that would help him wipe out all of God's children who remained loyal to him. He commanded that all that worshipped the beast would receive a mark on their right hand or on their foreheads, as proof of such. And that no person would be allowed to buy or sell anything unless he had this mark. And I imagine there will be stiff penalties for selling food, medicine, and clothing to anyone without the mark; and a large reward for turning in people without the mark, or reporting someone selling to them. People will be turning in their own mothers, fathers, and children in order to get the rewards, which in turn will enable them to get food, which there will be a shortage of. Some will be so taken in by Antichrist that they will feel it is their duty to turn in their own children to be killed! How terrible these three and one half years will be; you won't be able to trust anyone! And how tempting it will be to give in and accept the mark, if you are starving or sick. You won't have much of a choice left then; either beg, starve or be killed. If you choose to receive the mark, you will be branded with the mark of hell. If you choose to die, the instrument of death will be the guillotine (Revelation 20:4). And the newspapers will contain a list of the names of those beheaded the day before, to frighten the people into obedience to the law. These will be terrible days for Christians who insisted on staying in a "lukewarm" condition towards Christ, until it was too late. But this must take place before Christ returns to gather His own; which is the only ray of hope for these people. If you can survive for three and one-half years without getting the mark, you will be rescued by our Lord.

Luke 21:25-28. And there shall be signs in the sun, and in the moon, and in the stars; and upon the earth distress of nations, with perplexity; the sea and the waves roaring (this describes the trumpet judgments, after which Christ will return for his people; but does not describe the vial judgments after which Christ will return

213

as King). Men's hearts failing them for fear, and for looking after those things which are coming on the earth: for the powers of heaven shall be shaken. And then shall they see the Son of Man coming in a cloud with power and great glory. And when these things begin to come to pass, then look up, and lift up your heads; for your redemption draweth nigh.

Rev. 13:18. Here is wisdom. Let him that hath understanding count the number of the beast: for it is the number of a man; and his number is six hundred three score and six.

In this verse we are told that the number of the beast is 666. And it is certainly true that more people have put forth more effort and time on this verse than on any other one in Scripture. Who will this beast of a man be?

It has been pointed out that the ancient people had no figures for numbers, and that the letters of the alphabet did duty for numbers as well. Thus any name given its numerical value could be added up to a sum in figures as well. By using this idea, many are convinced that 666 stands for Nero. Many names have been suggested, and for many reasons. But the number 6 is the number for man. 3 is the number for divinity. So the beast will be a man who claims to be God. Three sixes imply that he is a false god and a deceiver. I don't really think that it will make any difference as to who he was before—Nero, Hitler, or Judas Iscariot; because I don't really believe that he will use the same name again. So you won't be able to identify Antichrist by any name that he has used in the past. Remember, Elijah came back as John the Baptist, not Elijah. And Jesus says his name will be different when He returns as King.

So you will have to identify Antichrist from other things which we can learn about him. Keep in mind that Satan will imitate God as much as he possibly can. First we see the Satanic Trinity—Satan, Antichrist, False Prophet—imitating our trinity of God, Christ, and the Holy Spirit. God sent His Son into the world 1972 years ago, which we all know about. And I believe Satan sent his son into the world at that time also, in the body of Judas Iscariot. Paul called Antichrist the son of perdition; and the only other time this title is used in the Scriptures is when Jesus speaks of Judas in John 17:12. And in John 6:70-71, Jesus referred to Judas as a devil; but this is not a known fact, and Satan will stick to the known facts when he is imitating God. As God was in Christ, born of a virgin by the Holy Spirit, so Antichrist will be born of a woman (not necessarily a virgin) by Satan. In Genesis, God said to the serpent:

> Genesis 3:15a. And I will put enmity between thee and the woman, and between thy seed and her seed.

Now, we know that the woman's seed eventually turned out to be Christ; so the serpent's seed must be Antichrist. Christ started his ministry when he was about 30 years old, and I believe it lasted for three and one-half years; then at 33 he was killed. I expect Antichrist to be 30 years old when he first becomes known and is elected to head the ten-nation federation; and after three and one-half years, at the age of 33, he will be killed. But after three days he will be brought back to life. I believe that both Antichrist and the False Prophet will be Jews, for it is not likely that the Jewish people would accept as their Messiah one who is not a Jew. I believe the False Prophet will come from the lands around Jerusalem; but Antichrist will come from out of the sea of nations which make up the federation of ten countries. To be exact, I believe he will be a Syrian Jew, whose descendants can be traced back to the tribe of Dan. It would require a long, detailed explanation of the three visions of Daniel to explain why I believe Antichrist will come from Syria (which includes Assyria). But here is another clue: The context shows that this prophecy is connected with the downfall of Antichrist and the restoring of Israel.

Isaiah 14:25. That I will break the Assyrian (Antichrist) in my land, and upon my mountains tread him under foot: then shall his yoke depart off them (Israel), and his burden depart from off their shoulders.

I picked the tribe of Dan because this tribe was left out when the 144,000 Jews were sealed.

CHAPTER 34

A VISION IN SIX PARTS

In the 12th and 13th chapters of the Book of Revelation, we have been introduced to actors who have played major parts in the Great Tribulations, thus far. Now the 14th chapter consists of one vision divided into six parts; and has to do with certain events that occur in the last part of the Tribulations, and the introduction of the New Age. The first part of the vision is that of the Lamb on Mount Sion.

THE LAMB AND THE 144,000 JEWS

Rev. 14:1-5. And I looked, and lo, a Lamb stood on the Mount Sion, and with him an hundred forty and four thousand, having his Father's name written in their foreheads. And I heard a voice from heaven, as the voice of many waters, and as the voice of a great thunder: and I heard the voice of harpers harping with their harps: And they sung as it were a new song before the throne, and before the four beasts, and the elders: and no man could learn that song but the hundred and forty and four thousand, which were redeemed from the earth. These are they which were not defiled with women; for they are virgins. These are they which follow the Lamb whithersoever he goeth. These were redeemed from among men, being the firstfruits unto God and to the Lamb. And in their mouth was found no guile: for they are without fault before the throne of God.

The first time we saw these 144,000 Jews in Chapter 7, they were being sealed with the seal of the living God. Jesus put His seal of ownership on the remnant, so Satan couldn't harm them. These Jews didn't believe that Jesus was the Messiah at that time. But their eyes were opened, and they realized their mistake when Jesus raptured all the faithful Christians at the 7th trumpet. Jesus shows us this with the vision of them gathered to the Lamb. Realizing what a terrible thing that they had done to God, this remnant of the chosen people will dedicate themselves to the service of the Son of God. And now the Father's name is being put on their foreheads, also.

Now we hear voices and music from heaven; and the volume is such as you might hear of a great waterfall, and of great thunder. There were great joy in heaven; not only had the faithful Christians been raptured, but at last the natural children of God had been redeemed from the earth through the blood of the Lamb—they had accepted Christ as the Son of God. His own children had come home, after being away for so long! You can tell by the way they sing before the throne—beasts and elders—how happy they are. There was such feeling and joy expressed in the way they sang that it sounded like a new song. And no one could sing that song like that, but those who felt such feelings, which were only the 144,000 Jews.

Remember, the age or dispensation of grace (church age) ended with the 7th trumpet, and we are now beginning the Age of the Kingdom. And those 144,000 Jews are first fruits of this kingdom. In describing their characteristics, I don't think we can say that they are 144,000 men who have never had any sexual relations with a woman. First of all, I don't think that the remnant of the chosen people are all men, or necessarily single people. I think they are better described as an undefiled, virginal, a band of people who have kept themselves from the wickedness and idolatry which is prevailing everywhere in those fearful days of Antichrist. They are a guileness company, which does not mean sinless; but they have nothing to hide. They have confessed their sins and repented; and, through the blood of Christ, are now without fault before the throne of God. So, to start off with in the New Age, we have 144,000 Jewish people who have dedicated themselves to Christ. And they are given the same job that the church was given in this age: to preach the gospel throughout the world. They will be the light of the world during the Millennium.

THE EVERLASTING GOSPEL

> Rev. 14:6-7. And I saw another angel fly in the midst of heaven, having the everlasting gospel to preach unto them that dwell on the earth, and to every nation, and kindred, and tongue, and people, Saying with a loud voice, Fear God, and give glory to him; for the hour of His judgment is come: and worship him that made heaven, and earth, and the sea, and the fountains of waters.

An angel brought the everlasting gospel which was to be preached to all the world, to the 144,000 Jews, who are now dedicated saints of Christ. This everlasting gospel or Gospel of the Kingdom, is really no different than that which has been proclaimed from the beginning. It is the good news of all ages—that God is sovereign and man's happiness consists in recognizing His authority. It will emphasize particularly the Lordship of Christ.

Understand, there is only one Gospel; but, as the world has passed through the different ages, the Gospel has passed through the different phases. There was the gospel of circumcision. Then, when the Lord was here on earth, ministering along with John the Baptist, they preached the gospel of the kingdom; but men rejected the kingdom. So for over 1900 years, we have heard the gospel of grace or faith, God gave the people of this age an undeserved favor (grace). God said—Okay, you don't have to do anything (and a lot of people have the idea that God stopped there), no circumcision, no more burnt offerings; just hear and believe my Word (Bible). If you know the Word of God, and you believe what it says, He will do what He promises! People today say they believe it in church every Sunday. They may pretend, and perhaps even want, to believe it; but the truth is, they don't really believe and love our Lord (generally speaking). And that is why the church as a whole is in trouble with God. Now, in the Age of the Kingdom, faith won't enter into it that much. Christ will be back as our King and rule over the whole world.

But right in the beginning of this age the saints are to warn the people still on the earth that the hour of God's judgment has come, and to turn and worship Him before it is too late. Remember, Antichrist and the False Prophet are still trying to play God and force people to worship their image. I imagine there are still a lot of people in the world they haven't gotten to, which don't believe in Christ either. I believe that there will be a lot of people left on earth alive that have been converted during this next period, when the tribulations are over. And this will be the results of these 144,000 saints preaching the everlasting gospel all over the world.

BABYLON IS FALLEN

Rev. 14:8. And there followed another angel, saying, Babylon is fallen, is fallen, that great city, because she made all nations drink of the wine of the wrath of her fornication.

220

I believe Babylon is a symbol of the Satanic world system, whose headquarters are in Rome. The church and the state have become one under Antichrist. And the angel proclaimed that it is fallen. Most people believe this is a foreview of the destruction of Rome, which will come after the seven vials. But I believe the angel is telling the saints that this Satanic System, whose center is in Rome, and everything connected with Antichrist, is beginning to crumble. It is in the process of falling. Consider these facts: Satan's three and one-half years of power has run out, which is what he gave to Antichrist. The faithful Christians have been raptured, the Jewish remnant now follows the Lamb and preaches the Gospel, and is protected with the seal. People will soon find out that he has lost his Satanic power. Yes, Babylon is beginning to fall because of her corrupting and seducing forces, which have lured the nations into a kind of insane immorality. We will get a fuller description of the total destruction of Babylon later.

Under all of this, there is a lesson to remember: any man, any church, any nation whose influence is to evil, who loosens the bonds of the moral law, who makes vice more attractive, sin more easy, virtue more difficult, will not escape the avenging wrath of God.

DOOM IS ANNOUNCED FOR THE BEAST-WORSHIPPERS

Rev. 14:9-12. And the third angel followed them, saying with a loud voice, If any man worship the beast and his image, and receive his mark in his forehead, or in his hand, the same shall drink of the wine of the wrath of God, which is poured out without mixture into the cup of his indignation; and he shall be tormented with fire and brimstone in the presence of the holy angels, and in the presence of the Lamb. And the smoke of their torment ascendeth up for ever and ever: and they have no rest day or night, or worship the beast and his image, and whosoever receiveth the mark of his name. Here is the patience of the saints: here are they that keep the commandments of God, and the faith of Jesus.

All three of these angels are giving their messages to the 144,000 Jews who are to preach the news to the world. They have been given the everlasting gospel, they have been told that this Satanic System is beginning to crumble, and now they are told what will happen to anyone that receives the mark and worships the beast and his image. This is the warning they are to give to the world.

The 7 vials, which are just ahead, are the Wrath of God. God is going to start cleansing the earth of all wickedness. And He says that whoever worships the beast and his image, and receives his mark on his hand or forehead, will feel the full fury of His Wrath. They shall be tormented with undescribable anguish in the presence of the angels and Christ. And this will not end with the 7 vials, this will be eternal punishment in the lake of fire.

Two questions come to mind about this. Why is the fate of those that fail this time of trial so fierce? And why has this warning come so late? Why wasn't it given before Antichrist came into power, which could have saved a few more Christians?

In trying to answer the first question, we have to remember that in John's day the Church was battling for its very existence. If the Church was to continue to exist, the individual Christian must be prepared to face suffering and trial, imprisonment and death. It was because so much was dependent on each individual Christian being faithful unto death that the doom on the men who denied the faith was so terrible and so tragic. Now, we have the same situation here; except we are not talking about the Church. We are talking about people who will repopulate the earth. There will be the 144,000 Jews and their converts, from what I can see; and some of the converts may be martyred. So the existence of the future populated earth depends on the people not worshipping the beast, at this particular time.

Now, as to why the warning came so late. It was not necessary to send an angel with this warning before the faithful Christians were raptured, which was at the end of the trumpets. John gave the warning to the Christians in the Book of Revelation in 96 A.D. The two witnesses probably spoke of it; but the Jewish people wouldn't have listened, at that time, to anything that came out of the New Testament. Besides, most of them believed their Messiah had come, in the person of Antichrist. So, after the eyes of the Jews were opened, it was necessary for them to receive the message; so God sent angels down to tell them.

It will take courage of a very high order to stand up against all the terrible trials ahead, and hold firmly to the truth of God which has been revealed. Remember, even though Antichrist has lost the power given him by Satan, he isn't dead yet. He will try that much harder to force the world to worship him, and to gather an army for his final battle with the Son of God. And John points out that it will require the patience of those who keep the Commandments of God, and the faith of Jesus, or the Jewish saints.

Rev. 14:13. And I heard a voice from heaven saying unto me, Write, Blessed are the dead which die in the Lord from henceforth: Yea, saith the Spirit, that they may rest from their labours: and their words do follow them.

Blessed are the dead which die in the Lord from here on. To me, this is a very puzzling verse; but, before I go into it, I will give you two other translations.

Some say that, since the worst of the Great Tribulations are still ahead, this means it will be better to die in Christ than to live. Then they will rest from their labors and be spared further trials. Times will be so terrible for those living on the earth at this time. This may very well be true, according to man's way of looking at it.

I would guess that most people believe that John is talking about those who die as martyrs in the Great Tribulation, who will be specially blessed because it will be harder during their lifetime to stand for the truth of God's Word than at any time in history. I agree that the martyrs will be specially blessed.

First of all, it doesn't indicate a special blessing, or that they are martyrs. And we know that everyone who dies in Christ, regardless of when, is blessed. But here it definitely states from henceforth, or from here on: and we are two-thirds of the way through the Great Tribulation. Even if John was only referring to martyrs, what about all the Christians martyred during the seven trumpets? And I'm sure that Jesus wouldn't instruct John to write that it is better to die in Christ than to live in Christ, at any time. Most of the time, we are more valuable to God as live witnesses. So I believe we have to look elsewhere for the true meaning of this verse.

Every person alive on this earth is either alive or dead in Christ. Every professing Christian who was alive in Christ at the seventh trumpet was raptured. The 144,000 Jews are now alive in Christ. So, as of this particular time in the tribulations, we have to classify the rest of the world as being dead to Christ. I think Jesus is proclaiming a new ruling, as of this point in the tribulations. We have just heard about the fate of those who get the mark of the beast and worship him. But what if in a moment of weakness, starvation, or sickness you gave in and were branded; and now you would do anything to undo this terrible mistake you made —is there no way back? A branded person preaching against Antichrist, and publicly confessing his wrongdoing and his love for Christ, would be very harmful to this Satanic System and helpful to the cause of Christ. He would be killed as soon as possible by the beast. I think this is an example of the dead, which died in Christ, and will be blessed. Jesus is telling the people that there is one way back for God's children who failed the test. They would actually be offering themselves as human sacrifices, knowing that it would mean their death; but then they would be able to rest from their labors, and know that their works follow them, which is what they will be judged by then.

Don't forget, this is not the dispensation of grace anymore, where faith is what counts. This is a new dispensation, in which God will deal with people a little differently. So it is not out of line, according to Scripture, for Jesus to declare a new ruling at this time.

VISION OF ARMAGEDDON

In this next vision we are given a quick glimpse of the beginning of the harvest, or the Day of Judgment. The seven vials work up to the battle of Armageddon. But from here on the reapers will begin binding the wicked with the rope of death, which will hold them till the harvest is complete; and then they will be thrown into the lake of fire at the end of the world, or at the end of the Kingdom Age.

Jesus talks about this in the parable of the wheat and the tares. The servants ask the householder whether they should go gather the tares from the field (or the children of the wicked one from the world). And they are instructed as follows:

> Matthew 13:29-30. But he said, Nay, lest while ye gather up the tares, ye root up also the wheat with them. Let both grow together until the harvest and in the time of harvest, I will say to the reapers, Gather ye together first the tares, and bind them in bundles to burn them; but gather the wheat into my barn.

> Matthew 13:40. As therefore the tares are gathered and burned in the fire; so shall it be in the end of this world.

> Rev. 14:14-16. And I looked, and behold a white cloud,

225

and upon the cloud one sat like unto the Son of Man, having on his head a golden crown, and in his hand a sharp sickle. And another angel came out of the temple, crying with a loud voice to him that sat on the cloud. Thrust in thy sickle, and reap: for the time is come for thee to reap; for the harvest of the earth is ripe. And he that sat on the cloud thrust in his sickle on the earth; and the earth was reaped.

First we see the victorious Christ, shown here as sitting on a white cloud, coming to judge the wicked and personally claim his possessions—the "white cloud" signifying the purity and absolute righteousness of the judgment that is to take place. And the golden crown on his head shows His divine Kingship. The judgment command comes from the temple, the immediate presence of God, and the call is for immediate reaping because the harvest is ripe. Christ is told that the time has come for him to reap, and he does so through the instrumentality of the angels, as we are told in Matthew 13:39 that the reapers are angels. So the earth is reaped: everything that is of God, Christ will claim for Himself. John shows us this by picturing our risen Lord reaping those who are for salvation, and another angel is shown reaping those who are for condemnation. The heathen nations will be gathered together outside Jerusalem, as described in Joel 3:12, for the great battle, and the reapers, who shall begin their job.

Rev. 14:17-20. And another angel came out of the temple which is in heaven, he also having a sharp sickle. And another angel came out from the altar, which had power over fire; and cried with a loud cry to him that had the sharp sickle, saying, Thrust in thy sharp sickle, and gather the clusters of the vine of the earth; for her grapes are fully ripe. And the angel thrust in his sickle into the earth, and gathered the vine of the earth, and cast it into the great winepress of the wrath of God.

And the winepress was trodden without the city, and blood came out of the winepress, even unto the horse bridles, by the space of a thousand and six hundred furlongs.

This pictures the coming battle of Armageddon and the judgment of the nations at the Second Coming of Christ. We will have a much more detailed description of this battle in the following chapters, so I won't spend too much time with it now. The vine of the earth refers to Antichrist and his followers. All the wicked nations of the world shall be gathered against Israel.

Zechariah 14:2. For I will gather all nations against Jerusalem to battle; and the city shall be taken, and the houses rifled, and the women ravished; and half of the city shall go forth into captivity, and the residue of the people shall not be cut off from the city. Then shall the Lord go forth, and fight against those nations.

And we can see by the description, that there will be a great slaughter, and it will cover a large area. The Wrath of God is fierce!

The action, once again, stopped in our story at the end of Chapter 11 in the Book of Revelation; and for the last three chapters, we have been given a lot of information concerning what has happened in the first part of the Tribulations, what is happening, and a glimpse of what will happen. Now, as we turn our attention to Chapter 15, the action is about to pick up again. The Wrath of God is soon to begin.

CHAPTER 35

THOSE WHO CONQUERED THE BEAST

Rev. 15:1. And I saw another sign in heaven, great and
marvellous, seven angels having the seven last plagues;
for in them is filled up the wrath of God.

This sign is described as being marvellous because these
angels have the seven last plagues, and in them the fury of
God is complete; and with them, Antichrist and the False
Prophet, the whole Satanic Empire will be destroyed. As terrible as these plagues are, they are great and marvellous because they will rid Christ's creation, the earth, of the bulk of
the wickedness that will rule over it at that time.

Rev. 15:2-4. And I saw as it were a sea of glass mingled
with fire: and them that had gotten the victory over the
beast, and over his image, and over his mark, and over
the number of his name, stand on the sea of glass, having the harps of God. And they sing the song of Moses
the servant of God, and the song of the Lamb, saying,
Great and marvellous are thy works, Lord God Almighty; just and true are thy ways, thou King of saints.
Who shall not fear thee, O Lord, and glorify thy name?
for thou only art holy: for all nations shall come and

worship before thee; for thy judgments are made manifest.

Once again John sees what looks like a sea of glass, which previously we interpreted to stand for the cleansing Word of God here on earth; in heaven, crystallized, as a glassy sea upon which the saints take their stand to praise Him who redeemed them, and made them clean forever. But this time, that which appeared as a sea of glass was mingled with fire, showing that those who stood on it had been tested and cleansed with the fiery persecutions of the beast. Gold is purified by fire, just as faith is purified by trials which may seem like fire. God allowed Satan to put on trial the "Lukewarm Christians" which are alive in these times, in order to prove their faith. And this group that we see here were victorious over the beast, as they didn't worship him or receive his mark. Does this necessarily mean that they were all killed? I'm sure the beast will be guilty of mass murder of Christians who refuse to worship him; but I do not believe that all those being tested, and who remain faithful to Christ, will die or be killed. How can they survive for three and one-half years? I have only one answer to that—"All things are possible through Christ."

Now we see those who conquered the beast, standing on the glassy sea, having the harps of God; and they are singing songs which symbolize their victorious joy as a result of their triumph over the beast, and their redemption. They praise and adore Him for His justice and truth, recognizing the righteousness of His ways and the holiness of His person. All nations shall come and worship before Him; but not as a result of man's efforts. It will be because the deeds and judgments of God will be disclosed. The world will never be converted by the preaching of the Gospel in this dispensation, or during the Church Age. It will, eventually be converted in the 7th dispensation, after the unbelieving portion has been purged out by judgment. Then the remnant left for the kingdom will give glory to the King of all nations, Our Risen Lord.

Many authors believe that this group of people standing on the sea of glass are Israelites, and are Tribulation martyrs—dying after the Rapture. I believe they are Christians who were tested by Satan during the 7 trumpets, and lived to be raptured along with the saints—which have been kept safe during this three and one-half years of the Tribulations at the 7th trumpet.

First let us take up the question, "Are they Jews or Christians?" To settle this question, we have to go back to the dispensations. Remember, this is the 6th dispensation. It ends in judgment like all the others; it deals with Christians and the church; and it ends with the 7th trumpet, which concludes 7 years of tribulations. We are being judged because of our "lukewarmness" and "coldness" towards Christ; just as the Jews were judged in the 5th dispensation because of their rejection of the Son of God. Their judgment resulted in them being scattered and persecuted throughout the world. It will be the judgment of the professing Christians of the 6th dispensation, to be tested by Satan for three and one-half years. So I conclude that it is impossible for this group to be anyone but Christians who proved their faith genuine during the 7 trumpets, and are now seen in heaven before the 7 vials, or the Wrath of God, starts.

Now we will take up the next question. "Are they Tribulation martyrs?" This is a convenient conclusion for most authors, because how else are they going to get them to heaven, since they have placed the Rapture before the Tribulations start? So they conclude that they were killed for the testimony of Jesus during the reign of the beast, and thus are victorious over him. But I believe that John would have been told to describe them differently, if they had been martyrs. Here they are standing on the sea of glass with harps and singing. Compare this with the following:

Rev. 6:9. And when he had opened the fifth seal, I saw

under the altar the souls of them that were slain for the word of God and for the testimony which they held (before Satan was cast to earth).

Rev. 20:4a. And I saw thrones, and they sat upon them, and judgment was given unto them; and I saw the souls of them that were beheaded for the witness of Jesus, and for the word of God, and which had not worshipped the beast.

In two different places John describes martyrs—he sees their souls—indicating that they haven't received their incorruptible bodies yet. In comparing the two descriptions, I have to conclude that they are not martyrs; and that the only way that they could get to heaven at this time —immediately following the testing period of the Christians, but before the Wrath of God—would be the Rapture at the 7th trumpet.

CHAPTER 36

THE WRATH OF GOD

Rev. 15:5-8. And after that I looked, and, behold, the temple of the tabernacle of testimony in heaven was opened: And the seven angels came out of the temple, having the seven plagues, clothed in pure and white linen, and having their breasts girded with golden girdles. And one of the four beasts gave unto the seven angels seven golden vials full of the wrath of God, who liveth for ever and ever. And the temple was filled with smoke from the glory of God, and from his power; and no man was able to enter into the temple till the seven plagues of the seven angels were fulfilled.

These final judgments originate from God's Temple because they are severer than the others which originated from His throne. The procession of the angels from the tabernacle symbolically shows that they are coming out from the resting place of the Divine Law to defend that Law, and to show that it cannot be disobeyed. The dress of those angels is the dress of the High Priest, of royalty, and one from heaven. They come to carry out their mission with the highest authority that can be given. God's glory is at stake; His righteousness demands the punishment of the wicked. And these angels are to administer this punishment. We see one of the four beasts, giving the 7 vials full of the Wrath of God to the angels. The beasts, as executors of the judicial government of God, perform accordingly.

Now the seven angels are about to begin their awful mission, of cleansing the earth. It is difficult for some people to believe that God would actually do away with all these people. But it must be understood that those are not God's people, but people of God's arch enemy, the Devil; and they have been trying to destroy God's children and take complete control of His creation. It is the end of the war between God and Satan, between good and evil. One of them will be completely victorious—would you prefer it be Satan? I can't help but day-dream a little, and try to imagine what a wonderful place this earth will be to live on, once all wickedness is taken away!

The temple is seen filled with smoke from the glory of God, and from His power; and no man, even though he has been redeemed, was able to enter the temple until the seven vials were poured out upon the earth. The temple was closed to man till after these seven plagues were administered. Why? I'm sure that in heaven at this time there will be many people who have wives, husbands, children and friends on the earth. And when they see what is to happen to them, even though they are wicked, it will cross their minds to go to the temple and pray to God for mercy for those on earth. So God is making sure that this is impossible. There will be nothing man can do to halt or turn back the Wrath of God. Even now we can't change what God has planned, so we must attempt to change man, with whatever tools God gives us to use.

As I have said before, I do not claim to be able to tell you how much we are to take as symbolic and how much is literal in these judgments. The Book of Revelation is a book of symbols; but there may be a great deal more in it that is literal than many of us believe. Really, though, I can't see that it is important that we know exactly what is going to happen, particularly this late in the game. But I can't help but notice that the outpouring of these vials shows, in large measure, the woes that were visited upon the kingdom of Pharaoh. Of course, the plagues during the tribulations will be more intense and widespread than in Pharaoh's days. Also we see a similarity to the seven trumpet judgments; but in the early trumpet judgments, the destruction was always limited; where in the vial judgments the destruction is complete. So let's examine each vial judgment briefly.

THE FIRST VIAL

Rev. 16:1-2. And I heard a great voice out of the temple saying to the seven angels, Go your ways, and pour out the vials of the wrath of God upon the earth. And the first went out, and poured out his vial upon the earth; and there fell a noisome and grievous sore upon the men which had the mark of the beast, and upon them which worshipped his image.

We hear the voice of God coming from the temple, sending the angels out to pour the Wrath of God on the earth. When the first vial was poured out, it caused all who worshipped the beast and who had its mark to get a very painful, foul-smelling, ulcerous sore. I believe this is literal; it will actually happen! The same Greek word is used here as in the sixth plague in Egypt, for the boils and blains. Maybe this is the result of some kind of chemical used when the mark was put on.

THE SECOND VIAL

Rev. 16:3. And the second angel poured out his vial upon the sea; and it became as the blood of a dead man: and every living soul died in the sea.

Here we are reminded of the first plague of Egypt, and

235

also of the second trumpet. I believe this refers to the Mediterranean Sea. The sea becomes as blood of a dead man and everything dies in it, before it was only one-third of it. It is also suggested that it may be a symbol of the complete moral and spiritual death of a godless society.

THE THIRD VIAL

Rev. 16:4-7. And the third angel poured out his vial upon the rivers and fountains of waters; and they became blood. And I heard the angel of the waters say, Thou art righteous, O Lord, which art, and wast, and shalt be, because thou hast judged thus. For they have shed the blood of saints and prophets, and thou hast given them blood to drink; for they are worthy. And I heard another out of the altar say, Even so, Lord God Almighty, true and righteous are thy judgments.

When the third vial is poured out, the rivers and the springs turn to blood. It appears as if the very source of life, water, is destroyed. We can plainly see that the sympathy of some in the heavens is with God. They feel that justice has been done, for the earth dwellers have shed the innocent blood of prophets and saints, and they deserve to drink blood. The altar adds its testimony, perhaps because the prayers of the saints under the altar are now answered.

THE FOURTH VIAL

Rev. 16:8-9. And the fourth angel poured out his vial upon the sun and power was given unto him to scorch men with fire. And men were scorched with great heat, and blasphemed the name of God, which hath power over these plagues: and they repented not to give him glory.

When the fourth vial was poured upon the sun, God gave

the angel power to scorch men with fire. And men were scorched with great heat, which did not cause them to repent; instead, they cursed the name of God. This is the only plague for which there is no Egyptian parallel. Notice, John makes it clear that God has power over these plagues; He is controlling them. If we believe that God made the sun, we can believe that God can darken the sun or increase its brilliance and heat at will. The laws of nature were made by God, and only He can set them aside. He has done so before.

> Joshua 10:13-14. And the sun stood still, and the moon stayed, until the people had avenged themselves upon their enemies. Is not this written in the book of Jasher? So the sun stood still in the midst of heaven, and hasted not to go down about a whole day. And there was no day like that before it, or after it, that the Lord hearkened unto the voice of a man: for the Lord fought for Israel.

Of course, if you want to look at it from another point of view, astronomers know that the earth is being drawn gradually toward the sun. Some interpreters believe that the earth's nearness to the sun may be the physical cause of this plague. But I doubt that, because that would be a gradual and irreversible warming trend.

THE FIFTH VIAL

> Rev. 16:10-11. And the fifth angel poured out his vial upon the seat of the beast; and his kingdom was full of darkness; and they gnawed their tongues for pain, and blasphemed the God of heaven because of their pains and sores, and repented not of their deeds.

God now strikes at the very center of this Satanic Empire, and fills his kingdom with darkness. We see that darkness and anguish do not tend to soften men's hearts, or to lead them to confess their sins. Their suffering seems to stir them up to curse God even more. Many believe that the city of Rome will become the capital of the world and the seat of the beast, the last great world dictator; just as it was the capital of the Ancient Roman Empire. I believe the image of the beast will be put in the temple at Jerusalem, and watched over by the False Prophet—thus making Rome and Jerusalem the two most important cities of the world at this time.

THE SIXTH VIAL

Rev. 16:12. And the sixth angel poured out his vial upon the great river Euphrates; and the water thereof was dried up, that the way of the kings of the east might be prepared.

Here we see the great River Euphrates, which is 1,780 miles in length; and I understand that it is ten to thirty feet deep, and several miles wide in many places. In other words, it isn't a small river; but when the 6th vial is poured out, this river is dried up. This is done to prepare a way for the kings of the east to reach the battleground, where the last great battle will take place. Many believe the dry riverbed will become a great highway which will play an important role in bringing together the armies of the world. I definitely take this literally. I have to, or disbelieve all the other instances where God used His power to part waters and dry up the ground, such as the Red Sea or the River Jordan.

Rev. 16:13-14. And I saw three unclean spirits like frogs come out of the mouth of the dragon, and out of the mouth of the beast, and out of the mouth of the False Prophet. For they are the spirits of devils, working miracles, which go forth unto the kings of the earth and of the whole world, to gather them to the battle of that great day of God Almighty.

Rev. 16:16. And he gathered them together in a place called in the Hebrew tongue Armageddon.

John sees three unclean spirits come from the mouths of Satan, Antichrist, and the False Prophet—the Satanic Trinity. To say these unclean spirits were like frogs was to say that their words were like plagues, that they were unclean, that they spoke empty words, and that they were the allies of the power of the dark. We know that the Satanic Trinity "breathed forth evil influence" that was responsible for the gathering of the nations of the world for this great battle. Some say that the mouth is the organ of speech, and speech is one of the most powerful influential forces in the world. But it is brought out in the Bible that unclean spirits are demons which can enter a person's body, and take possession of their minds. And they were to go forth unto the kings of the earth to gather them to the battle of that great day of God Almighty. And Satan gathered them together at Armageddon, which is on the greatest natural battleground in the world, in the valley of Jehosaphat, to the north of Palestine, among the hills of Megiddo. The word "Armageddon" means "the hill of the slaughter." We have seen that the blood will run to the horses' bridles; and in Chapter 19, we will be told of the unprecedented slaughter of Satan's army.

Let's go back to Verse 15 now. Just before the end of John's vision concerning the unclean spirits, John hears the voice of the Lord Himself.

Rev. 16:15. Behold, I come as a thief. Blessed is he that watcheth, and keepeth his garments, lest he walk naked, and they see his shame.

This verse is like the voice of the Lord Jesus Christ, breaking through the horror for an instant, calling warnings to rebels and encouragement to those who trust Him. Picture yourself as one of the 144,000 Jewish witnesses for Christ, or even worse, one of their converts, whose faith may not be as strong. The days will be filled with darkness and deception; the earth's armies are gathering against Israel, which will be God's faithful ones who have gathered in Jerusalem. Perhaps Satan has convinced the world that if Jerusalem were destroyed, these plagues, which are worldwide, would stop. Anyway, the word is that hordes of armies are getting ready to march toward Jerusalem. But, remember, you can't defend yourself with the sword! What a frightening experience, unless you have complete trust in Christ. So you can see why Christ felt it necessary to give both a warning and encouragement at this point. He tells them to trust Him, and keep the faith; and to watch their conduct so they won't be put to shame before the ungodly, when Christ comes. He says—Watch for me, as I come as a thief, unexpected, quickly, from out of the darkness of the night. Faith will be their only protection against Satan! How many will throw over their faith at this time. Would you?

Here is the final test for the professing faithful, just before our Lord returns. Will Jerusalem be saved?

> Romans 12:26-27. And so all Israel shall be saved: as it is written, there shall come out of Zion the Deliverer, and shall turn away ungodliness from Jacob. For this is my covenant unto them, when I shall take away their sins.

Many people interpret this to mean that all Israel as a nation will be saved. This is incorrect. Not even all those in Jerusalem will live, and the city itself will be taken.

> Zechariah 13:8-9. And it shall come to pass that in all the land, saith the Lord, two parts therein shall be cut off and die; but the third shall be left therein. And I will bring the third part through the fire, and will refine them as silver is refined, and will try them as gold is tried; they shall call on my name, and I will say, It is my people: and they shall say, The Lord is my God.

Two-thirds of the Jewish nation will die as a result of this battle, but all of Israel will be saved. All of those who prove their faith is genuine, whether they be Jew or Gentile, are God's "True Children"—ISRAEL. *How* will God save the faithful? I don't know; but He will.

Rev. 16:17-21. And the seventh angel poured out his vial into the air; and there came a great voice out of the temple of heaven, from the throne, saying, It is done. And there were voices, and thunders, and lightnings; and there was a great earthquake, such as was not since men were upon the earth, so mighty an earthquake, and so great. And the great city was divided into three parts, and the cities of the nations fell: and great Babylon came in remembrance before God, to give unto her the cup of the wine of the fierceness of his wrath. And every island fled away, and the mountains were not found. And there fell upon men a great hail out of heaven, every stone about the weight of a talent: and men blasphemed God because of the plague of the hail; for the plague thereof was exceeding great.

The 7th vial judgment shows by what power God will use to destroy the wicked, and save the faithful—nature. When the 7th vial judgment is poured into the air, nature is turned loose to smite the wicked. And the seven angels have completed their mission. Then a great voice, the voice of the One who cried on the Cross "It is finished," will cry "It is done." There must have been a brief minute of excitement in heaven before it started to happen, as voices were heard. But the storm warnings came; then this great earthquake, worse than any since man was put on this earth, which announces the return of Christ. As I have pointed out before, an earthquake signals an important happening; and the more important it is, the greater the earthquake. And this one will change the appearance of the earth! Jerusalem, the great city, is divided into three parts. This sounds terrible; but actually it will be a blessing to the faithful ones, as I believe this will separate them from the enemy, or in some way protect them.

> Zechariah 14:4-5. And his feet shall stand in that day upon the mount of Olives, which is before Jerusalem on the east, and the mount of Olives shall cleave in the midst thereof toward the east and toward the west, and there shall be a very great valley; and half of the mountain shall remove toward the north, and half of it toward the south. And ye shall flee to the valley of the mountain; for the valley of the mountains shall reach unto Azal: yea, ye shall flee, like as ye fled from before the earthquake in the days of Uzziah, king of Judah: and the Lord my God shall come, and all saints with thee.

This earthquake will not be limited to Jerusalem; it is a worldwide earthquake. Cities all over the world will fall. Islands will disappear and mountains will be leveled. God also remembers Rome, and she will get special treatment. This earthquake will claim its share of lives, but now God turns to hail, which He has used quite often in the past. We know that it was the 7th Egyptian Plague. And the Bible tells us that he used it on the enemies of Israel at Bethhoron in the days of Joshua.

> Joshua 10:11. And it came to pass as they fled from before Israel, and were in the going down to Bethhoron, that the Lord cast down great stones from heaven upon them unto Azekah and they died; they were more which died with hailstones than they whom the children of Israel slew with the sword.

I don't think that there is any question as to whether we

are to take this earthquake literally or not. Other prophecies tell of such an earthquake at this time, and indicate results that only a literal earthquake could cause. The Mount of Olives will be split in half and leave a valley running east and west. And I'm just as sure that there will be large hail. It says every stone will be about the weight of a talent, which is one hundred pounds. Perhaps they just seemed that large. But, regardless, the blasphemers of the End Times shall be stoned from heaven. In the Old Testament times the Law required that the blasphemer be stoned by all the congregation. (Leviticus 24:16)

We have now reached the time of the Second Coming of our Lord Jesus Christ; but John stops the story again, in order to tell us more details of what is happening.

The next two chapters of the Book of Revelation can be very confusing, unless we clear up a few things, and learn something about the history of Babylon. First of all, when John speaks of Babylon, he is referring to another city of the future, which will be like the great city of Babylon that was destroyed at least 100 years before Christ. There are a few who think that Babylon will be rebuilt; but I believe that Scripture supports the theory that it will be Rome. Ancient Babylon was not just a beautiful city; it was Satan's city, just as Jerusalem is God's city. It represents a Satanic system through which Satan hopes to conquer the world and set up a kingdom for himself. Of course, God has about the same thing in mind. And that is what the war that started in Genesis and ends in Revelation is all about. Before we try and trace Satan's footsteps from Old Babylon to Rome, notice the pattern of double meanings that has developed.

Remember that the beast of the sea that John saw has a double meaning: It represents the Revived Roman Empire, consisting of a ten-nation federation; and it represents its imperial head, Antichrist.

Also, the seven heads on the beast have a double meaning: they represent the seven hills that Rome is built on; and also seven kings which stand for the different world kingdoms from Daniel's day till the Stone Kingdom.

We will find that the ten horns, which are the ten nations, actually have a double meaning. When they are shown crowned, the kings have power, and when they are not crowned, they haven't received their power yet.

We will find that a woman, called Babylon, has a double meaning. She is the city (representing the Satanic systems) of Rome, and she is the False Church of Rome in the End Times. This will be the World Church of the future, which will compromise away any thread of truth that is left in exchange for power over the state.

CHAPTER 37

BABYLON

Now I will try to give you a little of the history of Babylon to help you understand the connection between Rome and Babylon. Babylon or Babel was built by Nimrod, the grandson of Ham, who was the unworthy son of Noah. This was the origin of nations, as God scattered the peoples after causing them to speak in different tongues; which was the result of their sins towards God. But before that Satan had implanted in their minds the "germ" of a doctrine that has been the source of every false religion the world has ever known. The "Babylonian Cult" was invented—a mystery religion originated in Babylon. Semiramis bore a son whom she claimed was miraculously conceived. His name was Tammuz, and he was hailed as the promised deliverer. This introduced the mystery of the mother and the child, a form of idolatry that is older than any other known to man. The rites of this worship were secret. And their image, the queen of heaven with babe in arms, was seen everywhere! Ezekiel protested against this in the days of the captivity. So, you see, this did not start with Mary and Jesus. The sign of the cross was sacred to Tammuz, as symbolizing the life-giving principle, and as the first letter of his name. It was from this mystery religion that Abraham was separated by divine call.

The city of Babylon continued to be the seat of Satan until the fall of the Babylon and the Medo-Persian Empires. Then he shifted his capital to Pergamos; which is where it was in John's day.

When Attalus, the Pontiff and King of Pergamos, died in 133 B.C., he bequeathed the headship of the "Babylonian Priesthood" to Rome. Thus the Babylonian religion and rites were brought to Rome and a pontiff was set up who was head of the priesthood, and later the Romans accepted him as their civil leader. In 63 B.C. Julius Caesar was made Supreme Pontiff of the "Babylon Order." Thus the Roman Emperor became the head of the Babylonian Priesthood, and Rome, the successor of Babylon. Later, in A.D. 378, the Bishop of the Church of Rome, Damasus, became the head of the "Babylonian Order." Thus Satan united Rome and Balylon in one religious system, and soon after, "rites" of Babylon begin to come forth. All the outstanding festivals of the Roman Catholic Church are of Babylonian origin. And as for the word "mystery," the Papal Church shrouded herself in mystery, particularly in its early years.

From this you can see how the connection of Babylon and Rome was made. But in John's day, the Papal Church hadn't developed yet, so he didn't know that he was speaking of future Rome instead of future Babylon. This must have been a real mystery to John; and no doubt he found it difficult to understand how the church could end up like that. And, to a lesser degree, it still is, because John speaks not of the church today, but as it will be in the End Times—one world church, closely connected with the ten federated nations and Antichrist; and playing a dominating role in the beginning.

Satan, starting with Nimrod, has sought to accomplish two objectives: a world political federation, and a world religious federation, both in opposition to God. Babylon represents this program of Satan, and because of its important role in Bible history, three chapters of Revelation are devoted to the end of this evil system.

CHAPTER 38

MYSTERY BABYLON THE GREAT

Rev. 17:1-7. And there came one of the seven angels which had the seven vials, and talked with me, saying unto me, Come hither; I will shew unto thee the judgment of the great whore that sitteth upon many waters: With whom the kings of the earth have committed fornication, and the inhabitants of the earth have been made drunk with the wine of her fornication. So he carried me away in the spirit into the wilderness; and I saw a woman set upon a scarlet-coloured beast, full of names of blasphemy, having seven heads and ten horns. And the woman was arrayed in purple and scarlet color, and decked with gold and precious stones and pearls, having a golden cup in her hand full of abomination and filthiness of her fornication: And upon her forehead was a name written, MYSTERY, BABYLON THE GREAT, the MOTHER OF HARLOTS and ABOMINATIONS OF THE EARTH. And I saw the woman drunken with the blood of the saints, and with the blood of the martyrs of Jesus: and when I saw her, I wondered with great admiration. And the angel said unto me, Wherefore didst thou marvel? I will tell thee the mystery of the woman, and of the beast that carrieth her, which hath the seven heads and ten horns.

One of the angels which had the seven vials told John that he would show him the judgment of the great whore that sitteth upon the many waters. The angel explains in verse 15 that the waters are multitudes of peoples, nations, and tongues. The great harlot, which is what the angel calls the world church, thus controls many peoples—multitudes, nations. And she has allured them into godlessness and immorality; she has intoxicated men by her doctrines and practices which violate the Word of God.

After hearing this unholy description of this woman, John is carried away in spirit into the wilderness, and there he saw her. She sat upon the beast which we have identified as representing the Revived Roman Empire and its imperial head, Antichrist. She is pictured here riding into power on the beast's kingdom. I think that this shows the church dominating the state in the beginning, probably for the first three and one-half years. She is clothed in purple and scarlet, the royal colors, denoting luxury and splendor. She is decked in gold, precious stones and pearls, showing that she is rich in worldly goods, and influential. She has a golden cup which is filled with abomination and filthiness of her adultery, which tells of her gross infidelity to God and His Word; and which she seduces others to drink from. On her forehead she has the harlot's frontlet with her name: Mystery Babylon the Great, the Mother of Harlots and Abomination of the Earth. Remember, Babylon, or the woman, represents both the church and the city of Rome in the End Times. But I think that "Mystery Babylon" refers to the woman as the false church. Some call her the "bride of Antichrist." Also, I believe that, since she is called mother, she has a brood of children. So this could be taken to mean that she is the mother church in Rome; and associated with her will be the people who make up the parts of God's Church today, which are represented by the letters to the churches of Thyatira,

Sardis and Laodicea. In other words, it appears that all the people, except those who make up the part of the church today, represented by the letter to Philadelphia, will unite with the world church. I believe there is a good deal of evidence that we are headed that way, at this time. It will appear to be a very good thing, and probably won't appear to compromise anything of importance—in the beginning. Some denominations say now that they will never join with Rome, and perhaps not; but those who don't will disappear. In those days it will come down to the individuals; what denomination you belong to won't matter, as the demands of the majority of the people will be met. And churches who do not join will soon have to close for lack of support. There will be those individuals who believe the prophecies in the Book of Revelation who will never join, as they will know what the outcome will be. Many believe that the Rapture will take place before this happens; but, as you know, I do not. What will happen to those who remain faithful to God and His Word? I'm only sure of one thing: you keep your faith, and God will keep His promise to keep you safe, just as He says He will.

John saw this woman drunken with the blood of the saints and martyrs of Jesus. This implies that Rome will not, or has not, simply persecuted the Christians as a police matter; but that she took a fiendish delight in it. She was intoxicated with the terrible joy it gave her. John is referring to the past as well as the future here. And John said that when he saw her he wondered greatly about her. Then the angel told John that he would tell him about the woman and the beast.

Rev. 17:8. The beast that thou sawest was, and is not; and shall ascend out of the bottomless pit, and go into perdition; and they that dwell on the earth shall wonder, whose names were not written in the book of life from the foundation of the world, when they behold the beast that was, and is not, and yet is.

249

We have said that the beast represented both the Revived Roman Empire and its imperial head, which is Antichrist, or the son of the Devil. We are now talking about the man, not the empire, as some believe. The angel said to John that the beast you saw was, and is not; which could describe the Roman Empire. But I hardly believe it will ascend out of the bottomless pit.

I mentioned before that I believed that Satan sent his incarnate son to earth in the person of Judas Iscariot, at the same time as God sent his incarnate Son to earth in the person of Jesus. Let me repeat: in II Thessalonians 2:3, Paul calls Antichrist "son of perdition." This name is used but twice in the Scriptures! Also, in John 6:70, Jesus said, "Have not I chosen you twelve and one of you is a devil?" This is the only passage in the Bible that the word "devil" or the Greek word "diabolus" is applied to anyone but Satan himself. In considering this, some may wonder if Satan has two sons. Without anything to go on, I would say no, because this would break the pattern of imitation. Going back to Revelation 11:7, it says that the beast that slays the two witnesses ascendeth out of the bottomless pit; and the beast is Antichrist. Now, how did he get there to begin with? My explanation is that he got there when Judas went to his "own place," according to Acts 1:25. Of no other person in the Scriptures is it said that he went to "his own place." So, the son of the Devil *was* here as Judas, but he is *not* here now, when John was writing this book. He shall ascend out of the bottomless pit, and appear as Antichrist; and later, we see in Revelation 19:20 that he will be cast into the Lake of Fire, or Hell. While he is here as Antichrist, the dwellers of the earth, whose names were not written in the Book of Life from the foundations of the world, will marvel when they look at him. We learned back in Chapter 13 that he received a deadly wound, the 7th head or king; but he was brought back to life! Thus he was, and then he was not, yet he is.

Rev. 17:9-11. And here is the mind which hath wisdom,

The seven heads are seven mountains, on which the woman sitteth. And there are seven kings: five are fallen and one is, and the other is not yet come: and when he cometh he must continue a short space. And the beast that was, and is not, even he is the eighth, and is of the seven, and goeth into perdition.

The seven heads represent two things. The woman which we have just identified as the "false church," the bride of the Antichrist, is located in the "city of *seven hills*" which is Rome. I believe the headquarters of the federation of ten nations and Antichrist will also be there. And since she is described as sitting on all of Rome, this indicates her complete power over the state, in the beginning. Also, the seven heads represent seven kings or forms of government which will rule from the time of Daniel till the coming of Christ: (1) Babylonian—Nebuchadnezzar, (2 & 3) Medo-Persian—2 kings, Darius and his nephew, Cyrus, (4) Grecian-Alexander the Great, (5) Grecian—divided into 4 parts and ruled by 4 of Alexander's generals at his death, (6) Roman—Caesar Augustus, (7) Revived Roman Empire (10-nation federation) under Antichrist during the first three and one-half years. The angel tells John that five have fallen; the 6th is, which is Roman in John's day. The 7th has not come yet, but when he (Antichrist, as the good guy) does, he will only reign for a short time (three and one-half years): and Antichrist, *which was, then was not,* because he was killed. But yet he became the eighth, because he was brought back to life. And because he has become a cruel dictator, he is counted as another form of government, the eighth, even though he is of the seventh. And later, he will go into perdition.

Rev. 17:12-14. And the ten horns which thou sawest are ten kings, which have received no kingdom as yet: but receive power as kings one hour with the beast. These have one mind, and shall give their power and strength unto the beast. These shall make war with the Lamb, and the Lamb shall overcome them: for he is Lord of lords, and King of kings: and they that are with him are called, and chosen, and faithful.

We have been given two pictures of the beast, one in the 13th chapter, and here in the 17th chapter. We see the beast, or Antichrist, pictured at the height of his power first; which would be during the last three and one-half years. This is shown by the fact that the woman or the church isn't sitting on the beast, and the ten kings or horns are seen already crowned in the 13th chapter. Here we have the empire or Antichrist, pictured as it was the first three and one-half years. The church is the controlling figure; and we see that the ten kings had not received their crowns or kingdoms as yet. They are to reign as kings one hour with Antichrist. This ten-nation federation will act as one under Antichrist, as they have given all their power and strength to him. In the end they shall gather and make war with the Lamb. And they shall be defeated because the Lamb is the Lord of lords, King of kings. He is Christ, our risen Lord, coming back as he promised, to set up his kingdom on earth; and with Him are the called, and chosen, and faithful. All of God's children are called, and if you are faithful, you will be chosen. But I regret to say that the Bible says that many were called but few were chosen to be present at the wedding feast, according to Matthew 22:14.

The angel told John that he would tell him about the woman and about the beast. He has finished his story about the beast, and now John is given more information about the woman.

Rev. 17:15-17. And he saith unto me, The waters which thou sawest, where the whore sitteth, are peoples, and multitudes, and nations, and tongues. And the ten horns which thou sawest upon the beast, these shall hate the whore, and shall make desolate and naked, and shall eat her flesh, and burn her with fire. For God hath put in their hearts to fulfill his will, and to agree, and give their kingdom unto the beast, until the words of God shall be fulfilled.

The whore "sitting on the waters" merely points out that she controls the peoples, nations, the whole empire at the beginning. But, after the first three and one-half years, the political power will rise up like a mad dog, led by Antichrist and the False Prophet. They will throw off the pretense of religion and substitute the worship of Antichrist. The ten kings which make up the Revived Roman Empire will grow to hate the church, and its demands and interference; and will literally destroy her. They will strip her of her gorgeous apparel by taking away her power and confiscating her great wealth; and burn her churches and cathedrals with fire. For at this time Antichrist, in his jealous hate, will not permit any worship that does not center in himself. And we see evil destroying evil. It certainly seems as if Satan is controlling things. But, unbeknown to them, even the evil ones are fulfilling the will of God. He has put it into their hearts, He is controlling them so they will agree to give their kingdoms to Antichrist until the Word of God is fulfilled—just like God controlled the mind of Pharoah during the ten plagues; just like God controlled the hearts of the Pharisees and chief priests in making them order the death of His Son. God has given us at least three examples of how he has made the children of the evil one do His Will. How much easier it is for Him to exercise control over His own children, if they permit Him to be their Father.

I say permit, because this is where you have a free will; He does not force Himself on you. You have been given a free will to choose—once and for all time! Are you going to serve God, or are you going to serve the world, ruled by Satan? Whose servant, slave, or puppet, for that matter, are you going to *choose* to be? Jesus says that you *cannot* serve two masters! If you have to decide everyday, on every problem, whether to play it by God's rules or to cheat a little, tell a few lies, or only God knows what, just to make a few lousy bucks or to impress this world; then you haven't used that free will, which you seem to hold so dear, to make the one and only decision which is necessary. Which side are you going to choose—which king are you going to serve? You cannot play by God's rules part of the time and Satan's rules the rest of the time; as that is trying to serve both kings, who are at war with each other, at the same time. No decision is a decision for Satan and this world, which shall pass away. You have to choose God as your Father, like he chose you as His children, in order to complete the agreement. If you believe in the Father, you will believe in the Son, and will receive all the promises that God gives to His children in the Bible, through our Lord Jesus Christ, and the Holy Spirit. The day is coming when our Lord is going to get tired of waiting for the "Lukewarm Christians" of today to make up their minds, and He will force them to choose in the tribulations of the End Times!

The last verse confirms that the woman is that great city, which I believe to be Rome. As the church, she will reign over the kings of the earth for the first three and one-half years. And politically she will dictate to the world for the next three and one-half years.

CHAPTER 39

BABYLON THE CITY

We have seen Mystery Babylon, the church, destroyed, and now we are shown Babylon the city (Rome) about to be destroyed.

Rev. 18:1. And after these things I saw another angel come down from heaven, having great power: and the earth was lightened with his glory.

After these things, or after the angel with one of the seven vials, had told John about Mystery Babylon, the false church, being destroyed by the ten kings, John saw another angel that came down from heaven. This angel seemed to be especially great. So recently had he come from the Presence of God, that he brings with him the light of God. In Exodus 35:29 Moses came down from Mt. Sinai with the second set of tablets, and his skin on his face shone. The people were even afraid to come near him. And we are told here that the earth was lightened with the glory of this powerful angel.

Rev. 18:2. And he cried mightily with a strong voice, saying, Babylon the great is fallen, is fallen, and is become the habitation of devils, and the hold of every foul spirit, and a cage of every unclean and hateful bird.

The angel proclaimed in a loud voice that Babylon is fallen—Babylon is still in the process of falling. In Chapter 14 we were told this, but not in a loud voice, at that time. But as I said then, I believe that it was beginning to fall, and I think what we learned in Chapter 17 confirms it: because, some time during the seven trumpets, which is Satan's three and one-half years of power, the religious part of Rome was stripped of its power and destroyed. Thus Rome had begun to fall.

> Matthew 12:25b. Every kingdom divided against itself is brought to desolation, and every city or house divided against itself shall not stand.

The best of the two evils was destroyed. And Rome became the natural place, or home, for all evil things and beings, including Antichrist and the False Prophet. This was still the center of this Satanic System, which tries to make the world worship Antichrist. Every foul spirit found a home here; every kind of sin was found here. No doubt many people were killed here in Rome, and it is reasonable to believe this would attract the vultures and every unclean and hateful bird.

> Rev. 18:3. For all nations have drunk of the wine of the wrath of her fornication, and the kings of the earth have committed fornication with her, and the merchants of the earth are waxed rich through the abundance of her delicacies.

For all nations have been corrupted by her intense immorality of this system, and particularly this city. And the kings of the earth have participated in these terrible sins against God. They have helped enforce these immoral laws, which were forced upon all peoples by Antichrist and the False

Prophet. This city which will be more sinful than any before, will draw people and money like bees to honey. And the merchants and businessmen of the world will grow rich, through the abundance of the delicacies that Rome will offer the people who come there.

Rev. 18:4-5. And I heard another voice from heaven, saying Come out of her, my people, that ye be not partakers of her sins, and that ye receive not of her plagues. For her sins have reached unto heaven, and God hath remembered her iniquities.

Before God pours out His wrath on Rome, all the righteous people will have fled. God warns them that this is an unsafe place, both spiritually and physically. Here, we see that God calls His people out of Rome so that they won't be tempted from fear, or by favor, to take part in her unholy sins, and suffer her punishment.

Many people compare this to God calling Lot out of Sodom, which was within a few hours of its destruction. Lot was told at a particular time to get out of Sodom. But I don't believe this call from God refers to a particular time. Actually, this call can be heard throughout the Bible. God is always telling his people to separate themselves from these sinful places. If God waited till right before He was going to destroy Rome to call out His people, I don't think He would have said, "So you don't partake in her sins." He would have just said, "So you are not destroyed with her." Remember, Rome became the home of all sin and evil, when Satan took over; and Antichrist became a cruel dictator, who claimed to be God, and demanded worship. Also, in order to buy or sell, you had to have the mark. It was at this time that Rome took a definite turn for the worse; and from this time on, I think God would be calling His people out. The sins of Rome have become so great that they reached heaven, and God is ready to judge her for all the terrible things that she has done.

257

Rev. 18:6-8. Reward her even as she rewarded you, and double unto her double according to her works: in the cup which she hath filled to her double. How much she hath glorified herself, and lived deliciously, so much torment and sorrow give her: for she saith in her heart, I sit a queen, and am no widow, and shall see no sorrow. Therefore shall her plagues come in one day, death, and mourning, and famine; and she shall be utterly burned with fire, for strong is the Lord God who judgeth her.

After it is noted that God has called his people out of Rome, He instructs the angel as to her punishment. Remember, the angels are the ones who administer these plagues. These instructions are not given to men to carry out; vengeance is mine, says the Lord. He tells the angel to repay Rome with the same evil rewards as she paid others, only double it. He said to mix her a double portion in the cup in which she mixed her portions. She has lived in much luxury and pleasure—now match that with torture and sorrows. She is proud, arrogant; she believes she is so powerful, strong, rich, and self-sufficient that she doesn't need God. And because of this her plagues shall come in one day: death, mourning, and famine. And she shall be consumed by fire, because mighty and powerful is the Lord who judges her.

Rev. 18:9-10. And the kings of the earth, who have committed fornication and lived deliciously with her, shall bewail her, and lament for her, when they shall see the smoke of her burning. Standing afar off for the fear of her torment, saying, Alas, alas, that great city Babylon, that mighty city! for in one hour is thy judgment come.

The kings of the earth, which refer to the ten kings which made up the Revived Roman Empire, have participated in the terrible crimes against the people, and against God; they also have shared in her wealth, and lived in the luxury of this great city. Now they weep and grieve for her, seeing the smoke of her burning. But they do nothing to help her; in fact, they watch from a distance, trembling with fear. She was such a mighty city, which needed nothing; but now look at her, utterly destroyed in just a little while, by the power of God.

There are some who believe that both Chapter 17 and 18 are referring to the city. Thus the kings are said to have hated and destroyed the city. If that was the case, I doubt that they would weep and grieve for her now. No. they destroyed the church, and now the judgment of God has destroyed the city.

Rev. 18:11. And the merchants of the earths shall weep and mourn over her; for no man buyeth their merchandise any more.

Here we see another group that weeps and grieves, but not for the city or its inhabitants, but because they are concerned about their own welfare. Rome has been making them rich; now who will buy their merchandise?

Rev. 18:12-14. The merchandise of gold, and silver, and precious stones, and of pearls, and fine linen, and purple, and silk, and scarlet, and all thyine wood, and all manner vessels of ivory, and all manner vessels of most precious wood, and of brass, and iron, and marble. And cinnamon, and odours, and ointments, and frankincense, and wine, and oil, and fine flour, and wheat, and beasts, and sheep, and horses, and chariots, and slaves, and souls of men. And the fruits that thy soul lusted after are departed from thee, and all things which were dainty and goodly are departed from thee, and thou shalt find them no more at all.

Rome will become the greatest commercial city of the

world. It will be "fun city" for those who can afford it. And there will be a great market for the list of merchandise that we have been given in Verse 12 and 13. For Rome's fashionable society of that day will wear the most costly of clothes and jewels. They will fill their homes with the most costly of furniture, perfumes, foods, and servants of all kinds, and for all purposes. Because of all the terrible plagues that have been occurring all over the rest of the world, they see how sudden death can strike. And they lavish themselves with every possible thing that money can buy, and participate in a mad whirl of unheard-of pleasures, and ceaseless feasting and drinking; as they are trying to forget what is going on outside of Rome, and to hide the fear that pushes itself into their minds in unguarded moments. Women will sell their bodies, and men their souls, to gratify their lusts.

A city filled with people like this is a businessman's delight. When they looked upon the city before, they didn't really see the people—they saw all their money. Now all that money that they loved so much, and schemed to get, is gone. And the luxuries and pleasures that they enjoyed here are gone, and they shall never find them again.

Rev. 18:15-17a. The merchants of these things which were made rich by her, shall stand afar off for the fear of her torment, weeping and wailing. And saying, Alas, alas that great city, that was clothed in fine linen, and purple, and scarlet. And decked with gold, and precious stones, and pearls! For in one hour so great riches is come to nought.

The merchants who have become rich by selling her all these things shall stand off in the distance, fearing danger to themselves, weeping and crying. And finding it hard to believe that this great city, which they picture as the woman dressed in fine clothes and jewels, could be destroyed. They say, "Look, in one hour, all that wealth is gone." You can see that the only thing that they were interested in was money, wealth—now they are ruined!

Rev. 18:17b-19. And every shipmaster, and all the company in ships, and sailors, and as many as trade by sea, stood afar off, and cried when they saw the smoke of her burning, saying, What city is like unto this great city! And they cast dust on their heads, and cried, weeping and wailing, saying, Alas, alas that great city, wherein were made rich all that had ships in the sea by reason of her costliness! for in one hour is she made desolate.

First we saw the kings weeping over their loss, then the merchants; now the shipowners, captains, and the crews, stand off in the distance, weeping, as they watch the smoke ascending. They seem to be even more upset than the others, as they even throw dust on their heads. And they cry, saying, "Where in all the world is there another city such as this, that we can take all our merchandise to?" The shipping industry has flourished, all the way from the shipbuilder to the seaman and dock workers. Merchandise has been brought to Rome from all over the world; but now, in one hour, all that trade which brought them so much wealth is gone.

When a city is destroyed by an earthquake or some force of nature, it is not unusual to hear of feelings of sorrow and grief expressed for the people which lived there. But here, in every case, what grieves them is not Rome or the people that lived there and were killed; but the fact that they lost their source of wealth and luxury. To make money and material things your God is the way to the greatest tragedy of all.

Rev. 18:20-24. Rejoice over her, thou heaven, and ye holy apostles and prophets; for God hath avenged you on her. And a mighty angel took up a stone like a great millstone, and cast it into the sea, saying, Thus with violence shall that great Babylon be thrown down, and

261

shall be found no more at all. And the voice of harpers, and musicians, and of pipers, and trumpeters, shall be heard no more at all in thee; and no craftsman, of whatsoever craft he be, shall be found any more in thee; and the sound of a millstone shall be heard no more at all in thee; and the light of a candle shall shine no more at all in thee; and the voice of the bridegroom and of the bride shall be heard no more at all in thee; for thy merchants were the great men of the earth; for by thy sorceries were all nations deceived. And in her was found the blood of prophets, and of saints, and of all that were slain upon the earth.

All heaven, together with the saints, apostles and prophets, are summoned to rejoice over the destruction of this ungodly city, the headquarters of Satan and his followers. So, from the midst of the grief of the earth dwellers, there comes the voice calling for joy from heaven. For they will be glad to see the vengeance of God upon His enemies, and upon their persecutors. We are confronted with this picture more than once in Scripture.

Deuteronomy 32:43. Rejoice, O ye nations, with his people: for he will avenge the blood of his servants, and will render vengeance to his adversaries, and will be merciful unto his land, and to his people.

Every time we are told that those in heaven rejoice and are happy to see God avenge their blood by destroying their persecutors on earth, we have a tendency to make excuses for the writer for saying such things. Many believe this cannot be true, as it doesn't go along with what Jesus said about forgiving our enemies and praying for those who persecute you. Even Jesus, on the Cross said to forgive them, "for they know not what they do." So it seems reasonable to our human minds that the writer must have let his personal experiences influence his writing on this point; forgetting that the Bible has one author, the Holy Spirit, who told each man what to write. So, as in many other situations, because we cannot understand how this could be, we decide that it isn't true. This is a big mistake on our part! Accept the Bible as the true word of God, and do not doubt it just because you can't understand something, or you don't think it should be like that. When the faithful children of God are gathered in heaven to return with Christ, we will understand all those things. And we will rejoice when we see the enemies of God being destroyed. The time has finally come when good triumphs over evil forever!

Now we see that a strong angel shows John what the destruction of Rome will be like. He takes a great millstone, and throws it into the sea. And he said, "With violence shall she fall and be destroyed completely, never to rise again." Music shall not be heard coming from this place anymore. Never again will there be the sound of any craftsman plying his trade. Never again will the sound of domestic activity be heard in her, or will there be lights from a window or a street. Never again will there be the sounds of a wedding. Rome is to be completely destroyed, never to rise again. This will come about because her merchants were the great ones of the earth, who worshipped wealth and luxury. It will come because she deceived all nations with her sorceries. It will come about because the blood of the prophets was found in Rome, and persecution went out from her, and people all over the world were slain because of her.

Now the woman is dead, never to rise again. She represented the False Church and the city of Rome, which together made up the heart of Satanic System. This is a great victory for God!

CHAPTER 40

HEAVEN REJOICES

Rev. 19:1-4. And after these things I heard a great voice of much people in heaven saying, Alleluia; Salvation, and glory, and honour, and power, unto the Lord our God: For true and righteous are his judgments: for he hath judged the great whore, which did corrupt the earth with her fornication, and hath avenged the blood of his servants at her hand. And again they said, Alleluia. And her smoke rose up for ever and ever. And the four and twenty elders and the four beasts fell down and worshipped God that sat on the throne, saying, Amen; Alleluia.

The heavens, the saints, apostles, and prophets were called upon to rejoice over the destruction of Rome, and all it stood for, in Revelation 18:20. And here we see the response. John first hears the shouting of a vast crowd of people in heaven praising God; which, I think it is safe to say, is all the redeemed of every age. God is praised because salvation, glory, honour, and power belong to Him; and because He has exercised His just and true judgment on that Satanic System, Rome. He has punished her because she corrupted the earth, and seduced others into forsaking God and worshipping false gods. And He avenged the murder of his servants. And again they sing praises to God, because the destruction of Rome was final.

Then, of course, John sees the twenty-four elders and four creatures, who have been prominent in earlier throne scenes. They fall down and worship God, who sits on the throne, and say, "So be it, praise God." This is the last time we see them, as the scene will soon change and follow our King to his earthly throne, and the bride will take their place here on earth.

> Rev. 19:5-8. And a voice came out of the throne, saying, Praise our God, all ye his servants, and ye that fear him, both small and great. And I heard as it were the voice of a great multitude, and as the voice of many waters, and as the voice of mighty thunderings, saying, Alleluia; for the Lord God omnipotent reigneth. Let us be glad and rejoice, and give honour to him: for the marriage of the Lamb is come, and his wife hath made herself ready. And to her was granted that she should be arrayed in fine linen, clean and white; for the fine linen is the righteousness of the saints.

John hears a voice that comes from the throne itself, which is most likely the voice of one of the four creatures; but I believe it symbolizes God Himself, speaking from the center and source of His government. It said to praise our God, all you his servants, and you that fear Him, both small and great. This certainly refers to two different groups of people; but I think that everyone in heaven will fall into one of those two groups. Then John hears what sounded like a great multitude, and like the voice of many waters, and as the voice of mighty thunderings saying, Alleluia; for the Lord God, the one who controls all things, has entered into His Kingdom. Let us be happy and rejoice and give him honor, for the time has come for the marriage of the Lamb; and his wife to be, has prepared herself. She is permitted to wear the cleanest, and the whitest, and the finest of linens, because the fine linen is the righteousness of saints. The bride of the Lamb will be the "True Church" of this age, not the professing church, now. Only those who truly love, believe, and choose Jesus for their Master; and He in turn redeems and cancels out their record of sins, which makes them righteous before God. He gives them His Holy Spirit, which is a guarantee of salvation, and sets aside their white linen robes. Now, this is not something that happens over and over; it happens once, which is all that is necessary. All your sins from the day you were born, until God gives you the Holy Spirit, are cancelled out; the record is redeemed by Christ, and paid for with His blood. You have been made righteous by your faith. You were dead in sin; but now you are alive in Christ, and as sons of God, your salvation is guaranteed. Also, as far as the law is concerned, you are dead; it is not you who lives, but Christ who lives in you. So, through Christ, you have been set free of the law; and without the law, there is no sin!

The *purpose of the law was to show us that we were sinners,* and needed Christ, as we could not be made righteous through the law, since it is impossible for us to obey it. *We heard and believed the Gospel.* And *was given the Holy Spirit (rebirth),* who is your helper here on earth. The *law has accomplished its purpose and is discarded. No law, no sins hereafter.*

This shows why it is only necessary for Christ to cancel out your record of sins once, at the time of your rebirth. But we are also told not to use this freedom as an excuse for letting your human nature rule you; instead, love and serve one another. Even though you aren't subject to the law anymore, and your salvation is secure, remember that your works will be judged from here on. So you must walk in the spirit, so you will not lose any crowns or any extra rewards.

I have repeatedly said that you must hear and believe before you can be reborn with the Holy Spirit. And God, who can see into the hearts of all men, decides when that is. God baptizes us with the Holy Spirit when He thinks our faith is genuine. This is the one baptism that controls our future. Any other baptism, performed by man with water, is but a shadow of the real one; it is a symbol, perhaps a beginning. Just as Holy Communion is a shadow of the real rebirth, a symbol, which Christ said to do in remembrance of Him.

The following verses give you some information on what I have just discussed. You may not think that this is connected with the Book of Revelation; but your understanding of this could make the difference between you being tested in the Great Tribulations or being kept safe.

Ephesians 1:13-14. In whom ye also trusted (Christ), *after* that ye *heard* the word of truth, the gospel of your salvation: in whom also *after* that you *believed,* ye were sealed with that Holy Spirit of promise, Which is the earnest (guarantee) of our inheritance, until the redemption of the purchased possession (us), until the praise of his glory.

Galatians 2:19-20. For I through the law am dead to the law, that I might live unto God. I am crucified with Christ; nevertheless I live; yet not I, but Christ liveth in me: and the life which I now live in the flesh I live by the faith of the Son of God, who loved me, and gave himself for me.

Galatians 3:23-25. But before faith came, we were kept under the law, shut up into the faith which should afterwards be revealed. Wherefore the law was our schoolmaster to bring us unto Christ, that we might be justified by faith. But after that faith is come, we are no longer under a schoolmaster.

After the rapture, the true church will receive its fine linen robes. Everyone who died believing in Christ as their savior, the "True" Church, and those who have withstood the testing of Satan, and are still alive, will be in the Rapture or first resurrection. And they will receive white robes; but not necessarily fine linen ones. Some may have just gotten there by the skin of their teeth! We are told that the "Bride" has made herself ready; she has put on her fine white linen robes.

The marriage of the Lamb takes place in heaven. This is the visible bringing together of the "True" Church and Christ. We belong to Christ now through the Holy Spirit. We love, serve, and worship one which we cannot see now; but then—there our Lord will be in plain sight, and we will *know* all the things that we believed by faith before. What a great day that will be!

So, while God is cleaning the earth with His wrath, the 7 vial judgments, and preparing it for the saint's reign, the saints themselves are in heaven being prepared to reign with Christ upon the earth. They will have to stand before the judgment seat of Christ, and all their works from the time that they had received the Holy Spirit, through faith, will be judged. Their sinful record was destroyed when they repented and received Christ, so they are righteous before God; but what kind of rewards they will receive now depends on how their works stand the test of fire.

1 Corinthians 3:13-15. Every man's works shall be made manifest: for the day shall declare it, because it shall be revealed by fire, and the fire shall try every man's work of what sort it is. If any man's work abide which he hath built thereupon, he shall receive a re-ward. If any man's work shall be burned, he shall suffer loss: but he himself shall be saved; yet so as by fire.

There is only one way to heaven for the people of this dispensation or age. You must have genuine faith, belief, and love for Christ. It is only through the Cross that we obtain salvation—not through works. Works, which are done to glorify the Son, the Father, and the Holy Spirit, will with-

269

stand the test of fire; and you will receive crowns, and rewards accordingly. Works which are done to impress men, or because it is a tax deduction, or for just personal gain, even though it appears to be God's work, will not stand the test of fire; and you will suffer loss of your rewards. Your works will not be judged by amount or size; but by what you have done with what God gave you. The more that God gives you, be it money, abilities, or wisdom, the more you are expected to do with it. For instance, a lot will be expected from God's messengers, or caretakers of His Word—or, in other words, ministers or priests. One who has been given little, and does a lot with it to glorify God, will be rewarded greatly.

I'm sure our stewardship will be tested; but just when this judgment of works takes place is not clear to me yet. Some believe that it has to be in heaven, before Christ returns with his saints, in order for them to appear in white; but all who are in the first resurrection are saved and receive white robes, without question at this time.

> Rev. 20:6. Blessed and holy is he that hath part in the first resurrection: on such the second death hath no power, but they shall be priests of God and of Christ, and shall reign with him a thousand years.

So I don't believe that the judgment of works comes till after we arrive back on earth with Christ. We have just received our robes, as a guarantee of our salvation. We see that the saints that return with Christ do not have any crowns, so they haven't received their rewards yet. Perhaps our works will be judged after the judgment of the nations, which takes place when Christ returns to earth, and sits upon the throne of His glory. This is when Christ divides those that are still living on the earth into two groups; His sheep on His right, and the goats on His left—according to whether they had helped or ill-treated His people. But really, whether it is after this judgment, or before it, is something that we will just have to wait and see. But we do know that our King brings our rewards with Him, when He returns to earth.

Rev. 22:12. And, behold, I come quickly; and my reward is with me, to give every man according as his work shall be.

Rev. 19:9-10. And he saith unto me, Write, Blessed are they which are called unto the marriage supper of the Lamb. And he saith unto me, These are the true sayings of God. And I fell at his feet to worship him. And he said unto me, See thou do it not: I am thy fellow servant and of thy brethren that have the testimony of Jesus: worship God: for the testimony of Jesus is the spirit of prophecy.

Who will be present at the wedding supper of the Lamb? There is of course the bride (True Church), and the groom (Christ) who have been brought together visibly, never to be parted. Then there are the guests, who are all the rest of the people in heaven; all those from other dispensations; and all those who defeated the beast in the Tribulations before the Rapture.

John is told to write, which indicates that it is important. Here we are told that all those which are called to the marriage supper of the Lamb are blessed. And then John is told that these are the true sayings of God. It seems to me that there is a lot in this verse, to assure us that all guests, as well as the bride, will be blessed. All that have been raised to heaven in the first resurrection, including the Old Testament saints, which were raised at the resurrection of Jesus, are blessed because their salvation is secure. None of these people will be thrown into darkness. I think that Jesus is making sure that you do not confuse this joyful happening in heaven with the picture that is painted by the parable of the marriage feast in Matthew 22:1, where some were cast out because they had no wedding garment. This is similar; but not the same picture at all.

When John heard that these were the sayings of God, he fell at the angel's feet to worship him. And the angel made it clear that we should worship only God! No man or angel, regardless of how high a position he holds, should ever be worshipped. The angel said, "I'm a fellow servant with you, and your brethren that have the testimony of Jesus. For the testimony of Jesus is the spirit of prophecy." The testimony of Jesus is the witness which God gives to men; it is the gift of the Holy Spirit. It is through the Holy Spirit that man can accomplish all things.

CHAPTER 41

CHRIST RETURNS TO EARTH

Rev. 19:11. And I saw heaven opened, and behold a white horse; and he that sat upon him was called Faithful and True, and in righteousness he doth judge and make war.

The wedding of the Lamb has taken place. Now we see Christ returning to take the kingdoms of this world and make them His own. We have prayed for this for over 1900 years—"Thy kingdom come, thy will be done on earth as it is in heaven."

We have studied His first coming a great deal, and we have pictured Christ as a man who was patient, gentle, loving, tender, forgiving, merciful, peaceful, helpful, mild-mannered, and meek. In fact, in Him was seen all the qualities of a faithful servant and witness, which is what he was, then. He set an example for us to follow. Because this picture of the Lamb is so well imprinted on our minds, it is difficult for us to accept Christ, pictured as the Lion of Judea; and as a conqueror, a warrior king who smites and destroys the ungodly, who are his enemies. But you must remember, he is not a servant now; he is a righteous king who has come to possess what is rightfully his, and to destroy the enemy

—those who reject Him and kill His people. The days when evil triumphs over good are at an end!

Don't forget about the 144,000 Jewish witnesses and their converts, who appear to be in a hopeless position there in Jerusalem. Put yourself in their place—the armies of the world are beginning to take Jerusalem. Then all of a sudden a terrible earthquake begins to shake the great city. You begin to run towards the Mount of Olives, which is where the Lord Jesus ascended.

> Acts 1:11-12a. Which also said, Ye men of Galilee, why stand ye gazing up into heaven? this same Jesus, which is taken up from you into heaven, shall so come in like manner as ye have seen him go into heaven. Then returned they unto Jerusalem from the mount called Olivet.

Then suddenly the heavens seem to open up, and there on a white horse sat the Lord, who was called Faithful and True. Christ has been called this before; but I imagine these Jewish witnesses said it with more feeling than anyone else. The Greek word for faithful, *"pistos"* means absolutely to be trusted and relied upon. A man can stake his life on the faithfulness of Jesus; and these people had done just that. In Jesus and His words, we meet the absolute truth; there is nothing false about Him. He is real, He is genuine. And we are told that in righteousness he does judge and make war—justice shall rule in that day.

We have now reached the climax of Revelation; and also the climax of the entire Bible. One thing is very important here to remember. Jesus ascended to heaven, and he shall be seen descending from heaven; and all who come in any other way are not Christ!

> Rev. 19:12-13. His eyes were as a flame of fire, and on his head were many crowns; and he had a name written, that no man knew, but he himself. And he was

clothed with a vesture dipped in blood: and his name is called the Word of God.

Here we see a further description of our conquering King. His eyes are not a flame of fire; but they are like a flame of fire, able to detect and deal with all iniquity, through the intensity of His judgment. And on His head, which is white as snow, will be many crowns, showing that He is Lord of all the kingdoms of the earth.

He will not be called Jesus Christ, the Lamb of God. He will have a new name that no man knows. Many have tried to come up with His new name; but I am satisfied that we will not know this name until we join the Lord in heaven. He will be clothed with a long robe, the color of blood; and a golden girdle to the waist, which is worn by kings or a priest, of which he is both. His robe is said to be dipped in blood, telling us its color, and symbolized the blood of his enemies. The Prophet Isaiah foresaw this day:

Isaiah 63:1-4. Who is this that cometh from Edom, with dyed garments from Bozrah? this that is glorious in his apparel, travelling in the greatness of his strength? (And the answer comes back:) I that speak in righteousness, mighty to save. (This is Christ. Then the prophet asks:) Wherefore art thou red in thine apparel, and thy garments like him that treadeth in the winefat? (And the response is:) I *have* trodden the winepress alone; and of the people there was none with me: (the Cross) for I *will* tread them in mine anger, and trample them in my fury; and their blood shall be sprinkled upon my garments, and I will stain all my raiment. For the day of vengeance is in mine heart, and the year of my redeemed is come.

He is still called the Word of God. It is interesting to note that, to a Jew, a word was not merely a sound dropped heedlessly from unthinking lips. It was a unit of energy charged

275

with power. Most certainly this is true of Christ, because here in action is all the power of God's Word. The creating word, the word of condemnation, the word of Judgment, the word of Promise. In Him every word of God comes true.

> Rev. 19:14. And the armies which were in heaven followed him upon white horses, clothed in fine linen, white and clean.

Here we see all the saints, and the bride following Christ upon white horses, which is a symbol of a conqueror, for they conquered the devil through Christ. And they have the clothing of those who are righteous before God.

> Rev. 19:15-16. And out of his mouth goeth a sharp sword, that with it he should smite the nations: and he shall rule them with a rod of iron: and he treadeth the winepress of the fierceness and wrath of Almighty God. And he hath on his vesture and on his thigh a name written, King of Kings, and Lord of Lords.

The sharp sword which is seen coming out of the mouth of Christ is the symbol of the Word of God, which He shall use to smite the nations. The Word of God which stilled the wind, and calmed the waves in Matthew 8:26, will turn all the elements against man. Look at the destruction caused by earthquakes, volcanoes, water, hail, lightning, wind, and the diseases the follow, even now. Notice that the sword is not described as the two-edged sword, as it is in Revelation 1:16 and Revelation 2:12. The two-edged sword can either save you, or condemn you. There is no question as to which edge these nations, gathered against Jerusalem, shall feel; so we see only a sharp sword coming from the mouth of our Lord here.

He shall rule with a rod of iron. This shall be true throughout His earthly reign. He will rule with stern inflexibility. Sin will be judged instantly and righteously. He shall rule peacefully as a shepherd; but those who are rebellious will find His shepherd's staff a rod of iron; which is a symbol of unyielding severity against sin. You have a choice now, whether to follow Christ, or the Devil, or to try and sit on the fence somewhere in-between. To know that you will have no choice when Christ reigns must bother those people who hold "the right of free will" so highly and declare that they are not robots or puppets. But I tell you, children of God will be happy to do whatever their King asks, and look forward to this reign.

The picture of Christ treading the winepress of the fierceness and wrath of Almighty God merely pictures Christ rendering out the unsparing judgment on the nations which have come to fight against Jerusalem and kill his faithful witnesses. The name King of Kings, and Lord of Lords, denotes His full kingship and lordship over all the earth and men, which is His right as Creator and Redeemer. It is on His robe, and on His thigh. Various suggestions have been made as to just how; but I can't see how that could be important. But on his thigh is where one would expect his sword, the power with which he will gain victory. So this points to the fact that his absolute sovereignty is that which will be His by the "Word and Will" of God, not that which He must win through a literal sword. The armies from heaven will not take part in this great battle, as far as literal fighting is concerned.

> Rev. 19:17-19. And I saw an angel standing in the sun; and he cried with a loud voice saying to all the fowls that fly in the midst of heaven, come and gather yourselves together unto the supper of the great God. That ye may eat the flesh of kings, and the flesh of captains, and the flesh of mighty men and the flesh of horses, and them that sit on them, and the flesh of all men, both free and bond, both small and great. And I saw the

beast and the kings of the earth, and their armies, gathered together to make war against him that sat on the horse, and against his army.

The battle of Armageddon is about to take place. The outcome of this battle is never in doubt. For we see here an angel summoning all the birds of prey, calling them to the great supper of God. Preparations are being made ahead of time for the fowls of the air to eat the flesh of the vast armies who gathered against Jerusalem. This "great supper" certainly is a contrast to the marriage supper.

When the Lord returns in power, He will stand on the Mount of Olives, which will split, and a valley will be formed running east and west. And I believe that this valley that is formed will be an avenue of escape for the Jewish witnesses who are fleeing the city because of the earthquake, and also from the armies of the earth who are taking Jerusalem.

Zechariah 14:4-5a. And his feet shall stand in that day upon the mount of Olives, which is before Jersualem on the east and the mount of Olives shall cleave in the midst thereof toward the east and toward the west, and there shall be a very great valley, and half of the mountain shall remove toward the north, and half of it toward the south. And ye shall flee to the valley of the mountains.

So, with the Jews safe, our attention is drawn back to the whole picture again. John sees Antichrist, the Son of Satan, with the kings of the earth, and their armies, and all their weapons. They are regrouping, and gathering to make war against Christ, the Son of God, and His armies, who appear to be weaponless. This is not just an ordinary battle; this is the last great battle between good and evil, between Christ and Antichrist, between God and Satan. There will be another encounter with Satan and another army later; but not like this. Actually, there is very little description of the Battle of Armageddon given here in Revelation, because the important thing is not the battle, but the triumph of Christ. Through the power of the Word of God, Christ single-handed conquers the world's armies! The Old Testament prophets tell more of the details of this battle. We know that He used a terrible earthquake, and hail. Here is a plague described also:

Zechariah 14:12. And this shall be the plague wherewith the Lord will smite all the people that have fought against Jerusalem: their flesh shall consume away while they stand upon their feet, and their eyes shall consume away in their holes, and their tongue shall consume away in their mouth.

The great supper of the feathered fowl (and beasts of the field) is described in Ezekiel 39:17-21. And in the same chapter it says that Israel shall burn the weapons of this battle for seven years, and they will be burying the dead for seven months, that they may cleanse the land.

All in all, it appears as if this will be quite a bloodbath for Palestine. Remember, in Revelation 14:20, blood covered the ground for 1600 furlongs from this battle. And that is almost the exact length of Palestine from north to south. I believe this bloodbath (sacrifice) will cleanse the land and remove the curse from the lands of Palestine. It will be watered by the River of the Water of Life. It will again receive the spring and fall rains. The dried blood will also serve as a natural fertilizer. And this area will become the Garden of Eden during the Millennium, which will be divided among the twelve tribes of Israel, as described in the 48th chapter of Ezekiel.

Rev. 19:20. And the beast was taken, and with him the false prophet that wrought miracles before him, with which he deceived them that had received the mark of the beast, and them that worshipped his image. These both were cast alive into a lake of fire burning with brimstone.

Satan has had two chief representatives here on earth during the Tribulations. These two men, not a system or an empire, are seen taken alive here. The beast, or Antichrist, who actually had lost his Satanic power some time ago, but not his self-confidence, was taken. Also his right-hand man, the False Prophet, who used to work great miracles in front of him. This was how Satan had deceived the people of the earth, and caused them to receive the mark of Antichrist (Son of Satan), and caused them to worship his image. Both of these men were thrown into the lake of fire and brimstone—alive! Just as Enoch and Elijah were taken to heaven without dying, Antichrist and the False Prophet are cast into the Lake of Fire without dying. This is not a place of annihilation, but a place of eternal torment. From what I can gather, they are the first to inhabit this place. There seems to be another place called Sheol in Hebrew, and Hades in Greek, where some wait till the final judgment.

Rev. 19:21. And the remnant were slain with the sword of him that sat upon the horse, which sword proceeded out of his mouth: and all the fowls were filled with their flesh.

The remnant is not the Jewish remnant that we speak of; it is the part of Antichrist's army that has escaped the sword of Christ thus far. They are slain by Christ, with the power of the Word of God, which comes forth out of his mouth. And once more, we are given the picture of the great supper of the buzzards, vultures, and eagles.

CHAPTER 42

THE MILLENNIUM

Rev. 20:1-3. And I saw an angel come down from heaven, having the key of the bottomless pit and a great chain in his hand. And he laid hold on the dragon, that old serpent, which is the Devil, and Satan, and bound him a thousand years, and cast him into the bottomless pit and shut him up, and set a seal upon him, that he should deceive the nations no more, till the thousand years should be fulfilled: and after that he must be loosed a little season.

We have now seen our Lord return, as He promised over 1900 years ago. And we also see that He brings his saints with Him. We saw Christ destroy Satan's armies, and throw Antichrist and the False Prophet in the lake of fire alive. One other person remains as a threat to Christ's Kingdom on earth. Satan, who has been the prime instigator of earth's evils, and opposition to God, must be taken care of. Remember, this was the last great battle of a war that has been going on since Adam and Eve sinned. God is victorious; Satan has been defeated, conquered, as all his armies have been literally wiped out. As a defeated leader, he isn't to be destroyed now; just put in exile.

John sees an angel, the agent of God, come down from heaven, and by God's authority, symbolically put the Devil in exile in the bottomless pit. He has the key or the authority, and the chain, or the means to do it. John sees the angel take hold of Satan, indicating that he has control over him now. The dragon, the old serpent, Devil, and Satan are all used here, showing that they are all one of the same. Anytime one of these names is used it refers to the Devil, anywhere from Genesis to Revelation.

John sees the Devil bound for a thousand years, and cast into the bottomless pit; shut, and a seal set upon it, so that he could not deceive the nations for a thousand years. Just what method God uses to bound up spirits, is not necessary for us to know. Notice that the Bible does not say that the angel had an iron chain, as this is just symbolizing the means to do it. God is just telling us that the Devil will be restrained, and isolated from the earth for 1000 years; thus preventing him from deceiving the nations for that period of time. But after the 1000 years, he *must* be freed for a short time. This is not just something that will happen; it must happen!

Remember, Christ actually took possession of His creation at the blowing of the seventh trumpet. Also, the first resurrection took place then, where all peoples that were alive in Christ (whether they were actually dead or alive) were taken out of and from this earth; because they are His possessions, also. So the first resurrection comes just before the Millennium, or the Kingdom Age, starts. For about the first three years of this New Age, Christ is preparing the earth for his kingdom by clearing out evil. Any builder will tell you that before you can build your house, after you take possession of the land, you must clear the land, get your plans, material, and help organized first. And ever since the beginning of the seven vials, or the Wrath of God, that is what we have been seeing. But, as I have explained before, John can only write about one thing at a time, when actually several things are happening at the same time.

So at last the bulk of the evil has been disposed of. The King is now ready to take his place on his earthly throne and set up His Kingdom over the whole earth, with His saints as helpers.

> Rev. 20:4. And I saw thrones, and they sat upon them, and judgment was given unto them: and I saw the souls of them that were beheaded for the witness of Jesus, and for the word of God and which had not worshipped the beast, neither his image, neither had received his mark upon their foreheads, or in their hands; and they lived and reigned with Christ a thousand years.

First John sees the thrones, and to those who occupy them, the power of judgment is given. I think we saw these thrones represented by the twenty-four elders in Chapter 4. I believe the apostles and twelve Old Testament saints will occupy twenty-four thrones around the throne of Christ.

> Matthew 19:28. And Jesus said unto them, Verily I say unto you, that ye which have followed me, in the regeneration (New Age) when the Son of Man shall sit in the throne of his glory, ye also shall sit upon twelve thrones, judging the twelve tribes of Israel.

John also saw the souls of them that were beheaded for the witness of Jesus and for the Word of God. These would include all the martyrs, from the early church till the first resurrection, at the time of the seventh trumpet. Or you could say, all the martyrs of the Church Age.

And there were all those which had not worshipped Antichrist, or his image, or got his mark on their foreheads or hands. This certainly includes the bride, who wasn't tested in the Tribulations; this includes all those who conquered the beast by not giving in to his demands of worship, or receiving the mark, regardless of whether they were still alive or had died at the time of the Rapture or first resurrection.

283

And I think that this would include all those who had died in Christ before the Tribulations (born-again Christians), as they are in the first resurrection, and shall remain with the Lord.

I Thessalonians 4:15-17. For this we say unto you by the Word of the Lord, that we which are alive, and remain unto the coming of the Lord shall not prevent (precede) them which are asleep. For the Lord himself shall descend from heaven with a shout, with the voice of the archangel, and with the trump of God and the dead in Christ shall rise first: then we which are alive and remain shall be caught up together with them in the clouds, to meet the Lord in the air: and so shall we ever be with the Lord.

I would like to pause a minute to establish the fact that a lot of Christians have been taught to believe that there will be one general resurrection of all men at the end of the world, at which time, they believe, Christ will return. The Bible teaches that all men shall come forth out of the grave. But as you can see, in this resurrection, those which died out of Christ are not mentioned. The following verses imply two resurrections also:

Luke 14:14. And thou shalt be blessed for they cannot recompense thee: for thou shalt be recompensed at the resurrection of the just.

John 5:28-29. Marvel not at this: for the hour is coming, in the which all that are in the graves shall hear his voice, And shall come forth; they that have done good, unto the resurrection of life; and they that have done evil, unto the resurrection of damnation.

It is true that the Bible does not establish a time period between the two resurrections. But this is a common practice in the Bible. If there had been a single event when all the dead were raised at the same time, there wouldn't have been a reason to mention two separate resurrections.

I have no doubt that there will be two separate resurrections, and all that is in the first resurrection will return with the Lord and reign with Him over His earthly kingdom. And as I have mentioned before, I believe that the Old Testament saints were resurrected at the same time that Christ was, or at the end of their age; just as the first resurrection of our saints will be at the end of our age!

Some people believe that only a select few will return with Christ to enjoy this wonderful New Age. But I believe that all who are in the first resurrection will return to help their King turn this world into a good place to live in, where all will worship the true God, and eventually see all types of evil disappear. And all who return will live and reign with Christ 1000 years.

> Rev. 20:5-6. But the rest of the dead lived not again until the thousand years were finished. This is the first resurrection. Blessed and holy is he that hath part in the first resurrection: on such the second death hath no power but they shall be priests of God and of Christ, and shall reign with him a thousand years.

These who died rejecting Christ, or just not accepting Him as their personal Savior, and being born again, will not live again until after this 1000 years. They will not be in the first resurrection and get to help Christ set up and reign over His Kingdom on earth for the 1000 years.

> John 3:3. Jesus answered and said unto him, Verily, verily, I say unto thee, Except a man be born again, he cannot see the kingdom of God.

But blessed and holy are those which are in the first resurrection. Their salvation is guaranteed. When the time

285

comes for the Last Judgment, they will have nothing to fear, as it has no power over them. Instead, they shall be priests of God and Christ, and shall reign with Him a thousand years.

CHAPTER 43

DOCTRINE OF AN EARTHLY MILLENNIUM

Before continuing, it is important that we spend some time on the doctrine of an earthly Millennium. The Millennium is viewed by Christians in three major different ways. There are some who take the amillennial view, which teaches that there will be no literal kingdom of a thousand years established on this earth. They believe that the Kingdom promises are being fulfilled spiritually within the church.

There are also those who take the postmillennial view, which teaches that Christ will come to the earth after the Kingdom has been established and the church has experienced a thousand years of prosperity. And that He will judge the world at this time—Judgment Day.

There are also those who take the premillennial view, which teaches that Christ will come to establish and rule personally in His Kingdom here on earth for 1000 years; and that at the end of the 1000 years, He will judge the world.

These are the major views, but there are many variations of these. Also, I believe that there are many who really don't have any definite convictions on the Second Coming of Christ, or the Millennium, or anything connected with it.

It bothers some people that the word "millennium" doesn't appear in the Bible. For that matter, neither does the word "trinity," and other words which we use to describe a belief. And millennium is just the latin word for "a thousand years." In the first 7 verses of Chapter 20, "a thousand years" is used six times in describing the reign of Christ on earth after the Tribulations. Some believe that it doesn't mean 1000 years; but I believe that, if we weren't to take this literally, it wouldn't have been used six times in six consecutive verses.

Of course, this coincides with the theory of this being the seventh (1000-year-long day, figured from what God has given us—recorded Biblical history) day or Sabbath Rest for God's children, who believe in Him. Many say that this is actually the old Jewish belief in the golden age. Perhaps it is; but the Holy Spirit saw fit to have it brought up again in Hebrews 3 and 4. And why shouldn't it be a belief of both Christians and our Jewish brothers, since it will be great for both of us? I have shown you that at the beginning of the New Age the eyes of the Jewish remnant will be open to the Son of God, and their sins will be taken away. They will be brought safely through the Wrath of God, because of their faith and trust in Christ.

Romans 11:25-26. For I would not, brethren, that ye should be ignorant of this mystery, lest ye should be wise in your own conceits; that blindness in part is happened to Israel, until the fulness of the Gentiles be come in. And so all Israel (remnant) shall be saved; as it is written, There shall come out of Sion the Deliverer, and shall turn away ungodliness from Jacob.

This also coincides with the theory that this earth will go through seven ages or dispensations—the 7th fulfilling or completing all the plans God had for this earth and His people. I believe that Paul is referring to this in the following:

Ephesians 1:9-10. Having made known unto us the mystery of his will, according to his good pleasure which he hath purposed in himself. That in the dispensation of the fulness of times he might gather in one all things in Christ both which are in heaven, and which are on earth, even in him.

My own church doesn't believe in the Millennium because there is not enough evidence of it in the New Testament, so they say. But we have to recognize one thing; the Old Testament was given to man by God, and it deals mostly with the Age of Law. There is only one book (Genesis) that deals with all the rest of the ages that came before. One book out of thirty-nine was written to cover, according to the dispensational theory, four earlier ages. God could have given the prophets more information on the past ages; but it wasn't important for his people of the Age of Law to know any more. They were told a lot about the "Golden Age," as they call it, because they will be very much involved.

Now the New Testament was given to man by God, and it deals mostly with the Age of Grace, or Church Age. And only the 20th chapter in Revelation deals with the Kingdom Age; and only the 21st and 22nd chapter deals with the New Heaven and New Earth. This is because this section of the Bible was written for this age. And I fully expect there will be a third section added to the Bible in the Kingdom Age, which will be given to man by God, and will deal mostly with the Millennium.

We have to deal with this in the proper perspective, and look at the life of God's creation as a whole, not just our little portion of it. In the past, things were not the same as they are now; and they won't stay the same in the future.

It is true that these theories, which are accepted by some, rejected by others, cannot be proven or disproven until all things are made clear by Christ, Himself. I personally could never accept the idea that Christ was not going to return in bodily form. Acts 1:11 shows that He left in bodily form, and shall return in the same manner. And in the parables He speaks of Himself returning. And to say that Christ returned, as the Holy Spirit, is to deny the Trinity. It is an accepted fact that the apostles thought He was going to set up his Kingdom and restore Israel when he was here, particularly in the beginning. But He kept telling them, towards the end, of His coming death; and that He was going away but would be back. After His resurrection, but before Christ ascended, His apostles asked Him whether He was going to set up the Kingdom and restore Israel then. And He told them at that time that it was not for them to know when this would occur.

Acts 1:6-7. When they therefore were come together, they asked him, saying, Lord, wilt thou at this time restore again the kingdom of Israel? And he said unto them, It is not for you to know the times or seasons, which the Father hath put in his own power.

Never once did Christ discourage His own apostles from believing in this earthly kingdom, where they would reign with Him, and Israel would be restored. Now, I honestly can't believe that Jesus, Son of a righteous God, would leave letting His own apostles believe an untruth. And it is a well-known fact that the early church believed, waited, and watched for the return of their Lord Jesus Christ. They believed that He would return, and they believed in His earthly reign. It was this strong belief and hope that He would return soon that gave the church courage to stand up and even grow under the severe persecutions of Rome.

No, Christ did not let His apostles believe an untruth, because it was and still is the truth—there will be an earthly reign of our Lord; and Israel will be restored to their rightful place. Israel will be a light to the world, witnessing all over the world for our King, and God. Jerusalem will be the religious center of the world. And we, the saints from this age, will be reigning with Him in Jerusalem. The details of the Millennium are not as important to us Christians, which the New Testament applies to, as to Israel; because we will return with Christ with immortal bodies. And the Jews will still have mortal bodies. So the only thing that is really important to the born-again Christian is that there will be 1000 years in which we will reign with Christ on earth. And Jesus sent that message to us through John, in the 20th chapter of Revelation.

In the Millennium, God will be giving man another chance to become the kind of people that He wants for His subjects. This time it will be under the best possible conditions. No Devil to tempt them; hunger or sickness can't be used as an excuse for sin. There will be one church with one set of laws handed down directly from a visible King. There will be no excuse for any kind of wickedness, and when it occurs, it will be dealt with severely and swiftly. According to those who believe in the dispensational theory, this will be the 7th period of time that God has changed His method of dealing with man and their sins. Each period ends in judgment on the wicked. And the 7th or the Millennium will be no different.

CHAPTER 44

THE END OF THE KINGDOM AGE

Rev. 20:7-10. And when the thousand years are expired, Satan shall be loosed out of his prison, And shall go out to deceive the nations which are in the four quarters of the earth Gog and Magog, to gather them together to battle: the number of whom is as the sand of the sea. And they went up on the breadth of the earth, and compassed the camp of the saints about, and the beloved city: and fire came down from God out of heaven, and devoured them. And the devil that deceived them was cast into the lake of fire and brimstone, where the beast, and the false prophet are, and shall be tormented day and night forever and ever.

After being in prison or in exile for 1000 years, Satan is turned loose to test man's loyalty to God. Here they have lived in ideal conditions; you wouldn't think that there would be anyone who wouldn't truly love and worship our King. But this isn't the case! Because Satan successfully deceives the nations again. You see, even under these ideal conditions, some people just pretend loyalty to God. And as soon as Satan is loosed, he finds a host of these people ready to do his bidding and join him in the last rebellion against

God. This rebellion will be world-wide. The rebels will probably be individuals among the nations who, to a large extent, only pretend loyalty to Christ's iron rule. The number of these rebels will be like the sand of the sea: not just a few, but countless millions. These hostile armies led by Satan come up against God, the camp of His people, and the Holy beloved city of Jerusalem.

About the only thing that we are told concerning this revolt is the results. There will be a complete, supernatural destruction of these hostile armies, as they will be consumed by fire from heaven. And Satan, who deceived them, will be cast into the lake of fire and brimstone, where Antichrist and the False Prophet are. And Satan shall be tormented day and night forever and ever. Once again, it is not necessary for Christians to know the details of this final revolt. The only thing that is important to the saints of this age is God's victory; and that is important to all true believers, of all ages! Because as long as He wins, so do we!

THE FINAL JUDGMENT

Rev. 20:11-15. And I saw a great white throne, and him that sat on it, from whose face the earth and the heaven fled away and there was found no place for them. And I saw the dead, small and great, stand before God; and the books were opened: and another book was opened, which is the book of life: and the dead were judged out of those things which were written in the books, according to their works. And the sea gave up the dead which were in it; and death and hell delivered up the dead which were in them: and they judged every man according to their works. And death and hell were cast into the lake of fire. This is the second death. And whosoever was not found written in the book of life was cast into the lake of fire.

The scene of judgment which John sees closes the Millennium and marks the beginning of eternity. This judgment concerns all who were not in the first resurrection. The throne is great because it is God's throne, and it is white to show its divine purity and righteousness, which characterize God's decisions. God shall judge the wicked through the Son of God. Jesus Christ will occupy that throne, for to Him, all judgment is given.

John 5:22. For the father judgeth no man, but hath committed all judgment unto the son.

II Timothy 4:1. I charge thee therefore before God, and the Lord Jesus Christ, who shall judge the quick and the dead at his appearing and his kingdom. (Two different times.)

When John sees the great white throne, he also sees the earth and heaven shrink out of the picture. So I don't believe that the "Great White Throne Judgment" will take place on earth. Probably, during the renovation of the earth by fire, it could take place in the old heaven. This isn't really important to those who won't be there; and to those who are, it will be a frightening experience wherever it takes place. But we know that the renovation of this earth is reserved until the time of that judgment of wicked men.

2 Peter 3:7. But the heavens and the earth, which are now, by the same word are kept in store, reserved unto fire against the day of judgment and perdition of ungodly men.

John sees the dead, both small and great, standing before Christ, who sits on the great white throne. This tells us two things. First, that none will be great enough to escape the judgment of God, and that none are too insignificant to be overlooked. Understand that these dead are those who were not raised at the first resurrection, as well as those who

295

have rebelled against Christ, at Armageddon, or who sinned and died during the Millennium, or who took part in the last revolt with Satan. We have to conclude that the second, or the resurrection of the wicked, takes place right before the white throne judgment; and at the end of the Millennium. When one dies not believing in Christ (in this age), their body goes into death (the grave) but their spirit goes to hell, where they suffer torment until the resurrection of damnation. At this time their spirit and soul are united with a new body. Body, soul, and spirit reunited, the man will stand trembling before the judgment throne; and this is what John sees.

We see that two kinds of books are opened. One is identified as the Book of Life. This is the book where all the names of God's children were written, at the beginning of the world; but the Bible makes it clear that they can be blotted out. Remember also that the names of the earth-dwellers were never written in the Book of Life.

Rev. 17:8. The beast that thou sawest was, and is not; and ascend out of the bottomless pit, and go into perdition; and they that dwell on the earth shall wonder (marvel), whose names were not written in the book of life from the foundation of the world, when they behold the beast that was, and is not, and yet is.

So the Book of Life is now a register of all God's children whose names have not been blotted out, regardless of whether they are physically dead or alive at this time. The other books mentioned are the books of recorded works and deeds. All of the sins, as well as the good things that a man does, are recorded by God.

Some believe that there will not be a single person standing before the great white throne that is not thrown into the lake of fire; and that the purpose of this judgment is to determine the degree of punishment that one will receive in the lake of fire, which will be determined by the records that God keeps.

We have talked about who would be in the first resurrection, or the resurrection of the living—their salvation was guaranteed; but their works would be judged to determine their rewards. They had accepted Christ as Lord and Master, and had genuine faith in Him; and in turn He bought or redeemed their record of sins, and destroyed it. Therefore no sins appears against them on the books. And of course their names were not blotted out of the Book of Life.

Now, in the second resurrection, or the resurrection of the damned, generally speaking, their damnation is guaranteed. It is only the degree of punishment that is in question. Most of these people will be "earth dwellers," who look upon the Cross and salvation through Christ as foolishness in this age; and their records will probably show them to be evil people. And their names were never written in the Book of Life.

But there will be a lot of lost sheep of the Church Age there also. Their names were in the book of life; they had the chance to be in the resurrection of life; and maybe they weren't really bad people, either. But they refused to take God seriously; they put off hearing and believing the Word, or perhaps they attended church, and said all the right words, but didn't really believe them in their heart. They never had genuine faith in Christ, and refused to be His servant, or to let Him be Lord and Master of their life. Therefore they didn't receive the Holy Spirit, which is the free gift and guarantee of salvation that God gives when Christ redeems your record of sins and claims you as His possession. It is through the Holy Spirit that you receive the promises of the Bible while you are still living on earth. So they suffered a great loss while they still lived; but now they must stand before the great white throne, wondering if their works will keep them out of the lake of fire, and no doubt wishing that they had turned to Christ with genuine faith when they had the chance, back in the Church Age. They have stayed in the grave an extra 1000 years because they failed to do so. They failed the test of faith; will they fail the test of works too, and dwell forever in the Lake of Fire? What a terrible ordeal to have to go through!

Some believe that these people haven't got a chance, and that a good record of deeds will only get them a better place in hell. This would be true if they were judged by the rules that Christ gave the Church Age: the ones that we are familiar with. But this judgment takes place at the end of the Kingdom Age or Millennium; and Christ as King has given that age different rules to live by, which we are not familiar with now. So we don't know just how their works will be judged! I don't believe we can honestly say what chance a person has of getting to Paradise on the new earth if his name is in the Book of Life; but they weren't in the first resurrection because of lack of faith. I can say this with all honesty—it is a chance I don't want to take.

Most of the time in this book, we have been referring to the people living at the time of the Great Tribulations. But now we are referring to those persons who die without being reborn of the Spirit at any time during this age before the Great Tribulations. So, if you have taken this book lightly because you do not expect to be living in the time of the Great Tribulations, think about the Great White Throne Judgment.

We see in the resurrection of damnation that the sea gives up its dead; and that death (the grave) and hell, where all the unfaithful and wicked spirits and souls are, deliver up their dead. Now death and hell are cast in the lake of fire because there will be no further need of them. Those places were like prisons, used to hold the unfaithful and wicked who died. But now there shall be no more unfaithful and wicked, and no more death. All those who *rejected* God are in the lake of fire. The lake of fire is the second death, and is eternal. It is said of this age "that it is better to be born twice, and die once, than to be born once, and die twice!"

The Old Testament seems to imply that patriarchal years will be restored in the Millennium, and men shall live as long as, or longer than, they did before the Flood. That is to say that a person dying at 100 years would be considered a child. Only sinners will die young. It sounds as if one of the old laws will be restored: "Children, obey your Father (God) so that you will have a long life on this earth."

Isaiah 65:20. There shall be no more thence an infant of days, nor an old man that hath not filled his days: for the child shall die an 100 years old, but the sinner being 100 years old shall be accursed.

It is very difficult to tell whether some verses in the Old Testament apply to the Millennium or the New Earth; but since there will be no sin or death in our new world, this has to apply to the Millennium.

The Son of God has reigned over His earthly kingdom until all evil has been destroyed, which is the purpose of the Millennium.

I Corinthians 15:22-25. For as in Adam all die, even so in Christ shall all be made alive. But every man in his own order: Christ the first fruits; afterwards they that are Christ's at His coming. Then cometh the end, when he shall have delivered up the kingdom to God, even the Father; when he shall have put down all rule and all authority and power. For he must reign, till he hath put all enemies under his feet. The last enemy that shall be destroyed is death.

Death has to be last, because it can't be destroyed until all of the enemies of God have been killed. And this is accomplished when the final revolt against Jerusalem takes place.

CHAPTER 45

THE NEW HEAVEN AND THE NEW EARTH

Rev. 21:1. I saw a new heaven and a new earth: for the first heaven and the first earth were passed away and there was no more sea.

This earth that we live on was once cleansed with the waters of the Great Flood. At that time, God provided the righteous family of Noah and the animals a place of safety while this was being done. And, after the cleansing was complete, God set his people back on the earth and told them to multiply and replenish the earth.

Now, several thousand years later, the earth and the people are getting just like they were in the days of Noah, except worse. We have now polluted the atmosphere, or the air that surrounds the earth. So this time God has to be more complete, so He uses fire. Peter describes this in these two verses:

II Peter 3:7. But the heavens and the earth which are now by the same word are kept in store, reserved unto fire against the day of judgment and peridition of ungodly men.

II Peter 3:10. But the day of the Lord will come as a thief in the night; in which the heavens shall pass away with a great noise, and the elements shall melt with fervent heat, the earth also and the works that are therein shall be burned up.

What happens to the people living on the earth at that time? God does not tell us that, because to the reborn Christians of the Church Age it really doesn't matter. We will have our indestructible, glorified bodies, which we were given at the first resurrection; and we shall follow the Lord wherever He goes. And the unbelievers of the Church Age will be thrown into the lake of fire. So, to the people of this particular age, this is all the information that they need. But to the people living in the Millennium (God will probably give them more information when the time actually comes) this is something to think about. I believe that the righteous mortals of the Kingdom Age will be transported off the earth while it is being cleansed with fire, then set back down on the new earth, surrounded by the new, clean atmosphere (heaven) just as Noah was. A modern-day Ark could be a huge spaceship. A couple of hundred years ago, that idea would have been laughed at; but now it is certainly conceivable.

One thing that we are told here about the new earth is that there will be no more sea. Just exactly what this means is not clear. Many believe that there will be no oceans or large bodies of water on the earth, then. But I think that we will have to wait and see about that.

Rev. 21:2-4. And I John saw the Holy City, new Jerusalem, coming down from God out of heaven, prepared as a bride adorned for her husband. And I heard a great voice out of heaven saying, Behold, the tabernacle of God is with men, and he will dwell with them, and they shall be his people, and God himself shall be with them, and be their God. And God shall wipe away all tears from their eyes; and there shall be no more death, neither sorrow, nor crying, neither shall there be any more pain for the former things are passed away.

John sees the Holy City, New Jerusalem, coming down from God, out of heaven. She is as beautiful as a bride dressed for her husband. Old Jerusalem has always been built by man, and is earthly. But New Jerusalem is built by God and is heavenly. This city is the place Jesus said He was going back to heaven to prepare for His Bride, the "True Church."

> John 14:1-3. Let not your heart be troubled: ye believe in God, believe also in me. In my Father's house are many mansions: if it were not so, I would have told you. I go to prepare a place for you. And if I go and prepare a place for you, I will come again, and receive you unto myself; that where I am, there ye may be also.

The church always follows Christ. We were here to help during the Kingdom Age, and we left with Him while a new earth was being created. Now John sees the glorified Church and her home, a literal city coming down from heaven. The city and the bride are so closely identified that they are here spoken of as one. It is a holy city because its occupants are righteous before God.

John is told by a loud voice out of heaven that the home of God is among men again (God dwelt with Israel in Solomon's temple in the Old Testament). And He will dwell with them and they shall be His people. The voice said that God Himself shall be with them, which seems to indicate that he is not referring to the Son of God, but the Father. The visible God, Christ, ruled until God put all things under his feet —that is, Christ was supreme ruler over everything. Now Christ places himself under God, and God will rule completely over all.

I Corinthians 15:28. And when all things shall be subdued unto him, then shall the Son also himself be subject unto him (God) that put all things under him, that God may be all in all.

Now God shall wipe all the tears from the eyes of his people. There will not be any more death, sorrow, crying, or pain. That all passed away with the old earth. This was already true for the resurrected saints who reigned with Him during the Millennium; but not for His people who still had corruptible bodies.

Rev. 21:5-8. And he that sat upon the throne said, Behold, I make all things new. And he said unto me, Write, for these words are true and faithful. And he said unto me, It is done. I am Alpha and Omega, the beginning and the end. I will give unto him that is a thirst of the fountain of the water of life freely. He that overcometh shall inherit all things: and I will be his God and he shall be my son. But the fearful, and unbelieving, and the abominable, and murderers, and whoremongers, and sorcerers, and idolaters, and all liars, shall have their part in the lake which burneth with fire and brimstone which is the second death.

He that sat on the throne said—Look, I make all things new. Then He commanded John to write because all these things are true and trustworthy. Because God is who He is, the believer can rely on His promises. The voice from the throne said to John, "It is done"—in other words, the old earth has come to its end; He has made all things new. It has been accomplished, as of now! He also said that He was the Alpha and Omega, the beginning and the end. This means that God, through Christ, created all things and ends all things—in His own time!

Now God extends an open invitation to all that thirst or who are eager. He says that He will give, as a gift, to those that thirst, the fountain which brings forth the water of life. Jesus said the same thing in the Sermon on the Mount.

Matthew 5:6. Blessed are they which do hunger and thirst after righteousness: for they shall be filled.

Here we see God the Father, and God the Son, both promising the Holy Spirit to all that eagerly seek righteousness through Christ. And God says that those who do this shall inherit all things; that He shall be their God, and they shall be His sons.

But then, on the other hand, God also says that cowards who turn from following Him, and those who are unfaithful to Him—the corrupt, the murderers, the immoral, those conversing with demons, idol-worshippers, and all liars—shall be doomed, because they will be cast into the lake of fire, which is the second death. Notice that Verses 3-8 here are not the words of John, or the Holy Spirit, or Jesus, or an angel: but they are from God Himself!

CHAPTER 46

THE NEW CITY, JERUSALEM

Rev. 21:9. And there came unto me one of the seven angels which had the seven vials full of the seven last plagues, and talked with me, saying, Come hither, I will shew thee the bride, the Lamb's wife.

The last time John met one of these particular angels, he was the bringer of the vision of the destruction of Babylon, the great harlot. Now he shows John the New Jerusalem, the Lamb's wife. Possibly the same angel brings the message of doom and the message of bliss. It seems as though we are being shown something here. Some believe it is the fact that a servant of God does not choose his task; sometimes it may be a pleasant job, other times an unpleasant one. Regardless, the true servant is obedient and willing to do whatever God sends him to do.

But I find, in comparing the two messages, that they complete a picture which is of vital importance to us all. The destruction of Babylon, which was the professing church, and a literal city housing the headquarters of Satan, is part of the picture. The other part is the glorification of Jerusalem, which is the True Church, and a literal city housing the headquarters of God. The real message that this angel carries is "Complete victory for God!"

Rev. 21:10-11. And he carried me away in spirit to a great and high mountain, and shewed me that great city, the holy Jerusalem, descending out of heaven from God, Having the glory of God and her light was like unto a stone most precious, even like a jasper stone, clear as crystal.

John is carried away in spirit to a very high mountain, to view the beauty of this huge city that is coming down out of heaven. Remember, this is a literal city made by God. It has the radiance of the glory of God. I imagine it looks like a diamond with the sun shining on it.

Rev. 21:12-16. And had a wall great and high, and had twelve gates, and at the gates twelve angels, and names written thereon, which are the names of the twelve tribes of the children of Israel. On the east three gates, on the north three gates; on the south three gates, and on the west three gates. And the wall of the city had twelve foundations, and in them the names of the twelve apostles of the Lamb. And he that talked with me had a golden reed to measure the city, and the gates thereof, and the wall thereof. And the city lieth foursquare, and the length is as large as the breadth: and he measured the city with the reed, twelve thousand furlongs. The length and the breadth and the height of it are equal.

Before going any further with the description of this great city, let's try and visualize what we have so far. The city will be 12,000 furlongs or 1500 miles long, wide, and high. Can you imagine a square city stretching from Boston to Miami southward, to Denver westward, and being 1500 miles high? Jesus said that his Father's house had many mansions! Many believe that this city has to be a cube in shape; but it could be a pyramid, and still have equal dimensions. Even when tall buildings are built, they get smaller as they go up; so I believe it will take the shape of a pyramid, but no one

308

can be sure till we see it. It has a wall around it with twelve gates, where twelve angels stand. There are three gates on each side of the city, and on these twelve gates are the names of the twelve tribes of Israel. And the wall has twelve foundations, and on them are written the names of the twelve apostles.

Rev. 21:17-18. And he measured the wall thereof, an hundred and forty and four cubits, according to the measure of a man, that is, of the angel. And the building of the wall of it was of jasper: and the city was pure gold, like unto clear glass.

The wall around the city is 216 feet high, which is actually not very high. The wall of Babylon was 300 feet high; but this wall is not for defense. The wall is made of jasper, and the city itself is made of pure, transparent gold—clear as glass!

Rev. 21:19. And the foundations of the wall of the city were garnished with all manner of precious stones. The first foundation was jasper; the second, sapphire; the third, an achalcedony; the fourth, an emerald; the fifth, sardonyx; the sixth, sardius; the seventh, chrysolyte; the eighth, beryl; the ninth, a topaz, the tenth, a chrysoprasus; the eleventh, a jacinth; the twelfth, an amethyst. And the twelves gates are twelve pearls: every several gate was of one pearl: and the street of the city was pure gold, as it were transparent glass.

The wall is built on twelve layers of foundation stones, which are inlaid with precious stones. Each layer is inlaid with a different precious stone. And looking at them, they give a rainbow effect of indescribable beauty. Each gate consists of one vast pearl; and the streets are paved with pure gold. This is a special kind of gold; it is transparent, clear as glass.

Do I really believe a city like that will come down from

heaven on the New Earth? I certainly do! If man can make great cities with towering skyscrapers, cannot God build greater ones? He who created the jewels, and the precious stones, the gold and silver, even the universe by the word of His mouth—is He not able to do with it what He wants?

I'm sure God had some meaning in mind when He designed His city and decided on its materials. But I do not know what He had in mind, and I'm not going to venture any guesses as some have done.

> Rev. 21:22-27. And I saw no temple therein for the Lord God Almighty and the Lamb are the temple of it. And the city had no need of the sun, neither of the moon, to shine in it; for the glory of God did lighten it, and the Lamb is the light thereof. And the nations of them which are saved shall walk in the light of it and the kings of the earth do bring their glory and honour into it. And the gates of it shall not be shut at all by day; for there shall be no night there. And they shall bring the glory and honour of the nations into it. And there shall in no wise enter it anything that defileth, neither whatsoever worketh abomination, or maketh a lie: but they which are written in the Lamb's book of life.

There are some who believe this to be a description of Holy Jerusalem during the Millennium, which they say is supended over the earth. But we find in the 40th, 41st, 42nd, 43rd chapters of Ezekiel what is believed to be a detailed description of the Millennium temple; and the river of life comes from under the temple, and goes to the sea. Also, we see that in the following:

> Zechariah 14:8. And it shall be in that day, that living waters shall go out from Jerusalem: one half of them toward the former sea (Dead Sea), and half of them toward the hinder sea (Mediterranean Sea): in summer and in winter shall it be.

This certainly is not talking about the past, because there is not, nor never has been, a river connecting the Dead Sea and the Mediterranean Sea. So this has to be the future; but before the New Earth! Because in New Jerusalem on the New Earth, we see here that there is no temple, and we were told back in Verse One of Chapter 21 in Revelation there was no more sea. And we are about to see that the water of life comes from under the throne of God. There is a great deal of similarity between the Millennium and Eternity on the New Earth. I think this is understandable, because the Millennium, even as great as it is, is only a shadow of the real thing. But remember, a shadow has to bear a good deal of resemblance to the real thing.

As we said, there is no temple visible in the city of God, for there is no need for a place of worship. Indirect approach through a temple is entirely unnecessary, because it appears as though both God and the Christ dwell in the midst of the redeemed. There is also no need for the light from the sun or the moon, for the radiant glory of God will illuminate the city. I don't believe this means that there will no longer be a sun or moon, as some do. It is true they will not be needed around the city; but the city cannot light the whole earth, not as long as the earth is round. We are told that there will be no night around the city; but I believe there will be in other parts of the earth.

The saved nations will walk in her light and the kings of the earth will bring their glory to her, and her authority will be universally acknowledged. Some think this is a Millennium scene because of the nations and kings being mentioned. But they are forgetting that it is only the "Bride" or the "True Church" of the Age of Grace, which lives in the holy city with God and the Lamb. There are still all the saved peoples from all the different ages: the Old Testament saints, the Tribulation saints, and those righteous people who were alive at the end of the Millennium; which I believe were transported to the New Earth. So all of us will have our duties as servants to our God, whether it is inside the city or out among the saved nations. Some believe that King David of old will reign over Israel. I believe that these are things that only time will tell.

We are told that the gates of the city shall never be shut, as there will be no night. And the glory and honor of the nations will be brought into the city. It seems as though that all will be free to enter the city at will. For everyone that is present on the New Earth has his name in the Lamb's Book of Life. It definitely stated that all those whose names were not found in the Book of Life were cast in the lake of fire, at the white throne judgment. So, if this is true, I believe that this does away with the idea that New Jersualem will be suspended over the earth in what might be called the "Perfect Age." It is also made very clear here that no evil of any kind will ever enter into the Holy City. So I believe that we can conclude that peoples of this age, which I believe to be endless, will remain true to God and righteous in His eyes.

THE NEW PARADISE

Rev. 22:1-5. And he shewed me a pure river of water of life, clear as crystal proceeding out of the throne of God and of the Lamb. In the midst of the street of it, and on either side of the river, was there the tree of life, which bare twelve manner of fruits and yielded her fruit every month: and the leaves of the tree were for healing of the nations. And there shall be no more curse: but the throne of God and the Lamb shall be in it, and his servants shall serve him; And they shall see his face; and his name shall be in their foreheads. And there shall be no night there: and they need no candle, neither light of the sun; for the Lord God giveth them light: and they shall reign forever and ever.

So far we have been examining the exterior of the Holy City; but now the scene changes to the interior. Somewhere in the midst of the city will be the throne of God, and the

Lamb. If the city is in the shape of a pyramid, I would think the proper place for the throne would be on the summit. But, regardless, we are told that there is a river of pure, crystal-clear water coming out from the throne of God. This wonderful river is called the River of the "Water of Life" because of its life-giving properties. It does not only sustain physical life but, more important, spiritual life. This will be a continuous flow of the Holy Spirit into all people and things which drink of this water. And since it brings out the fact that there will be no more seas, I feel this implies that the River of the Water of Life will be the only source of water. Thus all will drink from it, and all will be filled with the Holy Spirit: not only people, but animals, and all the land, and the trees and flowers—every living thing; and this will remove the curse from all the earth forever. And we will see the "Perfection of God" on the New Earth.

As great as the Millennium will be, it will not be perfection, because evil will come forth from it. We have seen where the River of Life comes from the temple and connects the Dead Sea and the Mediterranean Sea. In Ezekiel 47:8-12, we see that the River of Life heals the Dead Sea, making it fresh and pure. In fact, everything touching the water of this river shall live. Wherever this water flows, everything will live! And it flows into the Mediterranean Sea, which connects with the rest of the large bodies of water eventually. But there are some places that will not be healed.

Ezekiel 47:11. But the miry places thereof and the marshes thereof shall not be healed: they shall be given to salt.

So, even though the Millennium will seem like perfection, compared to what this world is fast becoming, it won't be. Not when you compare it with the New Heavens and Earth that God will prepare for his faithful servants.

The River of the Water of Life seems to flow down the middle of the street, and on either side of the river grows the tree of life. I believe this refers to a kind of a tree which grows on both sides along the riverbank. Some seem to think that this tree is so huge that it spans the river. One tree of this kind would have been sufficient for Adam and Eve in the Garden of Eden; but it wouldn't be sufficient for the whole earth. It will produce twelve different kinds of fruit, a different kind every month.

This tree grows right along the River of the Water of Life and drinks of this water, which is a continuous flow of the Holy Spirit. Thus the tree lives forever, and those who eat of its fruit are filled with life—the Holy Spirit.

Many try to symbolize this tree; but it is a literal tree, with literal fruit. Out of all the trees in the Garden of Eden, two trees were mentioned—the tree of knowledge of good and evil, and the tree of life. After Adam sinned by eating of the first, God drove him out lest he eat also of the tree of life, and live forever in his sinful lost estate. It was literal in the Garden of Eden, and it is here.

The resurrected saints already have immortal bodies; but those that have come from the Millennium have not, as far as we can tell. They have eaten the fruits of the tree of life and used its leaves as medicine on the old earth; but the Millennium is not completely perfect in anything. So it kept them from dying; but it didn't make them immortal. But possibly the tree of life on the New Earth, with its fruit and leaves, will complete the job, and make them immortal —thus the nations will be healed.

A curse was put on man, animals, and the land, when Adam sinned. Since then, the trouble, pain, suffering, distress, and death in the world have been caused by the curse. Remember, the land produced thorns and thistles, making it hard to cultivate. Now the cause of the curse (sin) has been completely removed. And in God's eternal presence, there will be no more curse. The redeemed will readily submit to and serve the Triune God. And they shall see His face, and His name shall be on their foreheads.

We are told again that there will be no night or darkness

here, probably because that was always connected with sin and Satan; which have been completely destroyed. We will need no candles or sun because the Lord God Himself supplies all our needs, resulting in complete happiness and fellowship with God; and we shall reign with Him forever and ever.

CHAPTER 47

THE CONCLUSION

The revelation of the future is now over. The last sixteen verses are closing testimonies. And it is often very difficult to be sure who is the actual speaker.

Rev. 22:6. And he said unto me, These sayings are faithful and true: and the Lord God of the holy prophets sent his angel to shew unto his servants the things which must shortly be done.

The first speaker is one of the angels; and once again he stresses the truth and the reliability of all that John has seen and heard. He adds that the same God who inspired the ancient seers has sent His angel to reveal these prophecies to His servant of the New Testament, because the prophecies are soon to be fulfilled. And we must accept this book of prophecy, the only one in the New Testament, as equally divine and treat it with equal seriousness as those in the Old Testament.

Rev. 22:7. Behold, I come quickly: blessed is he that keepeth the sayings of the prophecy of this book.

The second speaker is Christ, Himself, repeating that He shall come quickly; which means that when things start to happen He will come without warning. Then He pronounces His blessing on those who read and obey the words of John's book. Like I mentioned before, this is the only book in the Bible that starts and ends with such a blessing. And to think that, if it weren't for God Himself leading me to it, I would have missed those blessings! Because I have attended church fairly regularly for nineteen years, and until about one year ago, I didn't have the slightest idea what was in the Book of Revelation. And I'm deeply concerned about all the other people who are missing out on this blessing.

> Rev. 22:8-11. And I John saw these things, and heard them. And when I had heard and seen, I fell down to worship before the feet of the angel which shewed me these things. Then saith he unto me, See thou do it not: for I am thy fellow servant, and of thy brethren the prophets, and of them which keep the sayings of this book: worship God. And he saith unto me, Seal not the sayings of the prophecy of this book for the time is at hand. He that is unjust, let him be unjust still: and he which is filthy, let him be filthy still: and he that is righteous, let him be righteous still; and he that is holy, let him be holy still.

It is not surprising that our beloved apostle, overwhelmed by the abundance of the revelation given him, fell down to worship before the feet of the angel which showed him these things. John had made this error before, and again the angel forbids it. He tells John that he is only a fellow-servant of his, and of the prophets, and of those which keep the saying of this book. He says to worship God and Him only! Then he tells John not to seal up the sayings of the prophecy of this book, because the time is at hand. This is in contrast to the command to seal Daniel's prophecy.

Daniel 12:9. And he said, Go thy way, Daniel: for the words are closed up and sealed till the time of the end.

It concerns me to no end to see some of the churches of today listening to what the angel told Daniel, but refusing to pay any attention to what the angel told John concerning the coming days. (We were told that it was the same God who sent the angel to both men.) As a result, millions of people may have to face the latter days unprepared and frightened. The storm warnings are up, and they are for real; but some people are not being given the warning —because some churches claim that if you are prepared for today, you'll be prepared for tomorrow. After eighteen years of attending church, God showed me that I wasn't prepared. Are you?

The last part of this passage seems to say that men must remain as they are. Many believe that this describes the permanency of human destiny—that there is no second chance after death. I agree that neither your spiritual condition nor your record of deeds can be changed after death. They stand as is; but I don't really believe that this passage is referring to that. John has just been told not to seal up the prophecy of this book. And in relating the two I think we are told that the unveiling of this book will not change the true nature of a person. If a person is evil at heart, an interpretation of the Book of Revelation is not going to change him. On the other hand, it could help bring out the true nature of a good person who doesn't fully understand how important it is to play ball with God seven days a week. And, in order to do this, you have to know the rules, which God gave us through Christ, and the Holy Spirit—the Bible, particularly the New Testament, which was written for the Church Age. Man has only so long to establish his spiritual condition, which determines his destiny into eternity. And it may be later than you think! God appeals to you; but He will not force anyone.

Rev. 22:12-16. And, behold, I come quickly; and my reward is with me, to give every man according as his work shall be. I am Alpha and Omega, the beginning and the end, the first and the last. Blessed are they that do his commandments, that they may have right to the tree of life, and may enter in through the gates into the city. For without are dogs, and sorcerers, and whoremongers, and murderers, and idolaters, and whosoever loveth and maketh a lie. I Jesus have sent mine angel to testify unto you these things in the churches. I am the root and the offspring of David, and the bright and morning star.

Christ announces once again the certainty and the swiftness of which He will come the second time. There will be no time to prepare then. I'm reminded of the ten virgins who waited his return. It took a little longer than they thought. And five were prepared, and five were not. When they heard that He was here, the first five went out to meet Him; but the last five had to go get oil for their lamps, and when they returned, the door was locked! It is of the utmost importance that we get prepared to meet Christ, and make sure that we stay that way at all times. It is true that His return has taken longer than expected; and no one knows how much time there is left. But, as you can tell, many things point to the fact that it will be soon. Jesus also says that when He returns He will bring His rewards to the righteous for their works. All the saved will have to stand before the judgment seat of Christ and have their works tested by fire, in order to receive those rewards. Then Christ identifies Himself again by saying that He is the first and the last. He, the Rewarder, is the eternal Christ.

The 14th verse is believed to be a mistranslation —"Blessed are they that do his commandments"— because it is not doing that gives one title to the home of the saints. So it should read, "Blessed are those who have washed their robes," that they may have right to the tree of life, and may enter in through the gates into the city.

It is true that the salvation of the people of the Church Age depends on genuine faith in Jesus Christ; and not on doing works, or obeying the commandments. But I do not believe that this is a mistranslation just because it doesn't seem to have the proper meaning.

Christ begins to speak in the 12th verse, reminding us of His Second Coming, which will come at the close of the Church Age. He continues, and in the 14th verse, He is speaking of the people living in the Millennium or Kingdom Age. And we have to remember that the rules have been changed. The Age of Grace is over, and salvation is not based on "faith alone," as it was. They must obey the commandments and worship our King. Those with genuine love for our King will be permitted to enter Jerusalem and eat of the tree of life. This explains how the righteous people of the Millennium will be able to live a thousand years or more, and the wicked die young. The wicked will not be allowed to come into the city. Jesus goes on to say that outside the city are dogs (referring to immoral, unclean people), sorcerers, whoremongers, murderers, idolators, and those who love to lie, and do so. This is almost the same list that Jesus gave us in Revelation 21:8. He was speaking of those who were to experience the second death at the end of the Millennium, at the great white throne judgment.

It was the 15th verse which made me realize that Jesus was talking about Jerusalem of the Millennium now, not the New Jerusalem of the New Earth. There shall not be any sin or wicked people outside New Jerusalem, or on any part of the New Earth; as they shall all be in the lake of fire. The purpose of the Millennium is to harvest this earth, to completely separate the wheat from the tares; and burn the tares. And then this will certainly be true:

Matthew 13:43. Then shall the righteous shine forth as the sun in the kingdom of their Father.

But the Day of Judgment, the harvest, or the Millennium will last 1000 years! God will take His time, being careful not to destroy any good grain (His people); which are destined to live on the New Earth—the Father's Kingdom.

Then Jesus guarantees and certifies the truth of all that John has seen and heard. In the beginning of the Book of Revelation, it promises a revelation by Jesus Christ, sent by angels to John. Now, at the end of the book, Jesus guarantees it as being true. And Jesus indicates that His instructions are still the same as they were; John was to tell it to the "whole church." Jesus goes on to give further proof of who He is. In relation to Israel, He is the root and the offspring of David. He is the root of David because David sprang from Him—He was David's Creator and Lord. He is the offspring of David because, as man, He was born from a daughter of David. In relation to the church, He is the bright morning star. This presents Christ in His second advent, when He comes for His Bride before the dawn of the Millennium Day.

> Rev. 22:17. And the Spirit and the bride say, Come. And let him that heareth say, Come. And let him that is athirst come. And whosoever will, let him take the water of life freely.

Immediately the Spirit and the bride respond, saying "Come." This is an invitation to Christ to return to shine forth and gather His own to Himself. And all those that hear or understand this revelation are urged to join in this cry, "Come." The Spirit and the Bride appeal to Christ to return; and they urge others to do so. Then they encourage those which eagerly seek righteousness to come to Christ; and promise that, if they do, they will be given the water of life or the Holy Spirit. This shows that born-again Christians must not only be expecting and inviting Christ to return, but must also be encouraging others, who are eager, not to just accept Christ, but to come to Christ. There is a big difference between the two. And I think that it was this difference that I wasn't aware of that kept me from receiving the Holy Spirit. You can accept something and go on about your business until you are reminded of it, maybe seven days later in church. But you can't surrender yourself as a servant to a master and go on about your business as usual—the master won't let you! He gives you duties; but He also gives you privileges, and a rest from your worries, which is just great. Your life has to change!

Rev. 22:18-19. For I testify unto every man that heareth the words of the prophecy of this book, If any man shall add unto these things, God shall add unto him the plagues that are written in this book: and if any man shall take away from the words of the book of this prophecy, God shall take away his part out of the book of life, and out of the holy city, and from the things which are written in this book.

Christ Himself delivers a solemn warning to everyone who hears the words of the prophecy of this book. He warns against taking away or adding to the Book of Revelation. I don't believe that this is referring to each and every individual word; but a warning against tampering, interfering with, or distorting the teaching which the book contains. In Galatians 1:9, Paul said—If any man preach any other gospel to you than that which you have received, let him be accursed. It is the truth, and not the wording of the truth, which must not be changed. But I must warn you that the truth is sometimes hidden in words which don't appear to make sense; and in trying to make the Bible easier to understand, the truth can be altered.

Rev. 22:20-21. He which testifieth these things saith, Surely I come quickly. Amen. Even so, Come, Lord Jesus. The grace of our Lord Jesus Christ be with you all. Amen.

In His last message to the Church, Christ emphasizes His Second Coming. I think that He is really saying to us —Watch and be prepared at all times, for I shall come suddenly (rather than "I come soon").

Then John, representing all that look forward to this great event, says Amen. So be it—come, Lord Jesus. John, the beloved apostle, then adds a benediction: "The grace of our Lord Jesus Christ be with you all. Amen."

So ends this great, magnificent story of God's plan for His Creation, which started in Genesis; as well as this prophetic book, which zeros in on what may be the near future.

When I started writing this book, I did not set out to support any particular belief, or any particular church. I was seeking the truth through the Holy Spirit, and letting the chips fall where they may. I wasn't even aware that there were so many different views concerning particular things in the Bible. Many highly trained theologians have given arguments for and against all the different views; and I'm sure that they have made them sound as if they are right. But I know this; when it comes right down to it, it will only happen one way—God's Way! And it won't make any difference whether that way has been a popular or unpopular belief, an old belief or a more modern belief, whether it seemed reasonable or unreasonable to the human mind. It will happen just the way God has it planned!

I personally, from what I've been shown by the Holy Spirit, look forward with a great amount of anticipated joy to living in a world being perfected by our Christ, who will personally sit as King, and reign over it. I think it will be great to witness good triumph over evil, peace over war, truth over lies, love over hate, health over sickness, life over death; and to participate in whatever way my King decides.

Some have believed that man can accomplish this on earth. But how can anyone living in the world today believe that, when it is obvious that things are getting worse instead of better? No, only God can make this world a fit place for His children to live in. And He is sending His Son back to do just that. Just don't forget that the Devil is sending his son first, to con you into thinking that he can bring heaven to earth, and is the Messiah. And he will fool vast numbers of Christians and Jews because they have not been taught otherwise.

I thank God that for some reason He, Himself, has prepared me—not through my church, or through any other human being, or through any home-study course. Now I can face the terrible times ahead for this world without being frightened. Yes, it is true that I wasn't frightened last year about what was ahead, because I didn't know anything about it. But in this case, ignorance was not bliss, because I should have been frightened. I did not know, which I believe is the worst part, that I wasn't prepared! I was a good, lukewarm Christian, who let God have His way when it was convenient. And I was slated to be tested in the Great Tribulations, if I were still alive at that time. Are you?

CPSIA information can be obtained
at www.ICGtesting.com
Printed in the USA
FSHW011342041019